The 'ar·t, *of* Speeches *and* Presentations

Philip Collins is a columnist on *The Times*, chair of the Board of Trustees of the think-tank Demos and chief executive of High Windows Ltd, a speech-writing company. He was, until 2007, the Chief Speech Writer to the Prime Minister, Tony Blair. He has also worked as an investment banker and ran the Social Market Foundation, a political think tank. Since leaving Downing Street, he has written speeches for many chief executives in the corporate and voluntary sectors and for many senior government ministers. He writes a regular column analyzing important speeches for *The Times*.

The 'art, *of* Speeches *and* Presentations

The secrets of making people
remember what you say

Philip Collins

A John Wiley & Sons, Ltd., Publication

This edition first published 2012
© 2012 Philip Collins

Registered office
John Wiley & Sons Ltd, The Atrium, Southern Gate, Chichester, West Sussex, PO19 8SQ , UK

For details of our global editorial offices, for customer services and for information about how to apply for permission to reuse the copyright material in this book please see our website at www.wiley.com.

Wiley publishes in a variety of print and electronic formats and by print-on-demand. Some material included with standard print versions of this book may not be included in e-books or in print-on-demand. If this book refers to media such as a CD or DVD that is not included in the version you purchased, you may download this material at http://booksupport.wiley.com. For more information about Wiley products, visit www.wiley.com.

Designations used by companies to distinguish their products are often claimed as trademarks. All brand names and product names used in this book are trade names, service marks, trademarks or registered trademarks of their respective owners. The publisher is not associated with any product or vendor mentioned in this book. This publication is designed to provide accurate and authoritative information in regard to the subject matter covered. It is sold on the understanding that the publisher is not engaged in rendering professional services. If professional advice or other expert assistance is required, the services of a competent professional should be sought.

Library of Congress Cataloging-in-Publication Data
Collins, Philip, 1967–
    The art of speeches and presentations : the secrets of making people remember what you say / Philip Collins.
        p. cm.
    Includes bibliographical references and index.
    ISBN 978-0-470-71184-2 (pbk. : alk. paper)
1. Public speaking. I. Title.
    PN4129.15.C63 2012   2012004083
    808.5'1–dc23

A catalogue record for this book is available from the British Library.

ISBN 978-0-470-71184-2 (paperback) ISBN 978-0-470-71194-1 (ebk)
ISBN 978-0-470-71195-8 (ebk)   ISBN 978-0-470-71193-4 (ebk)

Set in 11.5/15 Adobe Caslon Pro-Regular by Toppan Best-Set Premedia Limited, Hong Kong
Printed in Great Britain by TJ International Ltd, Padstow, Cornwall, UK

CONTENTS

*To Hari and Mani, who are already teaching
me about the art of argument*

ACKNOWLEDGEMENTS

My professional thanks are due to three sets of people. First, my colleagues in Downing Street where I had the privilege of being able to enact everything I had learnt about writing a speech for the Prime Minister, Tony Blair.

Second, great thanks are due to *The Times*, whose generosity as an employer has allowed me the time off my duties there to write this book. I also owe a debt of thanks to *The Times* for granting me the space to analyse prominent speeches in its pages. It's a privilege to do so and the interest that these pieces have generated shows that rhetoric continues to fascinate people.

Third, to Brendan Barnes and the team at Speakers for Business who have helped to put together the speech-writing symposium at which I have tested the ideas contained in this book. My thanks are due to the people who came to those classes, for their stimulating thoughts and responses. For research assistance, my great thanks to Claudia Wood.

My personal debt of gratitude is much greater. Suffice to say that it is owed to an extended family but most of all to Geeta, Hari and Mani.

INTRODUCTION:
ATTENTION TO DETAIL

Speeches still matter, even in a technological age. The act of persuasion is ubiquitous in professional life and very many people need to master it. The act of making a speech is a medium that has remained essentially unchanged through the ages. The anthologies of great speeches are a reminder of the continuing power of well-arranged words but they are not necessarily the best guide to the task that you confront. A speech becomes memorable by virtue of the grandeur of the occasion it describes and most people are performing at a less exalted level. That does not mean that we cannot still write and speak well, or that there are not certain characteristics that all successful acts of communication have in common. This book will introduce the central argument that you need to understand your central argument. That is the most important precept of all good writing. This book will help you to master the basics of the craft with reference to the following mnemonic: D: effective Delivery; E: setting Expectations; T: the central argument, known as the Topic; A: understanding the Audience; I: making the speech Individual to you; and L: minding the Language that you deploy. Pay attention to detail. The precise details to which you must pay attention are the subject of this book.

Strange Isolation

A man steps forward out of the dark, alone, trailed by a spotlight. He walks slowly towards the podium which is the only thing that decorates the otherwise naked stage. He is being watched, not just by the two thousand people in the auditorium, all of whom are gripped by excitement, but by millions more watching as the event is broadcast live on television.

He walks into a strange isolation, for he knows, as does his audience, that he is about to beg their undivided attention for at least 25 minutes, probably more. There is no other setting in which we permit anyone to speak, uninterrupted, for so long. Yet this is precisely the exchange that we, as audience members, have licensed by our presence in the auditorium.

Some part of the audience is inquisitive, hoping to learn something; some part is sceptical, reluctant to be persuaded; and some part is eager, hoping to be inspired. Then there are audience members who are already bored, hoping, but not expecting, merely to hear something that retains their attention. Interest groups or rival firms or jealous colleagues are all paying particular mind, hopeful that the event will yield some advantage to their cause, even if that means you falling flat on your face, which will at least be amusing.

Soon enough, either simultaneous with delivery or very soon afterwards, the address will be enmeshed in a web of different technologies. If it is a major speech, it will be cut up and analysed for the news bulletins on television. It will be written up selectively for the newspapers the following morning. There may be a sketch of the speech, in which the writer picks out the one aspect that has gone wrong or is easily lampooned. Although the days in which speeches were published verbatim, without commentary, have gone for good, the speech may even be analysed in some depth with the best and worst passages highlighted and scrutinized.

Even if the occasion is not one that warrants the attention of the nation, it will rapidly be found in other contexts. The days when the speech existed solely as a transaction between the speaker and those in the audience are largely past. A transcript of the speech will probably be made available on an intranet, where the occasion will no doubt be broadcast. If it is not broadcast in real time, a recording of the occasion, certainly aural and probably visual, will be loaded onto the website later to the rest of the company sitting at their desks. Many speeches are multi-media events at the moment they occur. A transcript of the text may be circulated to members of an extensive corporate email distribution list.

And yet, for all the splicing that occurs in modern media, this event also retains the aura it has had since the first orator stood before the Athenian polis and tried out the trick of repetition. Perhaps the source of the fear that afflicts so many people as they contemplate speaking in public is an echo of the essentially primitive nature of the transaction. This is communication, to put it in modern parlance, which is one to many, and the last instance of the public speech will, in that sense, be the same as the first. In that loneliness, we can also find the perennial, visceral attraction of the moment.

The speech you are about to perform is therefore an echo of similar events held thousands of years before. It is hard to think of any other mode of communication that is essentially unchanged down the ages. The technological means of transmission is, at once, simple and sophisticated – the medium of speech. Let's go back to that man who is walking onto a stage. He approaches the podium where he stops, clears his throat and starts to speak. The normal rules of conversation are about to be suspended for the time it takes him to expound his argument. Against all the expectations and regular predictions of its demise, public speech still counts. It always will and it is a skill that needs to be mastered.

Speeches Still Matter

Open any anthology of great speeches and the chances are you will encounter a familiar litany (a selection of good anthologies can be found in the Bibliography at the end of this book). There are many speeches that feature in every one. They define the landscape of the tiny fraction of public oratory that we recall. Mahatma Gandhi's "There is no salvation for India" from 1916, Franklin D. Roosevelt's "The only thing we have to fear is fear itself" (1933), Winston Churchill's masterpieces in the House of Commons from the depths of 1940, John F. Kennedy's "Ask not what your country can do for you . . ." (1961), Martin Luther King's "I have a dream" (1963) and Nelson Mandela's "An ideal for which I am prepared to die . . ." (1964) are staples of the anthologies among modern speeches.

These are all in their way unique speeches, crafted and fashioned for the occasion by skilful writers. It is easy to suppose that they treat subjects long gone, that they are distant arguments whose eloquence remains, like a monument, even as

5

their relevance fades. Martin Luther King Junior's masterly preaching during the March on Washington DC in 1963. John F. Kennedy's great inaugural chiasmus ("Think not what your country can do for you"). Winston Churchill's memorable description of the effect of Communism after the war ("An iron curtain has descended"), which cast a shadow over the victory presaged in his justly famous war-time speeches, which are themselves exemplars of cohesion and economy.

But these speeches are more than the beautiful but ruined architecture that is a legacy of a lost age. They are still alive and they speak to us still. Pick up an anthology and enjoy the skill with which the words are crafted, the way the argument flows and vivid pictures form.

The continuing power of beautiful speech has recently had a powerful new testament. Barack Obama was carried to the Presidency of the United States on a tide of elevated rhetoric. Obama proved again what ought not to need proving – that clear prose in a poetic form still has the capacity to move an audience, both to tears and to action. Of course, the hopes that Obama excited in the process of rhetorical inspiration may yet give way to betrayal and disappointment.

That ambiguity is buried deep in rhetoric from the start. The popular connotation that words are "just rhetoric" suggests a duplicity at its centre. This accusation has a classical heritage. It was first levelled by Aristophanes in a celebrated passage in his play *The Clouds* in which he takes Plato to task for the fake nature of the words he uses as persuasion. This is a reminder that rhetoric is, after all, only words. Resolution must not lose the name of action; deeds will need to follow. We will find, as we proceed through the manual of writing a good speech, that this is an important principle. In learning how to speak we need constantly to attend to what we want people subsequently to do.

But it does not do to be too churlish or too much of a purist. There is always something enjoyable about hearing a great speaker convey a persuasive argument. Brilliance is a joy to behold. In these days of the easy availability of the great speeches, there is pleasure to be had in experiencing the mesmerizing effect that a great speaker, and Obama is an unquestionably great speaker, can conjure out of the rhythm of the words on the page.

The Importance of Not Being Barack Obama

But, if President Obama has helped to revive interest in the speech as an art form, he may be a bad guide to it. "All I have is a voice," said Auden and, much more than his text, Obama has a great voice with echoes of the black churches. Not everyone can sing a speech like President Obama can. Try the following experiment. Print out the texts of Martin Luther King's great "I have a dream" speech. Then print out the speech that Barack Obama gave on the occasion of his inauguration as President of the United States of America. Then perform them for yourself. You can hear the cadences if you are alone but, if you are not too embarrassed to do it, try to persuade someone to listen with you. Or, better still, get them to deliver the speech and you listen.

I am sure you will find that the King speech sounds pretty good. You might not have the lilt that he gives the words

7

but you will notice that the music is in the writing as much as in the speaking. It is hard not to deliver this speech in a sonorous way. The biblical imagery and archaisms more or less summon a command performance, even in your living room.

Then read the Obama speech. I'm just as sure you'll have far greater difficulty in making the rhetoric soar. The music is not intrinsic in the writing in the way it is in the timeless prose of the King James Authorised Version of the Bible, the only good book ever written by committee (of which more later). Read out by you, as you wander around your house, the Obama text sounds flat and at times rather dull. You begin to realize just how good Barack Obama is, as a performer. He has the ability to find the melody in his own words.

There is a second, even more intractable, way in which you are not Barack Obama. I suppose it is feasible you might learn to sing like he can. But no matter how well you train your voice, I am on safe ground when I predict that you are not currently the President of the United States of America and nor are you likely to be any time soon. The pressing questions that will assert themselves in your working life are unlikely to possess the grandeur of those which concern the leader of the free world. A speech about the attempt to establish universal health care, free at the point of delivery, is a major moment in American life. It warrants the use of the grand style and you cannot manufacture this pathos.

The context and occasion provide the grandeur, not the writer or the speaker. There is not a lot you can do about your context apart from accept it. The context in this case is that when you consider that Barack Obama is the first black man to be president in a country which, within the living memory of a large segment of the electorate, practised segregation in its cities, and, not long before that, transported black men to its shores in chains, then you have the raw material for some great speeches.

This isn't quite as true when you have to do a presentation on the quarterly sales figures to the senior management team who have gathered in a Travelodge somewhere off the Towcester ring road. It is not likely, as you make your way to the make-shift stage, that you are anticipating a slot in the next anthology of all-time great speeches. You probably think that just getting through the day without making a fool of yourself will do. You have to be more ambitious than that. You do have a specific purpose, which is to bind the team and inform them of the new, improved corporate strategy.

But the point is that it is crucial to get the register of a speech right. If you reach for poetry when the audience simply wants a clear account of the figures you will look and sound ridiculous.

This applies even to the best. As David Cannadine points out in his introduction to *Winston Churchill: Blood, Toil, Tears and Sweat: The Great Speeches*, Churchill had spent most of his career lavishing his verbal gifts on subjects that were not large enough to bear the weight. He had gained a reputation for verbosity and for being neither entirely serious nor entirely sincere. Churchill's early career is, in fact, an object lesson in what happens if you let the rhetoric run out of control. It was only with the failure of appeasement, the outbreak of war and imminent threat to British freedom that Churchill's words turned from bombast to brilliance.

The Purpose of this Book

Modern business cannot be conducted without effective public speech. Global technologies threaten to close the distance between locations but the importance of the clear presentation, done in front of a small audience in a given location, is still vital. It may now be web-cast, it may now reach an audience that would have been unimaginable a generation ago but clear speech is more necessary than ever.

It is also still true that speaking in public incites fear in far more people than it needs to. This book is designed to counteract that fear. It is written on the assumption that if people were more confident about the material they had in front of them, then they might be less fearful of delivering it. The central argument of this book is that you need to have a clear central argument, and this book is designed to assist you primarily in the task of working out what you want to say and how to say it well.

Some orators manage to say a lot without ever quite knowing what they are talking about. Churchill once described bad orators as people who: "before they get up they do not know what they are saying; and when they have sat down, they do not know what they have said".

It follows, accordingly, that there are several related types of book that this is not. It is not another anthology of great speeches. There is a voluminous literature on great speeches. A great deal of analysis has been lavished on why those speeches have survived the cruel test of time. There are some excellent guides to the technical aspects of rhetoric, which take you through the many tricks of the trade and introduce you to the classical language of rhetoric. This book isn't an attempt to rewrite those books, not least because that task has already been done very well. For example, the books by Sam Leith, *You Talkin' to Me? Rhetoric from Aristotle to Obama*, and Jay Heinrichs, *Thank You for Arguing*, both provide slightly more formal, but highly accessible, introductions to the classical techniques. But, as instruction manuals, the lessons in the art of persuasion are a little more buried than you might require, with that date in the diary pressing. This book is deliberately intended to be more immediately practical. It is also possible to write and speak well, obeying the dictates of classical technique, without necessarily knowing the name of every trick. For those who do wish to show off by naming the techniques they are using, there is a glossary at the back of this book.

There is a third type of book that this is not. There is also a huge choice, in any bookshop, for anyone seeking tips on how to present their material. Many of these books are full of wisdom and I recommend you seek some of them out. I would suggest that you look, in particular, at Graham Davies's *The Presentation Coach*, the final chapters of which set out some excellent tips on how to make the most of your material once you are up there on your own, ready to speak. Though the final substantive chapter of this book is about the delivery of the speech, as it is impossible to be comprehensive without considering the way that good delivery can enhance your material, the primary focus is on what happens before you arrive on stage.

That is because, somewhere in the gaps between these very different kinds of publications, there is something missing. Lots of people worry, reasonably enough, about the performance aspect of giving a speech. But they do not worry enough about writing the speech in the first place. It is not true that wonderful content can entirely supplant the need for good presentation – the two skills are complementary – but it can certainly help, not least because the nervous speaker will at least be confident that the material he is about to deliver is worthy of the occasion, even if he isn't. This book is designed to increase your confidence that your speech will be worthy of the occasion which, in turn, increases the likelihood that you will be.

But you do have to be realistic. Your task is not to put in a bid for being anthologized. Your job is to do your job as well as you can. It is to be the best speaker on the podium that you are expected to stand at, doing the best speech that you can do on the topic that you have been asked to address.

So that is what I propose to help you achieve. I do not propose to turn you into Martin Luther King as a speaker. I don't even propose to turn you into Neil Kinnock. Nor shall I suggest that, by the time you have digested this book, you will be in a position to imitate a writer like Ted Sorensen, who wrote some of John F. Kennedy's best lines, or Peggy Noonan, who wrote some outstanding speeches for Ronald Reagan. You ought not to try, even if you can do it. There are some lessons you can learn from great practitioners, and we will encounter some of the very best moments in the canon along the way, but part of the point of this book is to separate those attributes of high rhetoric that are relevant to you from those which are not.

The performer to emerge from these pages should be the best speaker you can be. There is little point in trying to construct an identikit speech maker, mouthing the words written by a skilled speech writer. A transaction of that sort will always be bloodless. It is no good a speech writer producing competent work with no personal cachet because rhetoric only comes alive when it creates a real personality. Good written work always has a distinctive voice. A speech without the voice of your character is not really a speech. It is just someone in a room, talking.

So, that's what we are looking for: the best possible version of you. I use the words "version of you" advisedly. The act of making a speech is an artificial occasion. You will never feel entirely as you do in the course of your everyday business and nor should you. This is a performance. The trick is to make it appear natural, to make the traces between you and your performing alter ego vanish. It is always tempting to hide yourself behind a cavalcade of visual aids. The purpose of this book is to help you avoid such a fate by enticing the vibrant person you know yourself to be to come out of the shell into which public speaking has consigned you.

So, with the reminder that you have to remain distinctively yourself, here are the generic things that can be said about all speaking engagements. Every occasion, from the main slot at a large public conference, down to addressing your colleagues in an internal meeting, will benefit from observing these basic precepts. These are the things that all acts of communication have in common and they also serve as a way of introducing the material in the rest of the book.

The Rule of Writing: Attention to Detail

In the art of writing a good speech, the person who has five priorities has none. This has the status of a law and it is a rule that no speaker can ignore.

Good writing has a structure. As the Duc de la Rochefoucauld said in his *Maximes*: "Good technique is what genius has in common with mediocrity." It's not clever to tear up the rules and declare that you are being creative. You are not being creative. You are being destructive. It takes a fundamental appreciation of structure and form to break the rules in an interesting way rather than a random way. Picasso managed it. The Beatles did a bit of it. But that's the company you are keeping. Good speech writing is about getting the basics right, time and again. Only when you have mastered the craft can you start indulging in some of the ornate flourishes.

No book like this is complete without a mnemonic. I have arranged the six generic tips on how to write a good speech to make them easy to recall, in a way that delivers a lesson in itself. The best way to remember the basics of writing is to recall the simple commonplace phrase: attention to detail.

Writing always benefits from being specific rather than general. A speech which is comprised of lofty abstractions, all joined up, is boring and meaningless. Referring to things in general terms leaves a speech curiously empty. It will always benefit from examples, from stories, facts, real things, arguments that are grounded. A speech which names culprits is better than one which dismisses mere arguments. A speech which gives precise numbers is better than one which makes do with general quantities like "a lot".

But the idea of paying attention to detail also contains the six basic precepts of good writing, which will be the basis of the advice offered in the rest of this book. Those six precepts are:

Delivery: the speech is written to be spoken. You need to think how you can make your delivery as effective as possible. This is not an essay; it's a performance.

Expectations: what do the people you will be speaking to expect from the day? Just as important, what do you expect? What do you want people to do once they have heard your speech?

Topic: what is your speech essentially about? Tell me in a single sentence. If you can't do that, you don't know. And if you don't know you aren't ready to do a speech.

Audience: who are you trying to reach? Who will be in your audience and what do they think about the topic that you are set to address? Will they be favourable or hostile to your approach?

Individual: a speech should be delivered by you. It should not just be any old speech. It needs to present the best possible version of you, which is subtly different from the hopeless advice to "be yourself".

Language: use simple terms and say nothing that an intelligent layman would not understand. It is not big and clever to use jargon and vocabulary that nobody would ever use when talking to their friends.

If you follow these rules nobody can promise that you will be a brilliant speaker. But there is a good chance you will not be a poor speaker. You will certainly be a more confident speaker and that is part of the battle for most people. If you look like you belong up there, the chances are that you will.

Let's take each one of the six briefly in turn. Though, for reasons that will become clear, I want to take them in an order that scrambles the word. I want to take you through the process of constructing a speech from start to finish. Some of the most common errors occur when people start the process either too early or from the wrong point. Methods of writing vary considerably but there are some basic guidelines that apply to all methods.

The Structure of the Book

Chapter One: Audience

As Alice advised us in Wonderland, the best place to start is at the beginning. So, you have a blank sheet of paper and you want to start. The temptation is always to start writing. But before you do anything as reckless as that, you need to think hard about the Audience you are going to be speaking to. Who are they and why have you been invited to speak to them? Before we can begin to work out what we need to say, and how we are to set about saying it, we need to know who we are going to be saying it to. What level of knowledge does your audience have? Are they likely to appreciate what you have to say or are they liable to be hostile?

Chapter Two: Expectations

Then it is important to know what the people in the audience expect. And also to work out what you expect from them. There are only three basic functions that a speech can serve and you must be sure what you are doing it for. Your speech will be informative, persuasive or inspirational. It may well have traces of all three functions but one of them will be the dominant strain. So, are you clear what you want people to believe or to do after you have finished with them? A speech is a remarkable event, probably a unique event in your life, in that you will be expected to speak, uninterrupted, for at least 20 minutes. Don't waste the opportunity by not being clear what you want to achieve from it.

Chapter Three: Topic

When you have surveyed your audience and established your expectations and purpose, you are ready to think about what you might say. But you are not yet ready to write. Before you start the long (and sometimes torturous) process of producing a first draft, you need to spend some time working out your central proposition. This is what Cicero, one of the great founders of rhetoric, calls the Topic. The most important thing for any presentation is that the speaker is utterly sure of the main idea that they have. Far too often the speaker is not entirely sure what it is they are there to say. You need to be entirely clear in a sentence or two what you are saying. What's the topic? That does not mean "what is the subject?" It means what do you have to say about it? Your material needs to follow inexorably from this central idea.

Chapter Four: Language

Now, with the Topic clearly defined, you can start the process which you no doubt thought was both the first and the most daunting task – the act of composition. You will find that once you have done the preparation required of you by the first three chapters, the actual writing will be much easier than you might have feared. That's because you now know what to write. It is a mistake to write with no plan. It's no wonder that writing is difficult if you do it with nothing in mind to say. In this chapter you will be taken through the process of building a resilient structure for a speech and then working on effective openings, main sections and closings. This chapter will also introduce some of the tricks of the rhetorical trade, many of which you will already be using.

Chapter Five: Individual

If you follow the process through this far you will be well set. But there is still a danger that you have disappeared in the process. It is important to remember that for every speech there is a speaker and the Individual in question is you. Or, the Individual in question might be the person that you are writing the speech for. There are many people who are perfectly good speakers but who contrive to disappear as soon as they are asked to do something a little more formal. You need to ensure that the confident person you are capable of being arrives on the stage when your moment in the spotlight arrives.

Chapter Six: Delivery

The spotlight is the subject of the final substantive chapter. Even after all this preparation the speech still has to be delivered and, although this book is concerned predominantly with the art of writing a memorable speech or presentation, it would be remiss not to end with some remarks about how to present that work as effectively as possible. You ought to be assured by now that your material will not let you down. But you could still let your material down.

Conclusion

After a reprise of the central argument and its components, the book then ends with the request that everyone who is called upon to speak in public takes the trouble to do it as well as possible. There are some chronic reasons why spectacular rhetoric is no longer as common as it once was. But that does not mean to say that speaking plainly and clearly is not still possible. To have the opportunity to make a speech is to be granted the chance to make your case to people who care enough to have attended. It is in your interests to do that well and yet it is extraordinary how often the opportunity is not taken.

The book therefore concludes with a rallying cry for good language. The standard of public language is not as good as it used to be. Yet, there is no reason at all why people cannot speak well and it is incumbent on anyone who speaks in public to be as plain and as clear as they can be.

CHAPTER ONE

AUDIENCE

In this chapter we will locate the start of the writing process long before composition. Everything is leading up to the central argument and there is much work that needs to be done before we get to that point. Before you are ready to begin you need to be sure that you really do want to make a speech, rather than take part in a panel session. You need to commit the time but, crucially, do not be tempted to start too soon. Once you have determined to proceed, you need to begin to get to know your audience. There are three ways of doing this – thinking, researching and asking. The best tactic, if you can, is to speak to people who are planning to attend. Then there are five questions you should ask yourself, as a further guide to what will be required of you.

1. What title have you been given?
2. How large an audience can you expect?
3. On what occasion will the speech take place?
4. How much does your audience already know about the topic of the day and do they have a prior prejudice?
5. Are you speaking to a larger audience than those who are gathered in the hall?

You will by now know enough about your audience that you are ready to think about what you expect from this speech.

Before You Begin

As the task of writing a good speech unfolds in this book, you will see that the pivotal moment, the fulcrum of the whole process, is the clarification of a resilient central argument. Everything prior to that point leads up to it and everything subsequent to that point follows from it.

In other words, there is a good deal of work to do before you start to write. Before you begin, you should stop and ask yourself the following question: how far away is the speech? Most people start their preparation far too early. The natural response to trepidation is to start working. Lots of people use activity to displace nervous tension. They think it will help to start writing two months before the event and have it completed and ready to be delivered with a week still to go.

This is a mistake and you will just need to be braver about it. There is no speech that has ever been delivered that could not have been done in a month, from start to finish. Starting too soon leaves too much time for your material to go stale and for you to lose confidence in what you have done. People start to make poor editorial decisions the more time that passes. You also run the risk that too many people get involved in the process and the speech loses its central thrust.

If that schedule sounds tight and you want to protest immediately that you are too busy for that kind of regime, then you need to ask yourself a more fundamental question: do I really have the time for this speech?

If you thought the speech was worth doing in the first place, then you will need to put aside the requisite time. Turning up poorly prepared is a discourtesy to your audience, as well as a foolish missing of an opportunity on your part. But perhaps your reluctance is pointing to a more basic concern. The sense of unease lurking underneath your bravado may be pointing to the fact that you have nothing to say.

That isn't quite the knock-down insult that it sounds. It doesn't mean that, if engaged on a topic of conversation, you would sit there in embarrassed silence. It means that you do not, just at the moment, have something sufficiently new and important to impart that it warrants organizing a whole event around it, to which people will be asked to interrupt their day to attend.

Be careful that your diary is not exercising a kind of tyranny over your time. Most speeches are just dates in the diary that you feel you cannot avoid. Many of these events will have been put into your diary by someone else, with only the merest indication to you. They probably thought it was corporate necessity that you attend and they may well be right. In other words, this is an event at which nobody involved actually wants to make a speech and this is a really inauspicious beginning. The annual industry conference is on the horizon and, as a big cheese in the trade, you can hardly not show up. But the obligation to attend is not the same as the need to make the keynote speech.

There are other ways to appear that release you from the obligation to be the main event. You could suggest a panel event in which leading figures answer questions from the audience. If those questions are submitted by agreement in advance of the event, you will not be ambushed by any nasty surprises. The presence of others on a panel always provides cover, in any case. You could arrange to have a structured conversation on stage, led by an interviewer, with whom you have discussed the course of the discussion in advance.

There are many occasions on which your task is simply to make the corporate case that you have made before. There is nothing wrong with that. The world does not change fundamentally for most of us in a matter of months. So, if that is the task you have, think hard before you accept the invitation to do a set-piece speech. You may be asking for a lot of hard work you will wish you had avoided. Not that you should automatically suppose that submitting to a structured interview, a panel or a question and answer session will release you from the requirement to prepare. Even if you are familiar with the standard material you have to impart, each of these occasions contains pitfalls that preparation can help you to avoid. It is also worth adding, too, that after you have done a few of these events you will have honed your answers and you probably have a set response to certain questions. That is fine as long as you are sure to interrogate your own patter every few months. Lines can date quickly and your delivery can betray the fact that you have become bored with saying it. You can be sure the audience will be if you are.

How Do I Get to Know My Audience?

A speech is sometimes known as an address and an address has to be addressed to someone. An argument has to be given to someone in particular. It is impossible to work out your speech in the abstract. So, the place to start is with an assessment of the occasion for your speech or presentation and the audience who will be there to hear you.

Before looking at what you need to ask of your audience, you need to think carefully about how you intend to go about unearthing the information. There are three ways you can get to learn more about your audience.

1. You can sit there and think
2. You can do some research from your desk
3. You can ask people

If you sit and think for a while you will usually find that you already know quite a lot about the speech you have been invited to give. It is likely that you know the occasion and the organization that has asked you to speak. If the presentation is internal you will probably know some, if not all, of the audience members. You will probably have a good sense of the educational level of your audience, its basic income and also know the context of the conference or occasion. Incidentally, there are some books and websites on speech writing which implore you to make a great deal of this kind of psychological musing. There are others too that ask you to do a certain amount of what they call "demographic" analysis of the audience. You should be careful with this. There is a limit to the psychological attitudes that can easily be read off from somebody's biography or the place you impute to them in the social structure. It's unlikely that extended study of this kind will repay the investment of time. There are events which demand a certain tone (such as a conference exclusively for women) but that will be clear in the title of the event and requires no great insight into demography. You almost certainly understand the purpose of the meeting you will address. It goes without saying that, if you don't know the answers to any of these questions, you certainly need to. But you will find that a clear picture of the event is already available in your mind if you just spend half an hour sketching it.

Now, the sketch you have ready-made in your mind is highly impressionistic. So let's paint in some of the details. If you know nothing else at all about the forthcoming event, you will presumably know who you have been invited by. Start by investigating who they are, if you do not already know.

The best way to begin this investigation is to ask what this organization stands for. As a guide, you can use the following questions:

- What question does this organization exist to answer?
- How would you characterize this organization, from what you can see on its website and the literature that you will find there?
- What problems do you imagine they encounter?
- Why do you think they are interested in the topic that you have been given?
- Imagine the meeting they had, at their headquarters, when your name came up. They had other options, yet they chose you. Why did they do that, do you think?
- Why did they imagine that you had any of the answers to what they need to know?

There is another way of ascertaining the answer. You could just ask them. You must have at least one contact at the organization that has issued the invitation, namely the person who contacted you. If they are at all efficient, they will already have attached some information about the event. In fact, it is more likely that they will have sent you too much rather than too little. Make sure that the accompanying material you have contains something about the prospective audience, a projected line-up of speakers for the day and something akin to the statement that sets out the purpose of the day.

If you are missing any of these elements, just ask. Then, while you are asking, inquire whether there is an archive of previous events online. You can usually watch speeches from previous years which will give you a sense of the type of occasion you have in store and of the type of speech to which this audience will be accustomed. Finally, ask your contact if there is anyone you could talk to at a later date for a fuller briefing on the nature and mission of the event. If you frame this as wanting to be sure that the organizers get exactly what they want from the event, people are invariably delighted that you should be so interested.

So far, you will have gained some useful information about the event but not very much about the people who really matter – the audience. Your contact may have been helpful but there is still a lot more you can do. The best strategy of all is to talk to the audience before the event. Of course, unless it is a small-scale event, it won't be possible to talk to everyone who will attend but that is not a counsel of despair. You can still unearth the information you need.

There are books on speech writing which suggest that you send a short questionnaire to the audience, assuming that you have been able to get hold of an invitation list from the organizer. The problem with this is that you are liable to annoy a large proportion of your audience, while gaining information of quite poor quality. Survey questions are usually too general and do not allow for the revealing follow-up question from which genuinely useful information often comes. There is something impersonal and perfunctory about a list of generic questions turning up in your inbox. As an audience member, I am apt to be more irritated than impressed.

There really is no substitute for actually talking to people directly. It will rarely be possible to talk to more than a small fraction of your audience. But assume that, on the day, you will be speaking to 100 people. If your research has yielded an account of the audience's character, you should be able to construct a small representative sample. Good research should allow you to locate five people who will be reasonably representative of the whole. Don't hesitate to contact them, if you can get their number or email address. Most people are flattered to hear from you, flattered that you should care at all and flattered in particular that you care what they think.

When you find these people ask them what single question they most urgently need you to supply the answer to. What single thing could they learn from your speech that they really need to know?

Though you are planning to talk to just five people, it is possible that each one of them will know others who are also planning to attend. You can be sure, too, that those five people will mention it to others, either before the event or on the day.

You will be appreciated for taking the pains to discover the needs of your audience, especially if someone recognizes a morsel of information which they think derives from the conversation that you had with them. Sometimes the people you speak to will not quite know what they are looking for from the day. They may be looking to you to answer that question. Sometimes the thing they are looking for is exactly what you know you cannot offer them, either because you don't know the answer or because you disagree with them. But at least you will know the ground on which you stand and that will help a great deal in the preparation of your text.

What Do I Need to Know About My Audience?

Now that you have steeled yourself to make contact with your audience, you need to make sure that you do not waste their time. The following section sets out what, ideally, you need to know. For ease of reference, the information you need to contemplate before you are ready to start writing can be broken down into five questions.

1. What is the title that you have been asked to address?
2. What is the likely size of the audience you will have?
3. What is the occasion on which you will speak and where will the speech take place?
4. How much does your audience already know and what is their view on your topic?
5. Are you speaking to more audiences than you can see before you in the hall?

Question One: The Title of Your Speech

To start with the title of the speech is such an obvious first question that it is remarkable how frequently people forget to ask it. You can make some basic errors at this point, which will ramify all the way through the preparation process, so it is as well to get the title of the speech correct from the beginning.

Your title ought to be narrow, clear and precise. It should not be "Developments in the delivery of milk over the last few years" or "Trends in the production of cricket bats". Those are broad subject matters, not topics for a speech. Your title needs to be one of two things:

(i)   an assertive statement, which you will set out to substantiate or confound, or

(ii) a clear question, which you will set out to answer.

"Five years from now, the rise of the supermarkets will have finished off milk delivery for ever" is a statement of intent, around which a speech can be organized. Likewise, "is the current consumer trend towards cheaper brands likely to persist even when the country returns to healthier growth rates?" gives you something to answer.

Beware the grand, vague title. It is a trap that will lead you to platitudes that, in the vain attempt to cover too much ground, cover too little. Saying nothing loftily is always easy but never impressive. If the organizers have landed you with a title without specific content, impose your own. Let them know early what you intend to talk about. Perhaps at this initial stage you will not be in a position to declaim the aggressive statement that you will prove on the day. If not, you should know the question that will need to be answered. A speech organized around a question always leads to a definitive statement in any case. The two approaches are, in fact, one. The question leads evidently to the answer.

There is one more word of warning needed. Be sure you do not set yourself a question that is unanswerable. You cannot hope to do too much in an address of 20 minutes (which is the time you ought to be aiming at). A good speech should rarely be longer than 25 minutes. Most allocations are longer than this but there is no need. It is a rare subject that cannot be explained fully and vividly in 25 minutes. Indeed, you should be quicker if you can be. Make sure the question you pose has clear and easy answers. You may not know which answer to choose but it is easy to identify a question that leads to such an answer. For example, in my speech suppose I set myself the task of answering the question: "Is the modern world changing faster than it changed in previous eras of history?" It is possible to envisage an endless seminar on this question which might occasionally yield some interesting insights. It is less likely that you have the time to assemble a crisp and coherent answer to this question by the time your annual conference comes around. It's just too big, too generic, too imprecise and too far removed from what you and your audience actually do. This question may well be the backdrop to the majority of your business activity and I am not suggesting it is not an important question.

It's just not the most important question for you right now, and that is what we are looking for.

Compare this question: "Does the financial crisis compel us to change course as a company?" You can tell a good, generative question when both the answer "yes" and the answer "no" suggest further lines of inquiry. To answer "yes" to this question invites us at once to say why such a change of course is necessary and what it will actually require of us in practice. That suggests a rudimentary speech structure straight away:

(i) What has happened? (Details of the crash)
(ii) Why does that mean our strategy has to change? (Set out the strategy and the elements that will no longer work)
(iii) What do we do next? (Set out the new strategy and why it will work in the new environment)

So, be clear, be precise and be narrow. Nobody ever complained that a speech was not general enough. If at a later date you decide, after you have learnt a little more about your audience, that you do need to range more widely, that is always easy to do. It is always true in the course of writing that it is easier to expand from a narrow subject matter than it is to winnow down from a general subject matter.

In philosophical terms, speech writing is a form of induction (moving from the particular to the general) rather than a species of deduction (deriving the particular from the general)

Question Two: The Size of the Audience

The rules of good writing and effective communication do not really vary. To this extent, the guidelines that we will encounter in Chapter Three (Topic) apply universally. The laws of good writing are akin to physical laws. They cannot be suspended. Clarity of argument matters if you are talking to three people in a room at work and it matters if you are leader of the Labour Party giving your speech to the annual conference.

But these two events do obviously differ markedly in every other respect and it would be odd if there were no requirements particular to either. There are relevant differences in the way you should approach the composition of a speech that depend on the size of the audience that you are about to encounter.

The degree of formality that is appropriate varies according to your relationship with that audience and the size of the audience. If you know the people in the room well, if you talk to them informally every day for example, then it would seem decidedly odd to come over all formal just because you are now delivering a presentation. The satire of your colleagues is usually enough to keep you honest on these occasions.

The other useful rule of thumb is that the greater the size of the audience, the more formal the presentation should become. Or, rather than say "should" become, it would be more accurate to say "could" become. There is no requirement to be very formal. Indeed, excessive formality of diction is one of the ways in which people lose their personality once they take to the stage. Formality here is not intended to suggest stilted prose. It just means that the speech is a little more crafted, a little more rhetorical.

Good speech writing is like ordinary speech, heightened. Imagine all the wittiest things you have ever said, spontaneously. Then imagine you managed to say them all one after another, tied up in a clever argument. That's a speech. It's not different from your everyday conversation; it's just better than you. It's you at just a bit more than your very best. It is you with the dull bits edited out. For some people this means that quite a lot of editing is required.

The smaller the audience the more that even rhetorical crafting of this kind will seem artificial and odd. Declaiming your text as if you were Ian McKellen reading the battlefield soliloquy from *Henry V* will really have you marked down as an oddball if your audience is Barry, Andy and Steve from the Weymouth office.

It is useful to distinguish three audience sizes, each one of which demands a subtly different response from the speaker.

1. Room: an audience of fewer than 10 people. This is the most intimate setting you will speak in. Every member of your audience will be individually visible. You will probably be closer to them than you would be in a grander setting and any reaction the audience betrays will be immediately obvious. Formality in this setting is going to seem strained and peculiar.

2. Hall: holding somewhere between 10 and 100 people. This is the most common type of address. As soon as the audience gets over 10 people, and certainly when it begins to climb close to 100, individual contact with each member will prove to be impossible. The audience, in a strange way, starts to become a single audience, rather than a group of identifiable individuals (which you should try to remember they remain).

3. Auditorium: over 100 people, all the way up to playing Madison Square Garden. This is the highest level of formality. The sort of performance required to play a larger venue is an exaggerated and heightened version of what is required in smaller settings. When you have a large audience there is the possibility of contagion. A good story can gain a laugh which can ring around a venue.

It needs to be repeated, though, that the basic precepts of writing do not change according to the venue. A large audience can spot a poor argument just as easily as a small audience.

Question Three: The Setting and the Occasion

The idea of the occasion is about more than the title of the conference. The occasion, which has some overlap with what, in his *Rhetoric*, Aristotle calls "pathos", is better described as everything in the background to the event which is relevant to the speech you might give.

It is important, of course, to think about the setting in which you will deliver the speech. The location, the town, a famous resident or historical event – they might all furnish a reference, even if it is no more than the courtesies and pleasantries that are uttered at the beginning. So, for example, a speech in Liverpool, in which a speaker has to make the case for investment in biochemical engineering, might profitably make use of the fact that the UK's first biochemical engineering department opened at Liverpool University in 1902.

It is also advisable to check when you are down to speak. Ask yourself where you are on the bill. The ideal spot in a conference is about 11am in the morning. The delegates have warmed up by then but they are not yet desperate for lunch.

Immediately after lunch is the worst slot, with people not yet ready to get going again.

Then, consider the particular context into which this event will fall. What has happened in the time since the last event? Or, if this is a singular conference, why has it been called? Why does the world need this conference at all? What question is it designed to answer? Try to imagine this conference in a wider setting and work out what relation it plays to larger issues.

The occasion is what gives your speech its resonance. Try to assess how momentous your occasion is. Do you expect that this will be an event which is remembered in years to come? Does it fall at a very important juncture in the development of your profession? Is there anything unusual about this particular moment that would demand something unusual from you?

Question Four: The Knowledge Level of Your Audience

The more you can learn about your audience, the better. There are two big things you need to know. First, how much do they know and, second, what do they think about your topic as they enter the hall to hear you speak? Let's take them in turn.

First, is this an expert gathering or a crowd of the uninitiated? Is this an audience likely to know a lot about the topic you will be speaking on or are they relative (to you, at least) novices? It is probable that the audience will be a mix, containing some members who know a great deal and some who know very little about the subject under discussion. Finding a pitch that interests the latter without patronizing the former then becomes your delicate task.

Getting the tone wrong because you are pitching your address at the wrong level of knowledge is a common error. An audience that already knows everything you are telling them will feel bored as well as patronized. An audience that cannot follow your technical exposition will switch off and feel alienated by someone who made them feel stupid. Of course, you will sometimes discover that the audience is made up both of people accomplished at a high level of specialized sophistication and those who are a good deal less familiar with the material.

In these circumstances you have three options. The first option is to summarize the more technical aspects of the presentation, with an explicit apology to those who already know what you are about to tell them. Your second option is to seek the highest ground which is common to both sets of people. This is not bad advice at all but it can be difficult to know what, in practice, it entails.

For that reason, the third option is much the best. That is to speak so plainly that you explain all the difficult concepts in words that an intelligent layperson can understand. This is a general principle which will recur frequently in this book. Try, as far as possible, to speak plainly, without unnecessary technical language or deliberate, pretentious flourishes and flights of poetic fancy like this one. It is always possible to talk about difficult things in a simple way and that way the initiated will not feel patronized and those who are new to the subject will feel that they have learned something.

Once you have come to some sense of what your audience will think, the second question is to consider that view in a little more detail. In particular, ask yourself about the general mood in the audience.

Is this a voluntary audience or a compelled audience? It is not uncommon for an audience to have little interest in the subject under discussion. This does not reflect badly on you as a speaker (well it might but it doesn't necessarily). Remember that some members of some audiences are attending the conference not because they especially want to but because it is expected of them. It's just a job and, frankly, they'd rather be somewhere else. The first task with an involuntary audience is to get their attention. Do not assume the audience is interested. It's your job to make them so.

If the audience is interested, or if you can prick their interest, they will either be favourable or hostile to your approach. You do not as yet have even a main argument, let alone a script. But in most cases you will already know whether, in broad terms, you are being cast in this setting as an advocate or a critic. You will usually have a good feeling for the sorts of things you think will find an echo in the views that will be present in the room.

Picture yourself before an audience, arguing the case for a high speed rail link between Manchester and Leeds. You have assembled your best possible case, replete with facts and projections about the future benefits. You have done your audience research well so you know what to expect. The man from the "No to High Speed Rail Campaign" is in the front row. He is sitting next to a rotund businessman whose lapel badge says he is from "We Need Better Transport". The two of them are making it easy for you but not everyone wears their allegiance on their lapel. Most members of the audience sit quietly and attentively, wearing badges that bear the names of organizations that sound studiously neutral.

However, your research has revealed that a large number in the audience object to the despoliation of the countryside between Manchester and Leeds, which is likely to be an incidental outcome of such a scheme. That is why the main burden of your speech has therefore been to reassure your audience that, contrary to misleading newspaper reports, the areas of outstanding beauty will either be tunnelled or bypassed altogether.

You had planned at first to make a speech in response to a paper by academics at Manchester University which purported to demolish the business case for the scheme. Your first draft contained a wholly different speech (which taught you the lesson of not starting before you know what you have to say). That first draft was more factual, full of the gains to economic growth that would be generated by improved infrastructure in the North West. It was a good speech, for a different occasion. It would have bombed if you'd done it, though. Your audience research has equipped you with a good speech for this occasion.

If you are faced with an audience which is sceptical, or even hostile, you may be in for a testing time. You will need to bear this latent hostility in mind as you select your arguments and supporting evidence. Conversely, you are not necessarily off the hook if you conclude that the audience will, in general, be favourable to your point of view. A speech that panders to the already-existing prejudice of an audience is usually dull and leaves people dissatisfied even as they concede that what you said was essentially right. You should still consider the following set of questions:

- What motivates this audience when it comes to this topic?
- What arguments will they find irritating and unconvincing?
- What are their biggest concerns and unanswered questions?
- How much of a factual basis is there for their general beliefs?
- Will those beliefs be based primarily on personal experience or on study?
- To what extent have they definitively made up their mind?

The first of these questions may offer a clue to the others. If you can locate the motive force of an audience you have a good chance of constructing a persuasive argument. For example, an audience of finance directors is likely to respond to a different emphasis than an audience of marketing executives. This will be true even if they work for the same company, with the same basic set of interests. Your basic argument will also be the same in both cases. But the manner in which you make it should correspond to what you have learnt about what motivates the people in question.

It is evidently a crude reduction of people to say that finance directors will automatically respond to a more arithmetical argument about the return on capital and marketing executives will require something a little more rhetorically polished and vivid. I know there are some creative finance directors out there (although not always in a good way). But there is plenty of time for adding layers of complexity and sophistication to the message. At this stage, we are just looking for pointers, assembling the information we need that will allow us to begin writing at the right place.

Question Five: The Problem of Plural Audiences

For almost every speech, there are two audiences. There is the audience you can see and the audience you cannot see. First of all, there is, of course, the set of people who are actually in the auditorium or the room before you and no speaker can afford to neglect them.

But something that has been true of political speeches for a long time has now become true of presentations more broadly. Ever since Roosevelt made the first political radio broadcast in 1924, the written word has travelled over the airwaves. Lots of speeches now have at least two audiences and by far the more important is the invisible cast of thousands, sometimes running into millions, who will see some part of the speech, or at least hear it reported, on television and radio.

The multi-media dissemination of the speech has spread from national politics into corporate life. Now that a presentation can be instantly uploaded onto a company intranet or even, if something especially intriguing or embarrassing has taken place, onto YouTube, the potential audience for your words far exceeds the numbers who receive an embossed invitation or the lucky bunch of colleagues who crowd into the presentation suite.

In many cases, the speech itself is merely the perfunctory performance that makes electronic repetition possible. Many political speeches have essentially happened before the speaker says a word. The best bits – or the least bad bits – are briefed to the newspapers and broadcasters in advance. That morning's newspapers will usually carry a report that Mr Brown will say that Mr Blue is a fool today. That will be picked up by the radio and television programmes, find its way onto political blogs and will start to be traded between the political obsessives. By the time the speech actually takes place, it feels like ancient history. Most people who ever know anything of the speech will have heard of it before it actually takes place. Some speeches are so well trailed that reading them out is like a chore. Everyone has already heard it.

Most corporate speeches are not like this but even the presentation in which there is no media interest can be made available to be watched at any point. The way that the speech is consumed is changing in a way that is beyond the control of the speaker. There is a lot less that we can do to anticipate how people will see the speech if we have no real idea when (or if) they will choose to watch it, who they will be with at the time, whether they will also be doing something else, what mood they are in while watching and so on. The usual ways of influencing the mood of a speech simply do not apply when the audience is fragmented into a long series of single people, watching a recording alone at their desk or later that evening at home.

At this stage, you just need to be aware of how extensive your audience will be. That requires you to know not just whether there is any prospect of the proceedings being disseminated as they unfold. You also need to know whether a transcript of the event will be circulated and, if so, to whom. You should also seek to work out whether there are any plans to put the event on film or videotape and upload it onto the website. Is that an internal site, which is protected and therefore will have limited traffic, or is it open, in which case the potential audience could be substantially larger? But who, in fact, is this uploading designed for? Who are the regular visitors to that site and which group of people would it be wise for you to number among your audience? It can be hard to count all these nameless, invisible people as part of your audience. It is natural to concentrate on those in the hall, and not unreasonable either. But you cannot afford to forget the rest of us, watching at home, listening to music at the same time.

Conclusion: You Know Who You Are Talking To

You may not yet know what you are talking about. But you will at least know by now who you are talking to. We are not done with your audience yet, as you will see in the next chapter. But we have done the basics and, if you have followed the argument so far, you should be well informed about who you can expect to have in front of you and what, in broad outline, they think.

It does not follow from this that you ought simply to reflect to that audience those things you feel it wants to hear. The material that an audience wants to hear is not always the thing that they need to hear or the thing that you specifically have to tell them. A speech which panders to an audience will usually be exposed. An audience rarely likes an obviously ingratiating speaker. If an audience feels that all you are doing is flattering them they will not, paradoxically, feel flattered.

They will feel patronized. Your audience research is designed to inform you of who you are speaking to and what they think. It is perfectly legitimate in some circumstances to then decide to tell them something they neither think already nor agree with. But that will depend on the expectations that they, and you, have for this speech, which is the subject of the next chapter.

CHAPTER TWO

EXPECTATIONS

It is nowhere near time yet to start writing. The next step in constructing a speech is to ask yourself what you expect this speech to achieve. Every speech has one of three functions. It will be primarily about transmitting information, or about persuading an audience of something, or about inspiring people to do something. Most speeches will contain traces of all three functions but one will always be dominant and you need to be clear on what your function is. The different types of speech impose different demands on the writer and speaker. You should work towards writing a statement of intent which sets out what you are expecting to do and to which you need to refer throughout the writing process. At this stage, you should think about whether you do, in fact, need to go on. Every step in the speech-writing process exercises a veto. If you cannot define your intent in making this speech then you ought to think about not doing one at all.

If you have followed the precepts in the first chapter, you ought to have a close appreciation of the audience that is no doubt eagerly awaiting your speech. You should have a reasonably accurate sense of who is expected to turn up and what they think. So, all set to start writing? Well, no, not yet. There are two more important steps to take before we begin the composition. You have spent some time trying to clarify what the audience wants from this speech. Now, using that information, it is time to work out what they can actually expect by clarifying what you expect from the speech.

Before we can begin to draft the speech, or even clarify its central thrust, we need to think about what kind of speech you are proposing to give. What will count as a success for this event? What are you hoping to achieve? In truth, many people are hoping just to get out alive. As long as they get onto the stage without falling over and get off without making a fool of themselves, that feels like a good day. The purpose of this book is to lift your sights a little and allow yourself more ambition. Set yourself a proper challenge because you can meet it. Confidence will flow from clarity about what you are trying to achieve.

The Three Functions of a Speech

Every good speech has a clear function. The function of the speech is not the subject matter, or even your precise argument. It is the reason that you are doing the speech at all. It is the desired outcome, the marginal way in which the world will be made different by your having prepared this speech.

The next task is to work out what you want this speech to achieve. We will not know what speech we are trying to write before we have clarified its purpose. The question here is not "what is my speech about?" It is "what is my speech for?" Your speech will also have a specific purpose. This is the actual subject matter you will address, which will be something like "how to reform housing benefit" or "the strategy for improved sales in the second quarter of next year in the Frome region". The specific content of your speech will occupy the succeeding chapter on the Topic of the speech.

All speeches can be divided into at least one of the following three functions:

1. **Information**: a speech whose principal function is to leave an audience better informed than they were before you began.

2. **Persuasion**: a speech whose principal function is to persuade an audience of a case that, before you began, had either never occurred to them or to which they had been actively hostile.

3. **Inspiration**: a speech whose principal function is to inspire the audience to do something that they had previously not considered doing or had been refusing to do or, occasionally, to carry on doing something.

Note the repetition of the operative phrase "principal function". The clear implication of this is that all speeches will have more than one function. The dominant motif of a speech may be to persuade but it is very difficult to do this without supplying any information and most persuasion leads, at some later point, to action. Persuasion is itself often designed to inspire. Large, substantive speeches contain all three functions in some measure. But one will always be the dominant strain.

There is actually a fourth type of speech. This is the ceremonial address that commemorates an occasion such as a wedding or the eulogy at a funeral. There is an enormous body of work, most of it not very good, that guides people through these speeches and the focus of this book is more on speeches for business and political occasions, rather than personal. That said, the basic principles of good writing apply everywhere and there is no reason to discard them on any occasion.

So let's look at speeches with each of the three functions in turn.

Speeches that Offer Information

The speech whose primary function is information can often turn out rather didactic and dry. The informative speech can be as much like teaching as it is like public speaking. If you really do have to do a speech in which your leading objective is to pass information from inside your head into the heads of the audience, then you will need to think carefully about how to make this potentially dull encounter come alive.

Examples of an informative address would be:

- A teacher telling students about the British Constitution
- A student describing her research into housing benefit
- A tour guide taking a group around the Palace of Westminster
- A manager taking the company through the new structures

The informative speech has a clear standard. When you have finished speaking you simply want people to know what you have said. It's a function so clear that you could test people as they leave the hall. But it won't work to adapt the persistent cliché about speeches, to tell them what you are going to tell them, to tell them and then to tell them what you just have told them. Unless the subject matter itself is intrinsically of great interest to your audience, you will never hook them. They won't listen.

The best teachers are those that engage the student. The learning takes place without anyone quite noticing. The best teachers are, in effect, persuading their audience to take the information on trust and persuading their audience to be interested in it. There must be an element of inspiration in this performance, even if that does not seem quite the appropriate word when you are discussing the new system for doing the payroll (actually people tend to care about that rather a lot, understandably enough).

So the informative speech is not a simple affair. Standing up and reading out the material is not enough. It will be even worse if, like the overwhelming majority of corporate presentations, you read out the material while standing with your back to the audience, looking at some slides on which you have printed the same information. I have, after a heroic effort of will, decided to excise most of the derogatory references to the standard corporate presentation from this book. There is a short, and hopefully not too intemperate, section on the pitfalls of PowerPoint in the chapter on how to deliver a speech well. Suffice to say, I don't ever use slides when I speak and I strongly encourage anyone I write for to ditch them too. They are usually a crutch, but a crutch that helps you to fall over.

Your audience may not realize they need to know what you intend to teach them. They may think they already know what they need to know. They may not want to hear what you have to tell them. Imagine that you have to announce to the company's employees that the senior management team has decided to merge two business units. You could baldly say that the primary function of your address to the whole company is to pass this information on. But you could have a riot on your hands if you don't think about it a touch more subtly than that.

The information it is your task to convey carries justifiable anxiety for your audience. You are talking to people who may be fearful for their livelihood and household income. When you coldly set out the new structure your audience will hear "they are shifting it all around so they can save money and that means getting rid of some of us".

So your speech will depend very heavily on a subsidiary function.

There is no scope for inspirational rhetoric here but you do have, in fact, a difficult act of persuasion to perform. You will need, if you can, to make a case for the merger, to make the audience see the business from the same point of view that has led the senior management team, reluctantly you should add, to their decision. If the people in the audience can see the rationale, if they realize this is not a capricious decision, then they are more likely to hear the information with equanimity. If you are especially good, some of them may even see the benefits for them in the proposed new structure. Here, in passing, is an object lesson. Remember how the information feels for the person in the audience. They will be less concerned about the overall company than you might expect. Their first loyalty is to themselves and you need to persuade them to take the larger point of view.

The speech which is at its heart informative is the dullest category. It will require unusual analogies and verbal pictures. It will require intriguing ways of describing familiar things. You will have to find at least three different ways of making your central point because if the audience leaves without grasping your central point, then the speech has transmitted no information and has to be judged a failure.

The speech which is genuinely more about conveying information than it is about anything else is the one exception to the general rule that a hand-out is the death of a speech. If you place something on a seat before you start, people will either read it and ignore you or not read it and ignore you in the knowledge that they can read it later (which they won't). So, never give out your speech to the audience in advance, but if the principal function is to ensure that they possess some information, it is entirely prudent to provide it for them in a digestible written form afterwards. In a small audience you can usually arrange for the organizers, or sometimes yourself, to email the relevant information later.

Speeches that Seek to Persuade

The information which is relayed in a persuasive speech has a purpose beyond itself. As the Victorian historian Macaulay once said "the object of oratory is not truth, but persuasion".

The persuasive speech is selected and ordered with a view to making people change their mind or change their behaviour. Inspiring people is a viable persuasive tactic but that too is a subsidiary aim. In a persuasive speech, the speaker has told himself before he begins that the measure of success is whether a significant proportion of the audience thinks differently at the end of his speech.

Examples of a persuasive speech would be:

- A lawyer conducting a defence in front of a jury
- A salesman talking about the virtues of a new product
- A manager trying to convince the workforce that change is in their interest
- The Health Secretary trying to persuade people to improve their diet
- The Prime Minister trying to get people to volunteer more of their free time under the banner of The Big Society

All of these different examples have one thing in common. The object of persuasion is specific. Don't be too ambitious and seek to change someone's whole worldview. You don't have either the time or the ability to persuade someone into a drastic shift of their *modus vivendi*. Even today, asking an audience of evangelical Christians to submit to my hedonistic utopia in which all religious belief has been banished and replaced by the playing of violent video games, purely on account of the twenty minutes I have spent in front of them, is a hope in defiance of all historical precedent. So choose something you know you have a chance of achieving.

You need to be able to define in no more than two simple sentences the idea that you want to change. What position is the audience in at the beginning of your speech and where do you want to move them to by the end? What is going to happen to these people on the day you deliver your speech, if you get your way?

Then, work out how many of the audience need to change their position. Do you know precisely who you are targeting? It may not be everyone in the room. Some of the audience may agree with you already. Some of them may not matter so much, for your precise purpose. And you can probably live with a minority not agreeing with you, even after hearing your persuasive rhetoric. So, set your ambitions, both for the change of heart you are seeking and the scale of that change of heart.

If you conclude that your speech is essentially designed to persuade and you are clear both who you are seeking to persuade and what it is you are keen to persuade them of, then you have three strategies at your disposal. First, you can persuade them by means of a tightly reasoned exegesis of the issues, whose inexorable logic leads the audience to a conclusion they do not like but cannot avoid. Second, if you have the rhetorical gifts, you can stir them to a change of view by the sheer ferocity of the passion with which you convey your argument. You can sweep them along. Or, third, you can do a bit of both.

But be careful. Reasoned argument is always the better option. If you already have the rhetorical capacity to persuade people by the sheer magnetism of your personality you are welcome to carry on reading this book but you perhaps don't really need to. As Bertrand Russell, the foremost mathematician and logician of his time, is reputed to have said soon after encountering his new student Ludwig Wittgenstein, "there is nothing more I can teach you." In fact, please get in touch because if you are that good there is a great deal I can learn from you. But you won't be that good and it doesn't matter. You're not trying to be a facsimile of the greats. You're trying to control the power and direction of your argument and that is perfectly achievable.

In particular, a persuasive argument needs to take its opponent seriously. If you caricature the opposing view you will not be able to mount a credible attack. You will be knocking over an attitude that nobody has. You need to pose the view you wish to criticize fairly and succinctly. Try to describe it in the way that a neutral third party would describe it – as coolly and factually as possible. Then, when you come to make your persuasive denunciation, you have credibility as a witness.

Remember that your starting point is that the audience does not agree and that it has good reason for disagreeing. Your audience is not full of idiots. Even if it is, it is a poor tactic to tell them they are idiots. Not many people actually identify themselves as idiots. So, acknowledge candidly what your audience thinks. A good speech is not really a monologue, even though it looks like one. A good speech is a dialogue in the form of a monologue. A good speech is an argument and an argument needs someone to argue with.

A speech that contains no internal dispute will never work. Gordon Brown's first speech to the Labour Party conference as Prime Minister was ruined for this reason. The account he gives of the opposing arguments is a terrible caricature. The audience knows that Brown is creating straw men for the express purpose of knocking them over. The rule of thumb for presenting the views of your opponents is this: whenever you criticize an argument, cite the name of the person who thinks it. That will concentrate your mind on giving a fair account. It is easier to caricature an argument in general terms than it is to attribute an absurd view to an individual. Most disputes are just genuine conflicts of value. The other person may disagree with you but they are not necessarily an idiot.

There is a paradox about effective persuasion. Even when that requires you to knock somebody else over, you can only manage that by being generous first. Try to tell a story that you do not believe with the same conviction as a story that you do believe. Then, when you come later in your text to demolish it, the demolition will sound authentic and important. If, by contrast, you have dismissed an opponent as a ludicrous fool whom nobody in their right mind could ever take seriously, there will be little satisfaction when you come to lavish your fury on them later. If you as the speaker don't take the opposing view seriously, why should I? Actually, if you think the opposing view really is that rubbish, then surely nobody will be fooled by something so evidently ridiculous? The fact that you still think it is worth demolishing such an obvious buffoon implies that you think I, the member of the audience, might actually fall for this person's tomfoolery. In which case, you are patronizing me and implicitly suggesting that I, your listener, am pretty stupid.

None of this is good. None of this is good at all. You have started by trying to knock over your opponent and within minutes you are knocking over your audience. And it all flows from your refusal to start your denunciation with a generous account of your opponent's real views.

Speeches that Seek to Inspire

Perhaps the most difficult of the three categories of speech is the address with the intention of inspiring an audience. The quality of charismatic inspiration is so much a matter of the chemistry between the speaker and the audience that it is less susceptible to good preparation of material.

If you conclude that the primary function of your speech is inspirational you need to ask yourself some tough questions: am I up to this? Can I pull it off? Not many people have the capacity to be inspirational and there is no shame in admitting that you are not among their number.

A speech which is seeking to inspire and yet falling conspicuously short can be excruciating to behold. The commodity that an inspirational speech distributes is confidence. You are trying to make the audience believe, through sheer force of personality, something that they do not believe at the moment. You will no doubt want them to act on that belief at some later point. That transmission of confidence will be impossible if the audience immediately loses confidence in you as a messenger.

Whenever people want an "inspirational" script they mean they want prose elevated to poetry. But the quality of inspiration can be quiet and exemplary rather than loud and declaratory. You don't have to do your impression of Robin Williams from *Dead Poets' Society* or start talking like Major Tim

Collins addressing his troops before they saw front-line duties in Iraq.

Examples of an inspirational speech would be:

- A protestor encouraging students to join an anti-capitalist vigil
- A politician generating enthusiasm from the party faithful at a rally
- A teacher instilling confidence in low-achieving students that they are good enough
- A football manager addressing his team when they are 3-0 down at half-time
- A boss producing an even better performance from her team of freelance buyers

It is hard to get past Winston Churchill when we are thinking of speeches of pure inspiration. When Churchill addressed the House of Commons on 18 June 1940, he gave the speech that we know now as the "Finest hour". His express intention was to inspire. The speech does contain aspects of information and persuasion. Churchill wants to inform the people of recent defeats and he wants to persuade them that fighting is the only option. But the basic function of the speech is inspirational. Inspiration in general, however, makes no sense. We need to be inspired for some specific purpose, to some end. The specific purpose of this speech is to ensure that the British people are ready to stand firm in the face of the impending Battle of Britain.

The best example of an inspirational speech from recent times is Barack Obama's brilliant speech in Grant Park,

Chicago, on the night that he won the Presidency of the United States of America. This beautifully crafted piece of work illustrates the danger of inspirational rhetoric, which is the same as its main virtue – it heightens expectations.

For you, the lesson learned from Grant Park is not to mimic Obama's language or his delivery. It is that the hopes that rhetoric excites need to be specified. If you inspire people in general but not to do anything in particular, people will supply their own account of what they believe they were promised. This is how disenchantment begins in politics and the same principle applies in other fields. You must make sure that, if you do manage to be an inspiration, you are a specific inspiration. Otherwise, you will find that, at a later date, nobody is quite sure what you promised would happen.

In Churchill's case the inspiration comes from the imminent threat of invasion and catastrophic defeat in war. In Obama's case it comes from the extraordinary meritocratic advance of a black man ascending to the highest office in a country in which his immediate predecessor generations did not even have full civil rights. These are not rhetorical advantages you are likely to enjoy.

But that doesn't mean that an inspirational speech is entirely out of the question. Leadership comes in many forms. You can, for example, inspire people in plain language by force of the case you make. An inspirational speech, for all but the most accomplished orators, is therefore best approached through the subsidiary method of relevant information and rational persuasion. Your own attitude can be eloquent even if your words are plain.

The Combination of Elements

These are the three functions of a speech and it will help you to be clear what your main purpose is. But, once you have done that, you will soon notice that the three functions are not entirely separable. As we have worked through them, other functions kept creeping in. This is inevitable and it will be rare that a speech has an exclusive function that does not rely to some extent on at least one of the other two functions. All good speeches combine the elements but they do so in a way that makes one function the consequence of the speech, which the subsidiary functions help to cause.

You can see the effective combination of functions at work in some of the great and most memorable speeches.

FDR's Inauguration Speech, 1933

In Washington DC on 4 March 1933, Franklin D. Roosevelt gave his inauguration speech as President at a time of economic peril for the United States. The prospect of a long and damaging recession was already stretching out in front of the nation. Roosevelt knew that his time in office would be defined by his ability to respond. The inauguration speech was his manifesto and his rallying call.

The principal function of the speech is therefore inspirational. He needs to rally the nation both to optimism, which seems ill-founded in the circumstances, and to action. This function is encapsulated in the famous line by which the speech has always been known: "the only thing we have to fear is fear itself".

But a closer analysis of the text shows that it works by placing the three functions in order. First, the listener is given the relevant information. Roosevelt's account of the state of the American economy is candid to the point of being gloomy. Without this candour he would lack credibility as a witness with an audience that is already experiencing the reality of recession. Any attempt to hoodwink them into believing that things are fine is doomed to fail. But Roosevelt then uses this account to persuade his audience that, with their engagement, recovery is possible, even imminent. This point leads naturally to the famously inspirational peroration.

All three functions that a speech can perform are combined in his text but the inspirational function is the dominant one. The information he provides and the persuasive argument he uses are both designed to lead to the concluding attempt at inspiring the nation. In this case, information and persuasion are the cause and inspiration is the effect.

Winston Churchill, House of Commons, 1940

The finest inspirational speeches ever made were those by Winston Churchill in 1940, when Britain faced catastrophe. The speech we know as "Blood, toil, tears and sweat" is heavily weighted towards its inspirational function. The information contained in the speech is not negligible but it is selectively deployed. The situation in the war was, in fact, truly dire and there were many times when Churchill teetered on the brink of untruth in what he told the House of Commons and the nation. In a sense, the persuasive function of this speech is directly in defiance of the information it contains. Churchill is trying to persuade the public to keep its faith even in spite of the accumulating evidence that such faith might be misplaced. It is from this combination that he conjures his central function, which is to inspire.

In both of the famous examples, information, persuasion and inspiration combine to make a striking rhetorical effect. The principal function of inspiration cannot be served without first supplying the right information. It is, in turn, difficult to imagine that anyone could be inspired without first being persuaded of the moral force of the case being made. The currency of that persuasion is information of one kind or another. The three elements clearly loop back on each other, relying on each other at every turn.

This will be true of your work, too, notwithstanding the fact that you are probably not trying to rouse a supine nation. But a speech which is designed principally to inspire an audience to give more money to charity will be an emotive and vivid text. Its imagery will tug at the heart strings as it conjures a sense of shame at the injustice that bedevils the lives of people who deserve no ill-fortune. In this case, as in most cases, the inspiration that something ought to be done can hardly be completed without supplying some information, both about the scale and the nature of the injustice that calls out to be redressed, and about the efficacy of philanthropy in rectifying it. The combination of relevant information and inspiring language will also, you hope, be persuading those members of the audience who think this is the job of government to widen their narrow view.

Your speech will have subsidiary aims. But they are in the service of the dominant function. You need to separate the one from the other because you cannot organize your material if you are unclear about this. To put the same point more bluntly, you need to know why you are doing this speech at all, rather than staying at home and doing something else. We all have that option and, if you don't know what you are hoping to achieve, you can be sure that I won't either.

Writing a Statement of Intent

If I were more prone to cliché, I would have called this section the mission statement. After you have worked out what type of speech you are delivering, try to capture your objective in some plain English. It will help you as you proceed to refer back to this statement of intent, to help to direct you in the selection of material that will follow. The next chapter is designed to specify this objective further, but it is important always to keep this general purpose in mind.

Here's one way to discipline yourself. Get a moderately sized Post-it note. You are going to write your objective for this speech on this Post-it note. The point of this is not that you can stick it to your computer as you write (though you can). It is to show you how tightly defined it needs to be. Your statement of intent cannot run to any more than two lines. It should say exactly what you want to accomplish with this speech. If you begin with the words "After my speech, the audience will . . ." you cannot go too far wrong.

Maybe, after your speech, the audience will be really well informed about the plans for a new email system. Maybe, after your speech, the audience will be persuaded that tuition fees were a great idea all along. Or maybe, after your speech, the audience will be inspired to walk straight onto the local nature reserve and start picking up litter.

Whatever it is that you have informed them of, or persuaded or inspired them to do, the instruction must be precise. So get the Post-it note. Don't stop writing until you've filled it. But do stop writing as soon as you've filled it.

Why Persuasion is Best

Your speech will have one of three functions, whether you know it or not. Or, rather, if you do not know it then your speech will have no function at all and there is no point in delivering it.

A speech with the principal aim of informing the audience is easy to construct but can be dull without the insertion of a little conflict. A speech with the principal aim of inspiring the audience can easily fall victim to your deficiencies both as a writer of poetic text and as an orator.

It thus follows that, wherever possible, you should try to turn your speech into an occasion on which you are planning to persuade your audience of something. In the course of persuasion, you will require plenty of information, and you will always be able to convey what you need to convey. You will, if need be, be able to inspire as you persuade, the latter being an effective means to achieving the former.

So, my concluding advice, as you gauge your own expectations for the speech you are about to deliver, is to turn it into a persuasive speech. Think about the question that lies behind the information you have and persuade people of the truth of the case you wish to make. Think about why it is you might want to inspire people and persuade them that you are right.

Are You Still with Me?

At this point in the proceedings there is one last thing. You need to confirm at this point that you really want to carry on. You have conducted extensive research into the audience and you have thought hard about what it is that this group of people needs to be persuaded of and why you are the person to do that persuading.

Then you are attacked by a horrible thought. You're not sure you're the right person to do this. You're not even sure it needs doing at all, by anyone. You are worried it's a bit late to come to this realization and, in truth, it is a bit late. But it may not be too late. It will be too late soon enough but perhaps not yet. It may still be possible to switch the invitation to someone better placed to fulfil the brief. Remember that the invitation was probably issued by someone the chief executive bumped into at a cocktail party. Your boss probably found himself eating sausage on sticks next to some dreadful bore and, in order to extricate himself, agreed to do a speech one day in the distant future.

For future occasions, remember the rule that applies to all engagements. When you are asked to do something, ask yourself "would I really like to do this tomorrow?" If your instinct is to say no, then decline. Don't kid yourself that, because the speech isn't for nine months, it will never come round. One day, the speech actually will be tomorrow and you will have to turn up. At that point you will fall back on your usual remarks, your stump speech, your stock of clichés, your heard-it-all-before banality. It will be two hours of your life that you will never have back.

So, if you have realized you ought not to be doing it and, if it is not too great a professional discourtesy to pull out, decline as politely as possible and make a mental note not to get yourself into such a tangle in future. This invitation needs you more than you need it, but you could and should have worked that out earlier.

If you do not choose to disembark at this last moment, everyone that is left is going through with the delivery. The date is in the diary. The tickets are booked to take you there. The hall is getting prepared and you are expected. You know, more or less, what kind of people are going to turn up to comprise the audience. You know, too, what you expect from this speech. You know you have a purpose in doing it and you know what it is. So, should you start writing now?

No, not yet. Not exactly. It is certainly time to start thinking about the specific content that will become the final text that you deliver on the day. But it is not yet time to commit your thoughts to paper for the good reason that you still don't know what you are talking about, and a speech that is written before rather than after you work out what you are talking about will never be a good speech.

So that is the subject of the next chapter, which is the most important of the book. What is your argument? What, in a nutshell, do you want to say? What is the Topic of your speech?

CHAPTER THREE

TOPIC

There is nothing more important than the main argument of the speech. It is impossible to write a good speech without clarity about the central argument. Too many writers do not know what they have to say. You need to isolate your main point. You should spend most of your preparation time sharpening this central argument. Speeches that have no central argument demonstrate just how important it is. The main argument needs to be placed conspicuously in the speech and threaded throughout it.

The Topic can be addressed in a process of five steps. The first step is to get to the point where you can write down your main argument in a single, clear sentence. This is equivalent to the wrongly maligned idea of the sound-bite, which is, after all, just the most vivid encapsulation of the speech in a single phrase. Alternatively, you can consider this to be the title of the speech. The second step is to write the speech in a paragraph, ensuring that everything refers back to the central argument. Once that paragraph is tightly written and contains no extraneous material, the third step is to take the text up to a page, introducing the very best of your supporting material and facts. At this point you are ready for step four, which is to write a detailed and thorough outline of the speech. This is good practice in itself but it may also help to persuade the speaker to engage properly in the process and accept the speech as his own, if you are writing for someone else. The fifth and final step is to take the outline to a full draft, which is the subject of Chapter Four on Language.

The Main Argument

There is a case for saying that there are three great thinkers in the history of rhetoric: Aristotle, Cicero and Peter Sellers. Aristotle and Cicero we will come to in due course but, as an example of how not to do it, take a look at the great Peter Sellers sketch called the Party Political Speech (you can see the sketch at http://www.wepsite.de/Party%20Political%20 Speech.htm). You will note that Sellers talks and talks, fluently and easily, without ever getting even close to a central argument. The comedy derives from the fact that he is breaking the cardinal rule of good rhetorical writing. He is refusing to get to the point. Or, rather, he doesn't have a point so he is skirting the issue. The reason we find this funny is not actually because it is a good satire of politicians who refuse to get to the point. It is deeper than that. Sellers is playing a politician who doesn't have a point to get to.

This is the most fundamental point in the process of writing a good speech. This is where we hit bedrock. The next two sentences should be carved in rock a hundred feet high. Get the main argument right and you cannot write a bad speech. Get the main argument wrong and you cannot write a good one. President Eisenhower put it well: "If you can't put your bottom-line message on the inside of a matchbook, you're not doing your job." You need to know your main point and be able to explain it, in language that is easily comprehended, by an intelligent person who is not a specialist in your field.

The great Roman authority on rhetoric, Cicero, gave the main argument of a speech the title of the Topic, which is what I shall call it from here on. Note at once that the Topic is not just the vague subject of the address. It is an argument about that subject. So, for example, "First World War Poets" is not a topic in this sense of the word. "Wilfred Owen is a better guide to the pity of war than Rupert Brooke" is a topic. As soon as you make a statement with which someone might disagree, you have alighted on a topic. Reverse the statement you have made – "Rupert Brooke is a better guide than Wilfred Owen". It still makes sense (although it is now wrong). You have found a Topic for your speech.

In an essay on Tolstoy's theory of history, the philosopher Isaiah Berlin once borrowed a famous distinction from the Greek poet Archilochus, which you might bear in mind. The fox, wrote Berlin, knows many small things. The hedgehog, though, knows one big thing. Lots of speeches are written, as it were, by foxes. They are full of very many small things. The better speeches are written by hedgehogs (I bet you never thought you'd read that sentence). They know one big thing and they argue it well. It seems like odd advice but it is good advice: try, as far as you can, to be a hedgehog.

The work on the Topic, to which you will be introduced in this chapter, will take up most of the time devoted to the preparation of the speech. Only after this is absolutely nailed down and completed can you start writing. Until you know what you want to say you do not know what research to do. You have no way of knowing what is relevant.

The work of a speech writer splits into three phases – before writing, writing and after writing. Before you write, you work out the argument. After writing, you refine and adapt the writing. Both of these phases are more important than the middle section. Indeed, good writing really is thinking and editing. Otherwise, you're just a typist.

Speeches With No Topic

The best way to see the Topic is to consider speeches in which the central message is either absent or obscured. In the examples that follow, the lack of a defining passage in the speech means that the speech lacks any definition. The writer has never quite got the point of what they were trying to say. There are some good lines, some good sections and some useful points. But the speech fails to take off because the speaker hasn't really got anything important to say. The speech becomes memorable for a negative reason. It is not as good as it needs to be and a poor speech on a big day is worse than calling in sick.

The best recent example of a poor speech on a big day was supplied by David Davis. In October 2005, Davis and his rival David Cameron both had to speak at the Conservative Party conference, to put before the assembled members their case for being leader of the party. Davis began the conference week as the clear favourite. By the time the week was out, his prospects of being leader were all but over.

Davis is not a gifted speaker. His delivery is wooden and he appears uncomfortable at the podium. His jokes fall flat. There is an old theatrical story about an actor who goes on stage every night and, as he enters, the action is such that the line "can I have a cup of tea?", delivered deadpan, elicits a big laugh. On the final evening of the run, the actor goes on and decides to milk it. He delivers the line with a flourish. Nobody laughs. A wise old actor tells him when he comes off that all through the season he has gone onto the stage and asked for a cup of tea. Then, on the last night, he went on stage and asked for a laugh. That is exactly what David

Davis did. Short of doing the mime of a drum roll and a crashing cymbal, Davis couldn't have made his gag lines more obvious. Unfortunately, that crushed whatever sliver of humour there was hidden in there.

The leaden comedy was not the only reason Davis flunked the speech. He died on stage, essentially because he had nothing to say. At the very moment that he had to articulate how he would take the Conservative Party to victory, he veered all over the place. The moment called for an inspirational speech. But genuine inspiration is not like a self-help manual. It requires more than the repetition of well-worn phrases. You can't give people confidence by telling them to be confident. You inspire confidence by being good. The stock piece of advice for writers applies here and it applies pretty much everywhere: show, don't tell.

You can see from the extracts below, which come quickly after one another in the speech, that Davis has no thread of argument. In its absence, he swings almost at random from terrorism to attacking Tony Blair, to stories about himself, then on, with no connecting tissue, to jibes about Gordon Brown. Then it's back to a bit more on terrorism and crime, an afterthought about schools and a few more stories about himself. It's like the opposite of a highlights package. It's an animal drawn on folded paper by several different people in the child's game. The overall effect is negative and destructive and even a partisan audience needs more than that. They need to know why they might be great – especially when they are struggling to win – not just hear it repeated that the political adversaries are horrible.

> "Maybe it sounded all right in Islington. But we know what it really meant in the most deprived areas of our inner cities: more drug pushers, and more ruined lives."
>
> "It's a policy so completely, so utterly ridiculous, I am amazed it didn't come from the Liberal Democrats."
>
> "I don't often say this, but sometimes the French get it right."
>
> "And we mustn't accept it when people living here can't speak English."

The contrast with David Cameron's speech is marked. A great deal of the attention on Cameron in the days that followed was on the method of delivery. Indeed, it was a theatrical coup to speak without notes and with no lectern. It was a bravura demonstration of confidence, a show of strength. The very fact of speaking like this was a statement in itself. It said that, at moments of importance and crisis, I will not only be calm, I will take calculated risks and I will be a different sort of leader.

Yet the speech cannot survive if it is nothing but the sum total of tricks of technique, no matter how good they might be. The trickery could have gone the other way. It could have gone down in folk memory as a desperate attempt to change the terms of the argument from a confident but essentially empty speaker.

Although it is hard to recall what Cameron said in any detail, the single message of his speech was very clear. His single sentence summary was "this party will keep losing unless it changes". As he expanded the message from a sentence to a paragraph he added that "I am the only politician in this race able to make that change. I am a winner and I will win for you." His method was the visual exhibit which showed the truth of his method. Showing and telling came together in a very effective performance of rhetorical theatre.

Turning Davis's partisan rubbishing of Labour to the opposite effect (to show how the Tories still couldn't win, even against that bunch of jokers), Cameron told the Tories what they knew they needed to hear:

> We meet in the shadow of a third consecutive election defeat, defeated by a government that has complicated the tax system, dumbed down the education system, demoralised the health system and bankrupted the pension system.
>
> It has made promises that no one believes, passed powers to a European Union that nobody trusts and set up regional assemblies that nobody wants and nobody ever voted for.
>
> And still we were defeated. We were defeated by a government that won fewer votes than any in history.
>
> But let's not blame the electoral system. Let's not take comfort in solid but slow progress. Let's have the courage to say: they've failed – but so have we.

This opening grabbed attention, which justified the need to change. The rest of the speech then went on to support that case and explain why David Cameron would be the one able to make that change. It ended on a positive and inclusive vision:

> So let's build together a new generation of Conservatives. Let's switch a new generation on to Conservative ideas. Let's dream a new generation of Conservative dreams.
>
> If we go for it, if we seize it, if we fight for it with every ounce of passion, vigour and energy from now until the next election, nothing, and no one, can stop us.

Reading Before Writing

When you sit down to think about your main argument, you already have a lot of knowledge at your disposal. You know your audience. You know what you want your speech to achieve. You now have to do the most important thing of all, which is to decide what you want to say.

Of course, an argument does not come from nowhere. You might be tempted to think that it would be better to begin writing so you can discover your argument, buried somewhere in your thoughts. There is no reason, in theory, why this cannot work. When a writer gets very practised at spotting the main point, it is possible. But, as a general rule, the inexperienced writer will be better advised to build upwards from a steady base.

This may be a speech on a subject that is very familiar to you, in which case you will already know the range of arguments that you might conceivably mount. But if the subject matter is relatively new, you will need to start reading. Or, to put the same point better, you should carry on reading. A good writer should always be reading. It shouldn't require the pressure of a looming deadline to force you to read. Absorbing good writing is how writers do their research and they never stop.

When he was asked how he got the idea that a toad could stand as a metaphor for work, Philip Larkin replied irritably that it was sheer genius. F. Scott Fitzgerald got closer to the truth when he said that a good writing style is an amalgam of reading at least half a dozen good authors every year. The short advice is: read as much as possible. And not the stuff you would normally read for work, the stuff you have no choice but to read. Try to select some material because it is well written. It doesn't much matter what the subject matter is. Just try to find some good authors, people who are good writers as well as people who share an interest with you. A speech is like a lyric but in speech writing the lyrics also create the music. The way we arrange the words has a musical effect and the only way to get their music in your head is to listen to it as much as possible.

Where Do I Put My Topic?

You will no doubt be familiar with the advice that you should begin your speech by telling the audience what you are about to say, then spend most of your time saying it before ending by telling them what you have just said. This isn't silly advice but it will make your speeches repetitive and, unless your phrasing is clever enough to dress up the same point in radically different garb, an audience will feel a little short-changed and very possibly patronized. So, you need to think in a slightly more sophisticated way.

The main point to grasp about your Topic is that this is your method of selecting material. If you are using the Topic correctly then everything you include will, in some measure, refer back to it. There is no harm in being explicit and making the central argument abundantly clear.

Here, the standard advice is not far from the truth. It does make sense to prefigure your argument. It is good practice to tell the whole tale in miniature in the first still. There is a case for presenting a version of your Topic almost at once. It grabs the attention of the audience and gives them a clear sense of where you might be proposing to take them. In this sense, the choice before the speech writer is the same as that which lies before the thriller writer. Do you reveal the mystery early on and then get the effect from the slow unveiling of how it came to be so? Or do you leave the mystery open, in which case the thrill for the reader is to discover the truth? In general, the first approach works better for the public speaker as your function is to enlighten the audience, not to tease them.

The main body of your argument will be in the middle of your speech. So you will certainly need a crisp statement of the main argument at this point. As I said earlier, there should be nothing in the speech at all which does not strike off this central thought but you do want to work towards the pithiest possible encapsulation of the speech. Try to think of a sentence that could stand as a summary or, even better, a few words that will be the title of the speech. Then, at the end of the speech, as you reach the conclusion, it is good to find a new way of emphasizing the central idea.

Many famous speeches have used this technique. The last line of Churchill's "This was their finest hour" speech was, indeed, "This was their finest hour". The last line of Obama's "Yes We Can" speech was "Yes we can".

But some of the more memorable messages have actually been put in the middle of speeches. Nobody really remembers how Martin Luther King's "I have a dream" starts or ends. The famous passage is right in the middle. The end lines are actually:

> that day when *all* of God's children, black men and white men, Jews and Gentiles, Protestants and Catholics, will be able to join hands and sing in the words of the old Negro spiritual:
> *Free at last! Free at last!*
> *Thank God Almighty, we are free at last!*

The virtue of these words though, quite apart from their biblical poetry, is that they are a different way of saying the same thing. The audience feels they have heard something new because the expression is so poetic. But the meaning has simply been repeated. We have been treated to the central argument again, without us quite realizing. That's because King knew exactly what he wanted to say. He had already said it and here he says it again, beautifully.

On 4 June 1940 Winston Churchill addressed the House of Commons at a critical point in the Battle of Britain. The speech, which is a masterpiece of economical writing, is known to us today by its most arresting phrase "we shall fight them on the beaches". This is, once again, not the final line. The speech actually ends like this:

> **we shall never surrender**, and even if, which I do not for a moment believe, this Island or a large part of it were subjugated and starving, then our Empire beyond the seas, armed and guarded by the British Fleet, would carry on the struggle, until, in God's good time, the New World, with all its power and might, steps forth to the rescue and the liberation of the old.

Churchill is pulling the same trick. He too repeats his central argument but finds a new way of saying it. The two instances of the argument are a complementary pair, separated in the speech but anchoring it into the meaning that he knows he wishes to communicate. By the way, Churchill is the best example of someone who worked at his speeches until he had them just as he wanted them. It would not be inaccurate to say that a political lifetime went into the production of Churchill's war time speeches.

What these two examples have in common is repetition.

> We shall go on to the end, we shall fight in France,
> **we shall fight** on the seas and oceans,
> **we shall fight** with growing confidence and growing strength in the air, we shall defend our Island, whatever the cost may be,
> **we shall fight on the beaches,**
> **we shall fight** on the landing grounds,
> **we shall fight** in the fields and in the streets,
> **we shall fight** in the hills;

The Five Steps Towards the Topic

But, before we can worry unduly about where the Topic fits in the speech, we need to write one. As this is the most important aspect of the whole process, it makes sense to break it down into clear units.

I have broken down this stage of the preparation into five steps. If you follow these steps you should arrive at the end of the chapter with a very good sense of what you are seeking to do as you begin to write the draft, which will be the subject of the next chapter.

Step One: The Topic Itself

Cicero called it the Topic. Aristotle called it "the seat of the argument". But, whatever you call it, you need to understand what it is. This shouldn't need saying, but it does. You need to know what your argument is. You need to be able to declare, in a single crisp sentence, what the essence of your speech is. Why are you moved to say it rather than not? Why should anyone give up any of their time to listen to you?

Experienced writers find it impossible to write without doing this. Their work is structurally sound just by sheer force of repetition. They no longer need to remind themselves to have a purpose and instructions to do so are patronizing. So, with apologies to the experienced writers to whom the following instruction will be superfluous, it may be a good idea to turn this into a formal process.

Write a statement in which you define your argument. Remind yourself of your conclusions about your audience and your expectations for the speech. These two pieces of information combine to produce your general purpose. Now it is time to focus on your specific purpose. What is the argument, in a nutshell, that you want to communicate? And what exactly do you want people to do after you have sat down? The very act of forcing yourself to write these things down will reveal the shortcomings of your speech. If you can't fill out this form with something convincing, you don't really have a speech.

Here are some examples of speeches in a sentence. See if you recognize them. The point in each case is that the speech did allow a simple summary. It would be wrong to say it lost nothing by being reduced to a single line, but the fact that the summary is possible shows you why the speech works when it is expanded to full length.

- It is intolerable that black people do not enjoy civil parity with white people
- We cannot afford to allow tyrants to stay in power in a world made more dangerous by stateless terrorists

- More government is not the answer to all your problems
- The British Empire will fight to the death to preserve its freedom
- Imperial power is unjust but we will resist only with peaceful means

These five speeches are, in order, Martin Luther King's "I have a dream", Tony Blair on the Iraq war, John F. Kennedy's presidential inaugural, Churchill in the House of Commons in the summer of 1940 and Mahatma Gandhi's philippic against colonial rule.

Then, below, I have attached some stylized examples of speeches that you might conceivably be called upon to deliver. All the descriptions below are short and pithy but not all of them work as a governing idea. It ought to be obvious which ones fall short, and why. The last one, which does work, will recur as a worked example as we proceed through this chapter and the next, culminating in a full speech for delivery.

- This company has a vibrant future if it can just stay true to itself
- The rise of more open communications platforms will suffer a backlash as people seek more privacy
- Wealth and income inequality are the biggest problem facing Britain today
- Britain will have to find a new way to make its living in the world in the future

- Obesity is more of an individual than a corporate responsibility
- A company which pursues profit alone will not achieve even that

There are varying degrees of specificity here. The second and fifth sentences are clear and precise. They are assertive and therefore could be the basis for a good speech. The third and fourth sentences are nearly good enough. They do say something but they are too broad. They leave too much open to question and do not narrow the field of inquiry in a way that is necessary for a good speech. The first one is awful. Broad, general, imprecise, close to meaningless. That doesn't stop similar speeches getting made, as they are all the time.

If it didn't strike you at once why the poor examples did not work, you need to stop and think more about this. The reason will always be essentially the same. The phrase you have written is too vague. It cannot be disagreed with. Try writing the opposite of what you have written. If it makes sense, you have a credible Topic. If it makes you laugh, you don't.

Take the following examples. If your main argument were "The British economy will not grow next year because the government does not have a plan", your diametrically opposing statement would be "The British economy will grow next year because the government does have a plan". It may be right or it may be wrong but it is certainly meaningful. Your Topic statement passes the test.

But imagine instead that you had written "The government intends national well-being to grow over the next five years", the opposing statement would read "The government intends the population to get more miserable over the next five years". Your Topic statement is banal because the opposition leads you to say something absurd.

The modern, derogatory word for these short descriptions is the sound-bite. Almost always associated with the maligned idea of "political spin," the sound-bite is often said to be a symbol of our diminished politics in which cynical politicians boil down meaningless expressions in an attempt to dupe the electorate.

A good sound-bite is much better than this. What is it if it is not a vivid encapsulation of the purpose of the speech? It's not a craven attempt to curry favour if you are able to capture your message in a memorable phrase. It's the art of good speech writing at the atomic level. It's a good discipline, the equivalent of the title of a book or the signature passage in a symphony. "To be or not to be" – that really was the question. That's the big dilemma posed by the play, beautifully wrapped up in a phrase. None of us are exactly Shakespeare, but that's who we are trying to be.

It is, as Mark Twain once said, "a minimum of sound to a maximum of sense". Good writing like this is poetic in the sense that it is a form of compressed meaning. A lot gets said very quickly. This is quite the opposite of the current connotation by which the sound-bite is said to refer to speech with no meaning or content at all.

The sound-bite as the title of the speech

Most speeches will not be contenders for coverage in national newspapers or the national broadcasters. But some are and many others may be covered in local newspapers. Anyone who has ever had a speech mediated by someone else will understand what happens. No matter how lovingly the words are crafted, no matter how tight the structure and how perfectly executed the speech is, most of it will not survive the brutal editing process of newspapers and television. Your speech is going to be reduced to a few phrases, like it or not.

It will end up as a sound-bite if it receives any attention at all. So you might as well try to get the right sound-bite covered. You might as well try to get the coverage to include the phrases that actually convey the broader meaning of the speech, rather than have the speech distorted by a phrase taken out of context that gives a misleading impression.

The resonant phrase is the one that sticks in the memory. In politics it's the one phrase journalists will take with them. In business speeches, a short phrase or fact may be the one thing your audience takes with it. If it's the only thing people remember, it has to be good.

Let's look at some examples to show how the crucial importance of the central message governs the rest of the speech and makes all the difference between a speech that works well and one that does not work at all.

The first example is the speech that Lyndon B. Johnson gave to Congress in March 1965. It has become known as the "We shall overcome" speech. The general purpose of this speech was to persuade. The specific purpose was to urge Congress to accept equal voting rights for African Americans. This is encapsulated in the central phrasing of the speech when Johnson says "to deny a man his hopes because of his color or race or his religion or the place of his birth is not only to do injustice, it is to deny Americans and to dishonor the dead who gave their lives for American freedom".

We can see with some examples that the sound-bite doesn't substitute content. It *is* the content. It is the distilled central message, a phrase that if read in isolation would give a person a sense of what the whole speech had been about. Does anyone recall Margaret Thatcher's 1980 Conservative Party conference speech? Not when it is described like that. But when it is recalled as "The lady's not for turning", the recall is instant. This was no idle slogan or empty proclamation. It was designed to assuage doubts within the party that a reversal of counter-inflationary monetary policy was imminent. It was the core of her speech and the rest of the speech supported this central message.

The best recent use of the sound-bite was Obama's campaign trail speech in South Carolina. This is the speech that will always hereafter be known as "Yes we can". This shows the importance of understanding your audience. In Britain, the culture could not support such boundless optimism. There is an irony and a cynicism in British political life that makes "Yes we can" sound rather banal, almost silly. The fact that it is the slogan of Bob the Builder doesn't exactly help either.

But it works for Obama for two reasons. First, the lilting delivery is appropriate to South Carolina and the sense of possibility he evokes taps directly into the idea of American possibility. Second, Obama is running to be President of the United States of America. There is, in fact, a lot more that you can do if you are the leader of the largest country in the world. A lot more than if you are Prime Minister of Britain, for example. But, more than anything, the catchphrase works because it is short, easy to remember and embodies the optimism that was the wellspring of the whole Obama campaign.

In the passage below, note how Obama specifies the issue. He gives an example of cooperation between whites and Latinos. His case is not abstract, it is concrete. Not just that we can – we already have. Change must be possible because even people who were once tempted by racial politics can see the light. By the time the refrain of "yes we can" arrives it functions like the chorus of a song. The chorus answers the verse. The case, by now, is unanswerable.

When I hear the cynical talk that blacks and whites and Latinos can't join together and work together, I'm reminded of the Latino brothers and sisters I organized with and stood with and fought with side by side for jobs and justice on the streets of Chicago. So don't tell us change can't happen.

When I hear that we'll never overcome the racial divide in our politics, I think about that Republican woman who used to work for Strom Thurmond, who is now devoted to educating inner-city children and who went out into the streets of South Carolina and knocked on doors for this campaign. Don't tell me we can't change.

Yes, we can. Yes, we can change. Yes, we can. Yes, we can heal this nation. Yes, we can seize our future. And as we leave this great

(Continued)

> state with a new wind at our backs and we take this journey across this great country, a country we love, with the message we carry from the plains of Iowa to the hills of New Hampshire, from the Nevada desert to the South Carolina coast, the same message we had when we were up and when we were down, that out of many, we are one; that while we breathe, we will hope.

Step Two: A Pithy Paragraph

Even with a clear sense of the central argument, we're still not ready to write. The next step is to take that crisp statement and work it up in stages. This will help you to ensure that everything you are writing derives from this argument. If you pitch straight into writing the script now you will get lost in the weeds. You will start worrying about "who should I thank at the beginning and will we need to have a word from the sponsor and I hope he isn't too boring and what about those parish notices that I have to include somewhere? Oh dear it's going to be awful."

Leave all of that for the moment. Let's keep our focus on the crystalline argument we have got to and let it flourish a little.

The next step is to write the speech in a paragraph. Think of this paragraph as the account of the speech that you would include in the conference brochure or the account you would like to see appear in subsequent reports of your speech. A paragraph is enough to introduce your Topic, to capture your central argument in the best phrase you can think of and then suggest how you will conclude the speech. You can do the set-up, the body of the speech and the way you play out all in a single paragraph.

Let's continue the example we began above. Remember that the single sentence Topic was that "A company which pursues profit alone will not achieve even that". If we take that proposition and expand it to a paragraph it could look like this:

> The dominant contemporary idea of the company is that it is an engine for the creation of shareholder value. This is actually a recent idea. The company has historically always had deep roots in its society. Today, in highly regulated product markets and with intense media scrutiny, it is impossible to argue that companies can ignore their social obligations. But more than that, it is poor business practice to do so. The commercial good and the ethical good are, in fact, married in the best businesses.

You can see there is already a lot there. You can see where your research might lead, what kind of facts you might require. You have a nice balance between the past, the present and the future and every sentence contains real arguments with which a determined opponent might disagree.

Step Three: A Speech in a Page

When you are happy that you have a paragraph that is a perfect précis of what you want to say, expand it to a page. Sweat over this page until it's absolutely right. Be sure that you have covered the whole arc of your argument and that you have referred to everything that needs saying and nothing that does not need saying. Make sure that you have one or two supporting arguments and illustrations. But waste no words. This is not the moment to breathe out with your favourite anecdote. Keep it spare and to the point.

Writing this single page should have been made somewhat easier by the fact that you have defined a clear Topic. If you are sure of your big point, all the material can be judged against whether it helps make that point or hinders it. In fact, the moment you know you have matured as a writer is when you delete a great line because it's not relevant. It's not easy to do but you will come to find a great satisfaction in the knowledge that your argument has kept its discipline and will not be interrupted by a digression, even if it is a funny one.

For example, imagine that at precisely this point in the flow of the argument I inserted an old line to the effect that this book will be read long after Milton and Shakespeare are forgotten. But not until then. It's a good line and it often works to raise a self-deprecating laugh in a speech (in fact, borrow it if it fits), but it didn't fit here. It's a funny line but, in this context, it's not a relevantly funny line and you should be disciplined about sticking to material that tells the tale you should be telling.

Let's return to the example we have been working with about the essential purpose of the company. Here, in a page, is that speech as it might look:

A good company is one in which ethical norms and commercial profit are allies. When the two are separated, bad practice ensues and the company will not only perform unethically, it will also perform poorly.

The common view of what makes a good company is that it is one that gives the maximum possible return to shareholders while keeping its customers happy and obeying the law. In this account, the company is a great vehicle for innovation and it achieves this by ruthless focus on what matters, which is what works commercially. This is a clear view with some distinguished advocates but it is fatally wrong. Right now, in the shadow of a terrible financial crisis and a recession, perhaps on the verge of a depression, we cannot afford to reinstate business as usual.

Historically, the company has always been deeply rooted in its local society. In the nineteenth century the best companies were seen as community organizations which gave their employees far more than the boon of occupation. The truth is that no business can ever truly succeed in a society that fails.

A reputation for being a good business, good in the ethical as well as the commercial sense, is hard won but easily lost. Think of the companies which have had serious problems. Long

(Continued)

after they have acted to rectify the specific issue, they find the problem sticking to their name. Corporate action that drags business into disrepute will no longer stay private or detached from the rest of society. The scrutiny of modern media is too intense for that. Our markets are too tightly regulated.

The change that we need is hidden in the dual meaning of the word "good". A well-run business creates jobs and offers products that satisfy people's demands. It contributes to the tax base in all the nations in which we operate. But "good" has a moral as well as a commercial meaning. Four years ago, at High Windows Ltd, we put in place a philosophy that guides how we do business. We believe that there is more to business than the earnings cycle. Our basic idea is that a company has to marry its performance with its ethical concerns.

We have an obligation to our environment and we have an obligation to the people who work for us. The good company offers employees a career, not just a job. Good candidates can pick and choose more between companies which make similar offers to them. The deciding factor is the kind of company that they want to work for.

Its economic health and its ethical well-being are not separate entities. They merge. They feed off each other. They need one another.

As you write your own page ask yourself if you have illustrated your main points with your best fact. Have you given the point the most vivid dramatization you have at your disposal? If so, you already have a good speech in miniature. The page above is a decent speech. It has the structure of a speech and it does the work of a speech. It's pretty taut and although it wouldn't be a hugely satisfying thing to listen to, it does say something.

It's not an entirely crazy idea to consider reading it out on the day. It might just be the best thing you ever write. Plenty of speeches get worse the more they expand. Perhaps the occasion really does warrant twenty-five minutes from you. Perhaps you are expected to speak for that long, whether you want to or not. But if a full speech is not imperative, and if you have already said what needs to be said in the seven or eight minutes that it takes you to read it out, think about doing that. Remember that the Gettysburg Address, at 256 words long, lasted little more than two minutes. Your page on software solutions might never go down in history as Barry's famous "simplicity is best" speech but it might do the job you have assigned to it.

But the chances are that a page will not be enough and that you will be proceeding to write and deliver a full speech. So, let's go on to the next step.

Step Four: Writing an Outline

Now that you have a good page, it makes sense to write a full outline of the speech. Until you know you have a strong enough argument you cannot be sure that this is the speech you will deliver, so you ought not to rush into your outline until you really are sure.

But now, you are clear about your main argument. That should be the body of the speech and you need now to fill in the material that will lead you towards that central argument and the material that will lead you out of it, towards your conclusion. You can indicate the facts you will need as supporting material and the anecdotes that might be relevant. The principal point of your outline is to allow you to discard irrelevant material. Try to get into the habit of constantly referring back to your main argument on the Post-it note.

The outline is also an external agent of discipline which forces you to yield to a structure. It will stop you as you embark on a passage of flowery prose that, as well as being too ornate, is not germane to the argument. It will stop you changing the subject halfway through a paragraph and prevent the speech drifting away into irrelevance.

There is a good classical guide to the outline. Cicero's five canons of persuasion function as a guide to writing a good outline to a speech.

1. **Introduction** – set your goal, decide your tense and tone of voice and get to the point
2. **Narration** – a statement of the most pertinent facts
3. **Proof** – the corroboration and illustration of the superiority of your point
4. **Refutation** – destruction of the opposing point of view
5. **Conclusion** – restate your case and lead to an emotional pay-off

Be careful you don't try to pack too much in, though. It is only an outline, not a speech. The outline should not run to more than a couple of pages. Don't set yourself questions that are too big; questions that it would take a lifetime to answer. For example, a section called "The Eurozone Crisis" could go anywhere. The subject is vast and you have not given any indication of which aspect you wish to consider, or why. However, a section headed "Poor Prospects for Exports in the Midst of the Crisis" is much more precise. It delineates an aspect of the subject and suggests a relevant interpretation.

Here is a checklist of things you need to include in your outline.

1. Something to introduce the subject and gain the undivided attention of the audience
2. A quick preview of your argument, contained in the best phrase you can conjure, the one you devised when you wrote your speech in a sentence
3. The introduction of the main argument which sets the question that your argument is the answer to, which you considered in some detail when you wrote your speech first in a paragraph and then in a page
4. The Topic of your speech; the body of the text which by now you should know perfectly
5. The case for why your argument is a compelling answer to the question you set yourself the task of answering
6. The peroration and your concluding remarks

When you come to write the full text, each paragraph will require supporting arguments. Each one will need to be illustrated and the outline should give at least a flavour of the facts that will uphold the claims you intend to make. It is also a good idea to write the connecting sentences that are like the tissue of a speech. An outline can look perfectly logical and rational and then you find, later when you come to write, that the transition from one section to another just doesn't work. It just doesn't flow. So give some thought now to how you will get out of Part 1 into Part 2. Why does Part 3 flow naturally from Part 2? You might find connections occurring to you that suggest a different arrangement of the material.

Below I have written an outline, following the template I have set out, for the speech that we have been working through on the good company. You will see that this outline has a clear direction. It could function as the detailed notes from which a speaker would learn their text. It's not yet a speech but it is a platform for a speech.

1. **Opening: The Good Company**
   The Topic: a company which pursues profit alone will not achieve even that
   - A good company is one in which ethical norms and commercial profit are allies
   - When the two are separated, bad practice ensues and the company will not only perform unethically, it will also perform poorly
2. **Argument: Today's Company**
   - Description of the dominant model of the company today: primacy of shareholder value and return on capital

- Some examples of this model and its successes and virtues
- But the crash means that we cannot go on as before
- Facts about the scale of the crash, brands that have disappeared

3. **Riposte: Yesterday's Company**

- It is a modern idea that the company is rootless; history of corporate obligations to society
- Examples such as Ford, Hewlett Packard and English Quakers

4. **The Topic: The Marriage of Ethical and Commercial**

- The facts about the investment performance of ethical companies better than their less ethical counterparts
- The loss of value that derives from the loss of reputation
- The intensity of regulation and of media scrutiny
- The environmental obligation (facts)
- The challenge of recruitment

5. **Closing: Tomorrow's Company**

- How we at High Windows are trying to embody these principles
- Recruitment, environment, ethical trading practice

The outline as contract

A good outline can have another, political, function. Many people have to draft speeches for speakers who are more senior than they are in the chain of command. Anyone in this position, which will be most people who work as a speech writer in an organization, will find that hierarchy is an enemy of good writing. It is much harder to write a good speech if, as the writer, you only have a distant relationship with the speaker, who may be an intimidating senior executive.

There is little point complaining about this. It is, very often, a fact of corporate life. The advice for the senior personnel in a company is "make your speech writer more senior". Or at least, treat them as if they were. You cannot get any kind of rapport with them unless you are prepared to engage with them personally, and quite frequently.

But until the day arrives that the status of speech writers reflects their true importance, you will need a device to bridge the gap in the hierarchy between you and the speaker. It is possible to work through an intermediary, usually a chief of staff, and this can be helpful. However, the more people that get involved in the speech-writing process, the worse it is. There is a linear relationship between the number of people involved and the poverty of the final effort. A speech written by a committee always erodes the effort that has gone into articulating a central argument in the first place.

Ted Sorensen, who wrote most of John F. Kennedy's best lines, was clear about this: "while consultation might be widespread, a single man must ultimately wield the pen . . . the boldness and strength of a statement is in inverse proportion of the number of people who have to clear it". You will find, for example, that there is no joke, no matter how good, that will clear a committee of six people. Peggy Noonan, Ronald Reagan's best speech writer, described the consultation process for speeches in terms which call to mind the bureaucratic processes of several large companies: "like sending a beautiful new born fawn out into the jagged wilderness where the grosser animals would pierce its tender flesh and render mortal wounds. But perhaps I understate."

It's therefore crucial of the speech writer to act as an editor-in-chief. You need to keep people at bay and retain the right to reject their suggestions. A flurry of tracked-change suggestions is the ruination of any speech. Even if every comment has something to commend it (which won't be true), they will not all fit together. The effect of taking every comment seriously is to disembowel the speech. Part of the art of being a speech writer is political. You need to make people feel you have taken their comments seriously – indeed, you should take them seriously – but in the end you have to trust your own judgement about whether that comment can be incorporated. Not everything can. Not everything will contribute to the articulation of the Topic and it is very easy for the track-change commentators to undo all the good work you have done.

The authority to hold critics at bay is also a function of your level of seniority and this is a recurrent problem. Gaining agreement on an outline and treating it as a contract is the best device to circumvent an inefficient and dysfunctional process.

If you are relatively junior in your organization, you may not have the option of engaging with the principal at every necessary point. The ideal way of preparing the speech is to have a series of meetings about the main argument which then lead, naturally, to the next steps in the process. However, in most organizations this will not be realistic. You just won't get that much time with the boss. In truth, engaging the principal at this stage, with the production of an outline, is not ideal. The best time is earlier than this. But it probably will not be possible and it is likely that it is at this stage that you will get the opportunity.

If you just have the one moment, use it to try to secure agreement on an outline of the speech.

Here an intermediary, perhaps a chief of staff, could be useful. If you write a good outline, you then have a reasonable chance that it will be signed off by the speaker. If you can engage the chief of staff to vouch that the chief executive really did read the outline, rather than just give it a perfunctory tick, then so much the better.

You need, as far as possible, for this outline to be a contract. When you subsequently write to it and select material according to it, you need to be sure that the chief executive bears the responsibility for those decisions. You need him or her to stick to it. If they don't then I'm afraid there is not a lot you can do except start again.

Step Five: From Outline Towards a Draft

Some writers like to build out from this point. It can work for some people to write the speech in a couple of pages, once they have their central argument and their detailed outline. This is a great discipline because it forces you to exclude extraneous material.

Then, when you have a really tight two-page version, think hard about which parts of the speech are too compressed.

Which parts now need to breathe a little? Where do you need more explanation? Where would an illustration or a story make the writing more vivid? Add in this depth at the next draft, taking the speech up to 2,000 words or so. At this point, if you have done the job well, you probably have a very good, well-structured, tightly argued speech.

But this is the subject of Chapter Four. Taking the text from outline to draft is exactly what we will consider next.

Not Just Another Brick in the Wall

Following my own advice, this chapter began with the imperative that you need to know what your Topic is and to make it run through the speech, before ending with a version of it. This chapter has been designed to follow and exhibit that advice as well as dispense it.

The Topic of this book is that no good speech can be written without a clear argument. Of course, it is still possible to write a truly awful speech even when you do have a clear argument. If that were not true this book would only require the one chapter. But the reverse is not true.

If, by some chance, you read and absorbed everything else in this book (or indeed any other book on speech writing) and you unaccountably forgot to read this chapter, you would hardly know what to do. The process is like an organism; as Arthur Miller once said about good writing: "take out any single element and something is lost from the whole."

In fact, the best illustration of the importance of the Topic is on view in the Science Museum in South Kensington in

London. Go to the fourth floor, to the children's section. In the play area, there is a bridge that appears to be held up by nothing. There are no arches or supports yet so long as the bricks are all in the correct place they stay up to form a bridge. Any single brick can be subtracted without undue detriment to the overall bridge. It will not fall over. It looks a bit depleted, with a brick missing but it still functions as a bridge and as long as you avert your eyes to the aesthetic subtraction, it is still recognizably and practically a bridge.

Any brick except one. There is one brick which, when it is taken out, brings the whole bridge down. It falls to rubble at once. It is the fulcrum of the whole structure. The whole thing depends, invisibly, on that single brick and as soon as it is removed the bridge crumbles. That brick is the Topic of your speech and you cannot hope to succeed unless you know which brick it is and make absolutely sure you fix it into place.

CHAPTER FOUR

LANGUAGE

After the preparation you have done, the time has arrived to start on the task that features in the job title – it is finally time to start writing. It is usually an error to start writing by piling up as many words as possible and then trying to boil the resultant mass down to speech length. But do start writing. Don't indulge yourself with the notion that you have a glamorous condition called writer's block. Just get on with it. Remember that writing is mostly editing and you need to be ruthless with your own work. The best source for good advice on how to write well remains George Orwell's classic essay *Politics and the English Language*. Inure yourself to the jargon and dreary language which infests every profession. Above all else, try to be clear.

How Writers Write

The final element of being a good speech writer is the one that appears in the job title: writing. The connection between thinking and writing has been noted many times. Writing is arguing silently. This is the origin of rhetoric as a classical discipline. It evolved as an act of persuasion but also of discovery. The classical philosophers believed the skilled use of rhetoric helped to unearth the truth.

Writing is essentially a matter of saying things in the right order. Lots of speeches call to mind Eric Morecambe's great response to André Previn's charge that he was playing all the wrong notes. "I'm playing all the right notes" he said, "just not necessarily in the right order."

People are endlessly interested in how writers write. The conditions, the circumstances, the location of the writer all exercise people's curiosity. It is as if novice writers are seeking to unlock a secret process that they will find in a shed at the bottom of the garden or in the feng shui of the study. Writing is an intrinsically solitary and individual experience. The choice of when, where and how to write is yours. The truth is that there are probably as many different ways to write as there are writers and there is no single way to do it.

Hemingway wrote 500 words per day without fail. Balzac would drink more than 10 cups of espresso a day. Alexandre Dumas ate an apple at 7am each morning under the Arc de Triomphe. Thomas Wolfe wrote standing up. Iris Murdoch would emerge from weeks spent cogitating in the study to announce: "It's finished, all I need now is to write it down." Stephen King goes through these motions when he sits down to write: "I have a glass of water or I have a cup of tea. I have my vitamin pill; I have my music; I have my same seat; and the papers are all arranged in the same places." He writes ten pages a day even on holidays. Charles Dickens walked twenty to thirty miles a day. He also placed objects on his desk in exactly the same position, always set his bed north to south and touched certain objects three times for luck. It depends what works for you.

I would counsel against one method, however, at least at first. Some writers follow none of the precepts I have set out in this book. They like to start from the other end. They write a lot and then boil it down. They edit ruthlessly, striking out passages that don't quite work and arguments that aren't quite pertinent enough. They enjoy the process of cutting; finding an almost physical pleasure in the slow revelation of the central argument. This is more like chipping angels out of marble.

There is a line attributed to the sculptor Jacob Epstein which illustrates the point. It is said that when Epstein was asked how he got such a good likeness of his subject, the Labour Foreign Secretary Ernest Bevin, he said that he took a block of marble and just chipped off any bit that didn't look like Ernest Bevin. You could approach the task of writing a speech as taking an enormous block of text and chipping away every bit that doesn't look like your central argument. Of course, to recognize that central argument when it is revealed, you still need to know what it was when you began. It should come as a great satisfaction but not as a surprise.

There will come a time when you are a good enough writer to be able to do this. You will learn to recognize the argument that is hiding there, amid all that superfluous material. But it is unlikely you will be able to do that at the moment. It is a skill that comes in time and after a lot of experience. So you would be better off, at least for now, clearing away the clutter and concentrating hard on getting your Topic straight before you cover yourself in information.

Starting Near the End

We have now arrived at the point at which most people, erroneously, begin. Having surveyed the audience, worked out what we hope to achieve with the speech and come to a clear understanding of the main argument that the speech is set to articulate, we are ready to write. In fact, we are going to discover that most of the hard work has already been done.

The full process of writing a speech does take time. As Mark Twain once said, "It usually takes more than three weeks to prepare a good impromptu speech." But it doesn't usually take longer than that. Don't start so soon that your material grows stale or out of date. You will also tire of material which is good. When you have read something for the fortieth time you become bored with it. That does not necessarily mean that it will sound bad to an audience which is hearing it for the first time.

It is perfectly commonplace, and nothing to worry about, to have nothing on paper at all with two weeks to go. If your preparation has been as good as it should be up to this point, you can write a good speech from here in a week, with plenty of time left for rehearsal.

That is because the term "writing" is only a partial description of the task we are describing. The really hard work has been done in the thinking that we have done prior to the writing. It's nowhere near as hard as you think to turn good thinking into good writing. If you do find the process difficult, it will not be (as you might be tempted to believe) that you are a terrible writer who cannot string two words together. It will be because your initial template does not quite work. You'll need to go back and refine it. Then, when you have got the thinking right, the writing will come more easily.

Writer's Block

It is worth a quick digression here on writer's block. This condition – the claim that something is occluding inspiration and preventing the words from flowing, some malign external force that has some inexplicable reason in wanting to stop a speech getting written – is something peculiar to writers. There is no corresponding plumber's block or electrician's block. Imagine someone turned up at your house to fix the roof and then claimed to have roofer's block when you gave him the job to do. Writing isn't quite as mechanical as fixing things that are broken in the house but there is still a lot of pretention in the claim that a writer is "blocked".

The only way to unblock is to write. Just start. Stop complaining. Stop saying you've got writer's block as if it were an identifiable illness and get on with it. This is not just hard-bitten hectoring from a pull-your-socks-up merchant. It is based on the insight that you never depart all that far from your average standard of writing. There will be days when it all flows perfectly and you leave your desk convinced that the world has no more need of F. Scott Fitzgerald. The eloquence and rhythm of the prose you have just tapped out will, in due course, when it is revealed to an astonished public, make *The Great Gatsby* redundant. Nabokov's amazing lyrical rhapsody in *Lolita* is all very well but is nothing when set against what you have just been doing, and on the subject of regional sales, too.

These days will be less frequent than those occasions when you are convinced that everything you have written should be shredded at once. Perhaps you have already acted and shredded the lot. Well, don't. The invariable rule is that nothing you wrote on your great day will be as good as you thought and nothing you wrote on your bad day will be as bad as you thought. Your variability around the axis of your central standard simply won't be very much. Even on days when he was not at the top of his game, F. Scott Fitzgerald wasn't that bad. Even on their very best days, some writers, unfortunately, will never get above mediocre. But it just doesn't happen for a terrible writer to have a magnificent day. Equally, somebody capable of brilliance will not really be able to write appallingly badly. That writer might have a day on which she is flat and uninspired. But the internal editing that a good writer always does will screen out the truly dreadful before it ever gets committed to paper.

That Speech in Full

We have worked through a speech and done a good deal of thinking about what we are trying to say. The outline we wrote in the last chapter was thorough and left us with surprisingly little to do.

As we compose the full draft, it is helpful, at least when you are an inexperienced writer (the experienced writer does this without thinking about it), to keep the following checklist in mind.

- Does each point contain a single clear idea?
- Does each point add to your main argument?
- Does each point link neatly into the succeeding point?
- Are your facts pertinent and memorable?
- Are your stories relevant?

From the outline in the previous chapter and with these questions in mind, the speech that would follow is written in full below. The text below is spare and written with no great flourish or adornment. But it is clear and has a direction. It also lacks personal character because so far we have not considered the fact that somebody in particular has to make this speech. Translating a speech from the general to the specific is the subject of the next chapter.

The Good Company

Good afternoon, ladies and gentlemen. It's a pleasure to be here and a privilege to be invited to address this gathering.

My subject today is one that, no doubt, everyone in this audience will have great experience of. I am going to argue that a company which pursues profit, to the exclusion of all other values, will not achieve even that narrow aim.

The good company has to marry its ethics with its commerce, its morals with its money.

When the two come apart, as they have done in many companies in recent times, we find that not just bad practice is unearthed.

We find that the unethical behaviour is commercially toxic. Irresponsible and reckless lending led directly to the near-destruction of the financial system.

We cannot continue as we are and I want to offer us a way out, a way to do business of which we can all be proud, and from which we all profit.

At the moment there is a risk that the shareholders profit out of the pockets of the public.

There are those who argue, like Bob Reich, that "capitalism's role is to increase the economic pie, nothing more". Private enterprise, they say, is a great vehicle for innovation. Our prosperity has rested upon it. As Milton Friedman said, the business of business is business.

If you take this view of the company, you say it should just concentrate on the efficient creation of shareholder value.

If you take this view, you give the business a narrow focus: make the return on capital as large as you can.

If you then tie this view to the short-term horizon of the stock market, you get a simple and brutal assessment of the role of the company.

Make as much as you can, now. Don't give any quarter because we want a return, this quarter and every quarter. You can see how the pressure builds and how people are tempted to cut corners.

You end up with your company as a source of value but not really guided by any value.

I'm sure you recognize this portrait. I'm sure you've been in these conversations.

It's a very clear argument. It's to the point and it's what a lot of people think.

But it's fatally wrong. And, with the world's major economies going backwards, with corporate profits down 8 per cent from this time last year, time has run out on this view of the world.

Just think of some of the famous names that have gone. Companies that were in every household, part of all our everyday lives. Charred and burned by a Great Fire that began in the City of London.

Think about the impact on living standards. People on the median income in this country have not seen their wages rise, in real terms, for five years.

Think about the overall effect on the nation. Growth has gone into reverse. Investment and infrastructure spending has not been lower for two decades. The very standing of the nation in the world is at issue.

If this is the way that modern capitalism works best then heaven help us when it starts to do some damage.

Fortunately, we can seek the solution to our present ills in our own past.

The German economist and sociologist Max Weber famously pointed out the connection between the rise of capitalism and the ethic of Protestantism. The Quakers, who founded some of the world's best-known banks and confectionery firms, built whole communities around the company plant.

In the nineteenth century, the best companies were all seen as community organizations, rooted in the society which gave them a home. They gave their employees far more than the boon of occupation. They often provided housing and other benefits. Workers tended to live very close to the factory. The whole ambit of the company, from supply through to effective demand, was usually local.

It was companies like Ford that built America's middle class by making products people wanted, lifting the purchasing power of working people by paying good wages, and strengthening the communities in which they operated by supporting libraries, schools, the arts.

Much of America's health and educational infrastructure has been built out of the wealth generated by capitalists. Hewlett-Packard has been arguing for half a century now that profit is not its principal motivation. Pharmaceutical companies have put millions into AIDS research. Avon is one of the world's biggest investors in breast cancer research.

All of these companies saw themselves as citizens. These are the roots of the joint stock company. It was based on the explicit understanding that there is no such thing as a market that is not underpinned by social institutions.

Think about my company, High Windows. The markets for our products are tightly regulated, and rightly so. We rely on the contractual and legal frameworks that are underpinned by legislation. Anyone who doubts this should try doing business in a country in which those safeguards are absent. We draw our employees from the society of which we are a part.

The man who drafted the law of limited liability, the former British Chancellor of the Exchequer, Robert Lowe, once described companies as "Little Republics". And he was right. Today, of the world's 100 largest economic entities, 37 are companies.

High Windows is one of those little republics. Well, maybe not so little. With nearly £4 billion in revenue and operations in 22 countries, employing 10,000 people, we are a serious presence in every nation we inhabit.

We have learnt that, all around the world, we are only as good as our reputation. A good name takes a lifetime to build and a moment to destroy.

That is why we take our environmental obligations seriously. This is not an issue that can wait. We need to act now. Water shortages are already a reality in some places, at the same time as other places are flooded. Energy prices have rarely been higher.

I am proud that High Windows is Britain's biggest corporate user of alternative energy sources.

And I am delighted to be able to announce that, this year, we won the Trumpton Sustainability Award for green business.

That is why we take our responsibilities to our employees seriously. The labour market for young talent is more competitive than it has ever been in my business life.

We are finding, and I'm sure you are too, that young people are using value judgements, not just arithmetic, as they make their career choice. They want to work for a company that does good, not just a good company.

Their passion is a reminder that, if we share the concerns of our people, we will get the best from them.

When our employees across Africa told us they wanted to join the fight against HIV/AIDS, we established health centres to provide medical check-ups. I have never seen a reaction like it.

The small good for the company came out of a larger good for the world.

When our employees saw that terrible earth-quake in Japan, they thought of those people as their colleagues. They wanted to help. So we did. We matched their fundraising efforts. It was one of the best things we ever did.

In the market for talent, being responsible is not added once the business is taken care of. It is taking care of the business.

You can see that fact already in the numbers. The Ethically Responsible Index has been out-performing the standard index of large compa-nies for five years.

Today, we are publishing a document which sets out all the evidence for the fact that com-panies regarded as responsible are better eco-nomic performers than those whose reputation is, well, shall we say, less complimentary?

It has never really been true that business and morality can be separated. Now the numbers are in and we can prove it.

And we take that responsibility seriously. Four years ago, at High Windows, we put in place a philosophy that guides how we do business. We decided we wanted to be known as a good company.

That means we give the word "good" two senses. It means economically successful, of course. Performing well is a mission all of its own.

And we shouldn't forget that a well-run busi-ness makes a major contribution in the course of its routine activity. As entrepreneurs we create jobs and offer products that satisfy people's demands. We contribute to the tax base in all the nations in which we operate. We sponsor commu-nity activities and make philanthropic bequests.

But it also means "good" in a moral sense.

Our basic idea is that a company has to marry its performance with its ethical concerns. Its economic health and its ethical well-being are not separate entities. They merge. They feed off each other. They need one another.

Somewhere in the development of modern business, something important got lost. Somewhere along the line, the advocates of the joint stock company began to believe they were running a sovereign entity.

They forgot that a company operates under licence and therefore has to give something back. They forgot that the company owes an obligation back to that society.

That amnesia had terrible consequences. The crash brought down a bad reputation upon us all. Whether we like it or not, whether we recognize it or not, we have to reclaim the title of a good company.

It's not sentimental. It's not an afterthought once you've repaired the balance sheet. It's the key to good business itself.

Ladies and gentlemen, thank you very much for listening.

The Importance of Editing

Much of the work that went into the text above is invisible. A lot of material ends up on the cutting room floor. This is an important point about getting better as a speech writer. All writing is editing. For a bad writer the editing has to take place after the rubbish gets written down. As a writer improves she will find that most of the editing is internal. The rubbish gets filtered out before it appears on the page. The good writer produces words that hang on a structure by instinct. It might look spontaneous in the act of creation but there is a structural integrity to it that would be hugely conspicuous if it were absent.

Churchill, for example, was a ferocious editor. He would go back over his words time and again until he got them just right. As befits someone who took rhetoric incredibly seriously, for him rhetoric really was his route to the top of politics. Churchill devised his own template for writing speeches: "(1) *Strong Beginning*; (2) one tight *Theme*; (3) *Simple Language*; (4) *Word Pictures* – think of 'Iron Curtain', for example; (5) Emotional *Ending*." But, above all else, he would edit, again and again. Lots of novelists read each sentence out loud a number of times to see how it feels. It is a great deal harder to allow a poor sentence to slip through if you have heard it said. Given that you are writing for speech, this is an imperative.

There is a story in which the protagonist is usually said to be Henry Kissinger. I have not been able to establish whether the story is apocryphal or not but for present purposes that does not matter. The truth in the story applies to speech writing whether or not the incident described has ever happened. Indeed, I strongly suspect this story is itself a piece of rhetoric, which is to say that something like this probably once happened but over time good storytellers have clarified it and embellished it, drawing out the central elements, relegating the irrelevant aspects and turning it from a fact into a story.

Most anecdotes have this quality. Just related exactly as they happened they will rarely work as a piece of rhetoric. A story is crafted in the way that reality is not. You will need to work at your stories. There is no point trusting to memory and just telling it how it happened. It won't usually be as funny and you will end up at an embarrassing section of your speech by saying apologetically "well, you had to be there".

This particular story goes as follows. In the days after he had ceased to be Secretary of State, Henry Kissinger employed a new speech writer, a veteran of the White House and an experienced and able writer, to help him as he toured the world making money out of his insights. Kissinger, who is a notoriously hard task master, set the new speech writer his homework. The speech writer set to work diligently and when he had finished he took the finished product, of which he was moderately proud, up to Kissinger's hotel room, as requested. The speech writer was unaccountably nervous as he approached Kissinger's room. He was an experienced practitioner, who knew what he was doing, yet he was nervous all the same. He wanted Kissinger's approval but, all the same, he felt confident that his work was good – it was certainly of his usual standard – and so his trepidation was mingled with excitement.

He knocked on the door and Kissinger answered. With no preliminaries at all, not even a how do you do, Kissinger said curtly "put it there. Then come back in two hours." The speech writer did as he was bid and went away, a little sheepish. He had a horrible two hours' wait for the verdict and, after pacing his hotel room for most of that time, went back to see Henry Kissinger, exactly two hours later. He knocked on the door. It opened, as if by magic; it seemed like Kissinger had been standing right behind it, waiting for him. Again with not even a gesture towards friendly small talk, Kissinger held out the speech and said simply "Is that the best you can do?" Which meant, of course, do it again and this time make it good. Chastened and a little surprised, the speech writer took the text from Kissinger's hands and, even more sheepish now, trailed back to his room to see what he could do.

When he got back there and read the speech out to inspect it he was surprised to discover that Kissinger was right. The main argument wasn't properly threaded through the speech, some of the prose was decidedly purple and certain passages were overwritten. He had allowed some favourite locutions to survive even when they were not justified by the context. Most of all, his Topic was not as clear as it needed to be. The speech tried to do two big things and, as a consequence, did neither of them brilliantly. Because he was a very accomplished writer, the speech served both functions quite well but it served neither brilliantly, and Henry Kissinger obviously wasn't satisfied with anything short of brilliance, which was fair enough.

The speech writer had to concede that he was being well paid for this gig. So he got to work. He deconstructed the whole speech, parsing every sentence and paring the argument down to its essentials. By thinking hard, as hard as he should have done in the first place, about what it was at root that he wanted to say, the speech writer turned round a second draft remarkably quickly, which he knew was a lot better than the first one. The majority of the text remained unaltered but the extra attention that he had been forced to give to the main argument had improved the finished article a great deal. He took it back to Kissinger with a certain satisfaction and swelling pride that he had the ability, which Kissinger would surely recognize, to turn round something so much better so quickly.

When he arrived at Kissinger's hotel room he got the same routine. Kissinger opened the door spookily and took the speech, telling the writer to come back in two hours. Doing exactly as he was bid again the writer went for a walk around the hotel gardens, thought about going for a run even though he hated running and somehow managed to while away two hours. As he approached Kissinger's room for the verdict he realized that his nerves were getting worse rather than better. He knocked on the door and Kissinger, taking a little longer this time to open it, arrived with the speech in his hands. Without looking up, Kissinger delivered the same verdict, verbatim: "is this the best you can do?"

Scuttling away with his speech in his hands and his tail between his legs, the speech writer was at a loss at what to do. He had the evening to deliver a text that Kissinger was happy with. He had no specific feedback about what was wrong and didn't feel able to ask for any.

So, he got to work. He took the speech apart line by line and, to his immense surprise and chagrin, he found a few weaknesses still left. Perhaps he had got too close to the text because, as he read it out loud, regretting instantly that he hadn't done this earlier, he realized that many of the sentences were too long. Many of the phrases, which looked great on the page, belonged in an essay and not in a speech. Some of the subsidiary points were dwelt on at too great a length and he still hadn't nailed down the central argument. As he spoke the speech he began to wonder what the main argument really was. No sooner had it appeared than the subject subtly shifted. He built in more illustration and support of his central thesis and made every single sentence strike off his definition of his Topic.

Then a superb metaphor occurred to him. It was one he had encountered years before and made a mental note that the day would come when it fitted. Every metaphor has its day and this was it. He used it near the beginning and it worked perfectly, allowing him to jettison some of the more pedestrian argument; it made the point beautifully, in language that was poetic but also precise. He continued all night in this vein, reading out every line until there was no flab left anywhere. Every line was as taut as he could make it. Every paragraph proceeded from premise to conclusion, by way of illustration. Every one contributed to the main argument. His account of opposing views was concise but accurate and his rebuttal of those opposing views was witty and devastating. He worked so hard and was so pleased with the results that he recovered some of the confidence that had been eroded by two false starts. This was just about the best stuff he had ever written. He went to Kissinger's room with his new text and slipped it under the door.

The following morning the speech writer presented himself early at Kissinger's door. This time he was dismayed and more than a little annoyed to get the same routine. "Is that the best you can do?" asked Kissinger, holding the text out to the speech writer with, it now seemed, a touch of contempt. Taking the prospect of secure employment in his hands, the speech writer shot back that "yes, it is actually. It is the best I can do." At which the merest hint of a smile appeared on Kissinger's lips as he said ruefully, "Good. In which case, I'll read it then."

That's what you ought to be looking for. You need to aim for the standard that Kissinger imposed in this story and the standard of the speech that the writer, under pressure, turned out. You should be trying to impose that level on yourself. Try to make the speech as good as you can realistically make it, from the beginning.

Mind Your Language

You will be enormously helped as a writer if you become sensitive to poor uses of language, examples of which unfortunately abound in the business world. The best place to go for tips on how to write well is George Orwell's brilliant essay *Politics and the English Language*. Everyone who has to communicate clearly ought to read it. Orwell's essay, like the rest of his work, is full of basic common sense and there is nobody who writes about writing who does not owe a debt to George Orwell.

The purpose that Orwell set out – to write clearly – is the function of good speech writing. We are trying to communicate something. It is remarkable how many speech writers manage to obscure their message behind a screen of incomprehensible jargon and dead language.

This is Orwell's main piece of advice: be as plain as possible. Don't grandstand and show off. Speak in a clear and accessible way. Imagine someone of your acquaintance who is intelligent but not versed in the field on which you are about to speak. If you pitch your remarks to that person you will find that you cannot resort to jargon because you will be aware how little of it they will understand. Keep that person in mind as you write and you will remain clear.

Orwell demands of us that we write simply, avoiding metaphor and similes that are too common. Below, in the section on jargon, is a list of modern phrases that have become tired and weary through repetition. Some of them mean next to nothing in the first place but even those which were once vivid have lost their lustre.

Orwell also instructs us to use short words wherever we can. It can take a long time to work out that it is not necessarily clever to use longer words. They certainly sound clever but Orwell points out that the truly confident writer does not need to put everything he has in the shop window all at once. This is a reminder of what Hemingway said when he was criticized by Faulkner for his limited word choice: "Poor Faulkner. Does he really think big emotions come from big words? He thinks I don't know the ten-dollar words. I know them all right. But there are older and simpler and better words, and those are the ones I use."

Try to write like you speak. This is a speech, after all. It's very unlikely that you will speak in ornate sentences, full of Latinate words, when you are talking to friends. So don't do it when you are preparing a speech. This leads to Orwell's next excellent suggestion. If it is possible to cut a word out, cut it out. When we are speaking, a person who tries our patience by never getting to the point is a bore. The same is true in writing and the same is true twice over when writing for speech.

The Abyss of Jargon

Every profession has its lingua franca. Every profession has its own private vocabulary. But you need to be very careful to distinguish between technical words that describe a phenomenon that occurs only in your world (such as the terminology of inorganic chemistry or molecular biology, which have no counterparts in common parlance) and the temptations of jargon.

The use of jargon is a particular failing and the bane of most business presentations. You can tell when someone is using jargon because the language manages to sound both familiar and distancing at the same time. On first hearing you think some meaning has been imparted – and jargon therefore has a comforting illusion – but, on reflection, the meaning seems to dissolve. Jargon is usually worn like a suit of armour for the speaker. It is a way of warding off controversy and genuine meaning. The use of what Orwell once described as "pre-fabricated hen houses" allows you to take up the time available while seeming to say something. For the listener, there is the temporary thrill of seeming to belong to the club of which the speaker is clearly a member. By using this dreary private language, the speaker is marking out his territory.

I would start to compile a list of phrases and words that you instantly recognize as jargon. Then make a solemn vow to yourself. Repeat after me: "I will never say any of these phrases, ever again, neither in private nor in public. Especially not in public where other people might hear me and conclude I am a dreary person with no imagination."

Everyone will understand the types of terms I am describing. Below is a list of my own current anti-favourites. But this chapter would extend to book length if I were to go into detail on every horror I have encountered.

Poor writers often find long-winded and uninteresting ways of writing in the false belief that it lends authority to their text. In fact, it just makes them sound insincere because nobody really speaks in the passive voice and you do need to remember that this is a speech. You are actually saying it out loud.

A Dozen Dreadful Jargon Terms, Dead Metaphors, Terrible Clichés and Assorted Horrors

Be careful to avoid jargon and needlessly obscure terms. Every industry has its own special language. People use it in order to feel like they belong. To use the correct terminology is also a way of signalling that somebody fits in. It shuts out others and closes the profession off, an important function for every profession which erects large barriers to entry. The test of language is whether an intelligent layman would understand. Some technical terms are unavoidable but ask yourself honestly: is there a common English equivalent for this word I am about to use? If there is, use it.

Below I have set out some jargon phrases which you really ought to avoid using, with a brief reason for each one.

The following assortment of disasters is just for starters. I could fill a whole book with similarly idiotic phrases. Think hard when you are tempted to use a buzzword and ask your-self whether you would ever speak like that at home or if you were out with friends. If the answer is no (which it will be) why do you suppose that an audience wants to hear that rubbish? Why do they not want to be spoken to as if they were normal people, too?

1. **Thinking outside of the box** – what were you doing in the box in the first place? What box, anyway?

2. **Touch base** – you are not American (unless you are, of course). Why do you need to smatter your speech with metaphors from American sport that you don't watch and your audience doesn't understand? This one is allowed only at the Annual Convention of Rounders Players.

3. **At the end of the day** – this has become so stale with repetition. Best used only if you are actually referring to the session at the end of the day. This is what happens to dead metaphors. Their literal meaning lives on long after the metaphor has died.

4. **Going forward** – rather than what, exactly? Which direction are the rest of us going in? Backwards? Time always travels forward, doesn't it? Or are you trying to distinguish your business from those other businesses that go in for time travel? Do you think gatherings of historians talk about the past as "going backward"? Of course they don't because it sounds silly. The thing is, it's no sillier than you saying "going forward". So stop it. There is an epidemic of this one at the moment and I make a point of refusing to listen to a further word

of anyone who says it, even once. I know at that point that they have stopped thinking because a moment's contemplation will tell you that it's silly.

5. **Blue sky thinking** – do you just mean clear thinking? In which case it might be better to have a metaphor that was itself clear. Or do you mean imaginative thinking? Well, what is imaginative about a blue sky? Would a great painter show the sky cerulean to denote extraordinary leaps of mental prowess? I doubt it. The sky is a useless metaphor for thinking, in any case, but if you were forced to use it then you would almost certainly suggest that something interesting might interrupt the blue sky. Black sky thinking? Rainbow thinking? The point where the sun ends and the rain begins? Sometimes, if you play around with a cliché you can end up somewhere intriguing. Not this time, though.

6. **Give you a heads-up** – meaning simply to let you know. So what possible circumstance can you imagine in which it would not be better to say simply "I thought I'd tell you" rather than "I thought I'd give you a heads-up"? Again, a pointless sporting metaphor which manages to make you sound blokey and ingratiating while saying something entirely commonplace.

7. **Singing from the same hymn sheet** – have you ever been in a church in which people have been singing different hymns because they have been given different sheets? No, it never happens. It would be a serious breakdown of organization on the part of the church wardens, wouldn't it? And even if it did happen,

people would just share the right hymn sheet wouldn't they? They wouldn't carry on, with half the congregation singing Onward Christian Soldiers while the other half belted out Guide Me O Thy Great Redeemer. It's a load of rubbish. It's a really stupid way of describing people doing the same thing.

8. **Proactive** – here is a competition you can enter. The winner gets a free copy of this book. Please supply me with an example of a sentence in which it would be better to say "proactive" rather than "active". People use "proactive" as an antonym of "reactive". They just mean that they did something in advance. If they mean anything at all they actually mean that someone was "pre-active". They mean they anticipated an event. They acted early. Those last two sentences show there are ways of describing what you mean without using this awful, unnecessary word.

9. **Pre-order** – not content with ordering things, people now like to pre-order them. But what is pre-ordering exactly? It is, essentially, ordering something before it is generally available. It is what, in the good old days, we used to call "ordering" something. So how much before an order does a pre-order have to be to qualify for its prefix? If I pre-order the tickets a week before the people who are merely ordering theirs (the fools), does that count? Or do I need some special knowledge in order to pre-order? Do I need to know about the existence of the tickets before anyone else, so I can pre-order them even before they actually exist? As soon as they exist, other people can then order them but I've got in there first. But then, when

the tickets are actually available, won't people just "buy" them, rather than "order" them? So what is the difference between "pre-order" and "order"? There is no difference at all. It is marketing rubbish and you've fallen for it.

10. **Thought shower** – this sounds more than faintly rude. Besides, the metaphor is misleading even if I could banish the unsavoury thoughts from my head (which I can't). In a shower every drop of rain is similar. It is not comprised of some raindrops which are good, useful raindrops which need to be developed into showers in their own right and really poor, rubbish raindrops which should never have been allowed to fall. They are just raindrops which together comprise a shower of rain. In a shower made of thoughts every thought is different. Some are useful and some are not. Some we need to retain and most we need to jettison. Just say what you really mean instead, which is that you have a chat about the subject with some people.

11. **Pushing the envelope** – this phrase has a precise lineage in aeronautical engineering. It means something to scientists; something specific and particular. But it translates terribly to ordinary speech because of the dual meaning of the unfortunate word "envelope". Listeners will not think of the envelope of sound and space. They will think of an envelope with a stamp on. And they will wonder why you would want to push it and, indeed, how you would go about doing so. Where are you pushing it to? Wouldn't you be better off posting it? Pushing the envelope seems

a very inefficient way of getting your thoughts to move. A bit pre-modern somehow.

12. **At this moment in time** – now. Just say "now". That's what you mean. There is no need to start talking like a comedy policeman in a bad drama. There are no moments not in time, are there? So the last bit is entirely redundant. But "at this moment" is pretentious in its own right. Just say "now".

I could, unfortunately, go on. There is a lot more in this vein. It originated on the corporate circuit and it has seeped into other professions. All I can do is to plead with you not to talk rubbish and every one of these phrases is spoken in the language of rubbish. As Eddie Izzard once said, this is arse and it is not even arse that is wearing the trousers of truth.

Redundant words add no extra meaning. Including redundant words in your writing can, in fact, obscure your meaning. Concise writing is much easier to understand. Redundant words distract the reader from your main point and diffuse the impact of your message.

Conclusion: Above All Else Be Clear

The axioms of writing for speech are obvious enough: avoid cliché, try to get a lot said quickly. Don't use phrases like "fast-changing world"; "twenty-first-century challenges"; "social partners"; "value added"; "hard working families". Never use the word "agenda" unless the word "item" appears in the same sentence. "Quality" does not mean good any more than quantity means seven. Whatever your field, become sensitized to its jargon and vow never to use it.

Above all else, try to be clear. Your style should seed the argument not supplant it. It is often tempting to write in a style which is different, more ornate and elevated, from ordinary speech. But this is supposed to be a speech. That is what you have been asked to write. So why abandon ordinary language? Why switch all of a sudden, like this, into a more pretentious idiom? Your task is to make yourself understood, as clearly as possible.

That is the single sentence of advice that you will ideally retain: be clear. If, when you read your work back, you find you get a little lost, redraft. If you get lost your audience will not follow either.

But, more than anything else, avoid the language that you no doubt feel is somehow more rhetorical. The upshot of writing like that is that your speech will lose naturalism. The person who appears on the podium will not be you, it will be some ersatz identikit speech maker. It is amazing how often people go missing when they appear on a stage to give a speech. That is, in part, a question of the way they write. But there is also more to it than that and the process of finding your speech personality is such a recurrent problem that it demands a chapter of its own. The Individual that you need to remain is the subject of Chapter Five.

CHAPTER FIVE

INDIVIDUAL

It is quite possible to have perfect technique and yet leave something vital out of the speech. That something is the individual personality of the speaker. This is what Aristotle called the "ethos" of the speech. Think about the character that you display when you speak. The dual meaning of the word character is instructive. It is simultaneously something that you have and something that you play. Enlist a friend to help you think about what you are like as a person and also how you come across when you speak in public. Get a video recording of yourself speaking and make extensive notes as you watch about the character traits that spring to mind. Then compare the account of your character that emerges with the person you actually judge yourself to be. You will then know which aspects of your character you need to find a way to communicate better.

Not Just a Speech But Your Speech

This is, you should remember, your speech. It is not just a speech that you have to deliver. It has to be your speech. It is possible to follow all the guidelines that have been set (even in a book as marvellous as this one) and yet produce something rather bloodless. In other words, it is possible to have a perfect technique and yet for there to be something important missing. That missing thing is you.

The aim of this book is not just to give you a technique for competent composition. It is more ambitious than that. The comprehensive aim is to give you a technique on top of which we can add something that is distinctive and peculiar to you.

Yet this is one of the hardest things to do. It is very common to see people go missing when they start to speak. There are many speakers, some of them highly accomplished in their professional lives, who simply disappear when they are asked to speak on stage. Many of the same people are, in fact, excellent communicators. In more intimate settings, they can be fluent, funny and informative. They do not go from excellence to incompetence when they transfer from one setting to another. But they do go from informal to formal, from flowing to solid, from loose to stiff. Something doesn't quite work. The personality gets ripped out.

You may recognize yourself in that description. You may feel that your ability to speak in public is not bad at all. You may be accustomed to addressing a team and do so in comfort and with aplomb. Yet, perhaps you do not quite transfer that confidence to a larger audience when you are delivering a speech. This chapter, on how to make your work individual, is for you.

The Character of Your Speech

After my tirade in the last chapter, you would not forgive me if I lapsed into jargon or technical vocabulary, even if it were the professional language of rhetoric. I continue to believe that it is possible to understand how to use rhetorical figures without necessarily knowing the Latin tags, still less caring about them. The academic study of rhetoric is, to my mind, fascinating but not everybody who needs to make a good speech agrees and a good speech is possible without a thorough grounding in the language of the classical scholars. For those who want to know the classical terminology, the glossary has all the main figures.

However, there now follows a partial exception to this self-denial. The greatest study of rhetorical technique is Aristotle's *Rhetoric*. The argument turns on Aristotle's distinctions between the three elements of rhetoric, which he calls ethos, logos and pathos.

So far, throughout this book we have been dealing with logos. Logos is the argument of logic. It is an appeal to the rationalist in the audience. It has been my case in this book that if the logos of your speech is good then you will never fail to deliver a competent speech.

But Aristotle rightly points out that there is more to a good speech than pure logos. A good essay can be rational all the way through. So can the solution to a mathematical puzzle. They don't have the same requirement to engage the emotions that a speech does (although you will find that the most revered and loved essayists are, in fact, those who do). There is no question, though, that an effective speech will add an emotional impact to the pure power of reasoning.

The two other aspects of Aristotle's trinity in their different ways remind us that a speech is a performance which requires a connection between the speaker and the audience.

Pathos is the method of arguing by appealing to the emotions of the audience. It is a form of argument in which the speaker deliberately departs from the rational calculation of advantage and uses arguments designed to evoke the sympathy or anger of the audience.

In most cases the pathos of an occasion is supplied by the backdrop and the occasion. The poetry, as Wilfred Owen once said, is in the pity. It is almost always a mistake to try to manufacture pathos. An intrinsically pathetic situation (in Aristotle's sense) will be obvious. You will understand that an emotional appeal has a chance of working. But most business settings do not call for such an appeal.

The third of Aristotle's elements of rhetoric is something that he calls "ethos". It can be hard to translate Aristotle's precise meaning into standard English but what he means, in essence, is character. Aristotle suggests three traits that the speaker needs to display in order to exhibit the necessary character: virtue, practical wisdom and disinterest.

An expression of virtue means that you make an explicit attempt to curry favour with the audience by a show of support of their values and beliefs. This can be done at a very high level of abstraction, such as George Washington trying to forestall military mutiny during the revolutionary war and drawing attention to his comparatively poor eyesight: "forgive me gentlemen for my eyes have grown dim in the service of my country". Abraham Lincoln warned people they wouldn't hear anything special before a great speech to lower expectations and convey sincerity.

Practical wisdom can be exhibited through the aural equivalent of a CV. An audience will be reassured, according to Aristotle, if the speaker shows that he or she has the relevant experience to resolve the situation at hand. In this respect, character is about experience.

The third quality of Aristotle's speaker of character is disinterest, by which he means the speaker shows that he is an independent voice, free from the wiles of special interests and able to speak freely. It was exactly this consideration that led the Roman authority on rhetoric, Cicero, to suggest that a speaker ought to argue reluctantly for something he ardently desires. If it appears that the speaker has been convinced by the evidence that he has himself presented, the conclusion will look like self-sacrifice, rather than something scripted in advance. To act as if this conclusion will neither harm nor benefit you will give you the attractive character trait of objectivity. Aristotle's advice can be summarized as the insight of the speaker who appears to be trustworthy and convincing will always be preferred by an audience over the speaker who appears the opposite.

From Being a Character to Playing a Character

Note already the artifice that is contained in the above heading. The very word "character" has an important dual meaning. A character in a play or a novel is a representation of something we recognize in the world around us, though it may be an idealized or heightened version of that reality. Even in realist fiction, in which we are meant to identify directly with the characters portrayed, they live a life which is, in fact, nothing like our own (for example, all the boring trivia of life have been deleted by the author).

In ordinary speech, your character is a description of what you are really like. The word has also acquired a sense of approbation. We do use "character" in a neutral sense to describe someone who is not especially likeable but it is also commonly used to denote someone of special virtue. A man or woman who "has" character is considered to be somebody of note, somebody who warrants respect. We also say of someone that they are a character, rather than that they have character. You could substitute the word character here with the word idiot. Being a character up on stage is rarely advisable. The task is to get you up there, not be somebody in the pub doing Ricky Gervais playing David Brent.

The kind of character we are seeking as a speech performance exists somewhere between the two dictionary definitions. It is not fictional, in the sense that it needs to be a character that is recognizably and authentically you. But it is not entirely realistic either, in the sense that a speech performance is an artificial moment and your essential character will need to be drawn in primary colours, sometimes in lurid colours, to make sure it is visible from the distant point in the audience.

Speeches Without Words

One way to think of the ethos of the speech is to imagine the emotional impression left if a speaker utters no words. The absence of a speech does not mean that nothing happens. Try watching a televised speech with the sound down (for some speakers this is the ideal way of watching). You will get a strangely clear idea of the speaker. The chances are that you will form an opinion of the speaker.

What is this opinion? You can't be judging the speech because you haven't heard it. You can't be commenting on the argument because you don't know what it is. And yet some transaction has taken place. The audience has experienced an intuitive sense of the character of the speaker. The way he looks, the way he holds himself at the lectern, the gestures he makes, the look on his face, the full complement of visual cues, all add to give something away. You will notice that some speakers are still and some are full of nervous movement. Some will hold a point of vision, like a ballet dancer spotting a turn. Others will look mechanically from side to side, as if they were watching a game of tennis. Some will look down, the lack of sound making them seem to be buried in notes.

Think of one of the greatest, and certainly the most maligned, orators of modern times: Adolf Hitler. Just recollect the awful effect he could conjure up theatrically. As the self-styled representative individual of the Reich, the embodiment of his depraved desire, Hitler is, in one sense, the best example of what Aristotle calls ethos. The sound is furious but coupled with the visual effect of the insignia, the iconography and, most of all, the wired anguish of the Führer's body language, the effect is a communication of coiled anger.

A good example of where the ethos of the speaker actually undermines the message is the speech that Margaret Thatcher gave outside 10 Downing Street after the Conservative victory in the 1979 general election. The words: "where there is despair may we bring hope" are delivered in a flat monotone, which empties hope with every poorly executed word. If you watch the speech, as well as listen to it, you will see Mrs Thatcher half on camera, smiling inappropriately. The impact of the written word is undermined first by the voice and then by the body. The ethos of the speaker has interfered with the language, rather than intensified it.

Writing for Someone Else

There are two types of speech that we need to consider in the rest of this chapter. Many people have to write a speech for someone else, usually their boss at work. That is a different task from writing a speech for yourself but both involve understanding a good deal about the person who is going to be doing the speaking.

Let's take the task of writing for someone else first. As far as possible, you need to establish a close working relationship with that person. It is, obviously enough, impossible to write personally for someone that you hardly know. You will have to make every effort to accumulate information about the person that you are charged with writing for. You need to know their full professional curriculum vitae. You need to know the full set of business issues that are currently occupying them. You need to know what they like to do outside work. You need to know their interests and extra-curricular activities.

The more time you spend with the person in question the better. Observe them, listen to what they say and take it in. Make notes about what you see. Think about how to make the most of the person you are working for. Try to imagine them in other settings (but be careful). Do they remind you of anyone famous or anyone else that you know? Is there any work of literature, any famous character that springs to mind? If you come up with Uriah Heep or Raskolnikov or Humbert Humbert, start again. Play parlour games about them in your head. If your boss were a car, what car would he be? If he were an animal, what would he be? The point of this is not to ridicule them (although it's good for that too). It's to draw a character sketch to aid you in the task of devising the character that you are going to help to put on the stage.

What is Your Character?

The second type of speech is the one that you write for yourself. It is not necessarily all that much easier to devise your own character (and you will need to devise it) than it is to devise the character of your boss. If it was as simple as just walking up to the podium and allowing your natural charm to vibrate around the room you wouldn't be seeking guidance in the first place.

You should do something at this point that you are not going to enjoy. You should start asking yourself some fundamental questions about who you are. The preparation of a speech can be a worryingly introspective process. This is, of course, the root of the fear it inspires. You are alone on stage and asking to be judged. It feels personal and that's because it is. It feels like your very character is being assessed and that's because it is. So brace yourself and consider the following questions:

- What am I like as a person? How would friends describe me? What words recur?
- What do people think of me on a first meeting?
- How does that impression change over time?
- If I were not in my current job, what kind of trade and profession would suit me?

Then, you need to do something else that isn't especially great fun. You should watch yourself on video. If you can bear it, get someone to watch with you. This has to be someone you trust to tell you the truth and you have to be happy for them to tell you uncomfortable truths. A candid friend is the only friend in this process, even if they are telling you that you are a dismal speaker. Getting to the bottom of this is the critical origin of improvement.

So, assuming you are psychologically ready for this, ask yourself, and get your friend to tell you, the answers to the following questions:

- Who do I remind you of, first before I speak and then after I begin?
- What do people say about me as a public speaker?

- If you didn't know what job I did what would your guess be, based on my performance?
- What are the main characteristics of the person on the video? Is the description the same as how friends describe you as a person? Do you recognize the person on the video?

It is very likely that the "real" you comes out of this exercise rather better than the odd, rather flat caricature of you that seems to have come out on the video. The effect is often like poor-resolution photography in which the character depicted is certainly yours and yet vital definition has been lost. In some instances, it is worse even than this. The character on the screen bears very little relation to the person you think yourself to be and the person your friends corroborate that you are. It is almost always the case that the "real" you is nicer, funnier and more engaging than the stilted and two-dimensional you that appears on video. It is as if you have suddenly lost your sense of humour or even your sense of self. It's not quite you, somehow.

Your Character as a Speaker

So, what should you do about this? How can you get the best possible version of you up on stage? Let's refer back to the questions that you asked yourself at the start of this chapter. The answers to those questions contain the clues to how you can write a character for yourself that is faithful to who you are yet actually works as a public speaker.

The first two in the first set of questions relate to the kind of person you are. Crucially, this is the kind of person that other people see, not the person that you simply think you are.

- What am I like as a person? How would friends describe me? What words recur?
- What do people think of me on a first meeting and how does that impression change over time?

The first two questions are designed to elicit a series of words that can reasonably be applied to you. Try to limit yourself to single words that describe a characteristic and a type of individual. Don't worry if some of the attributes appear to contradict others. It's likely that they will – we all have peculiarities. Some days you are more approachable than others. It's possible to be both friendly and not all that friendly, depending on who's asking. The best thing to do is to search your memory for social occasions and professional occasions that you have enjoyed (or endured) over the last month or so. Try to think of words that encapsulate how you came over on those occasions, both from your point of view, looking at your own performance, and from the point of view of people observing you. Try to imagine both people who know you well and who will therefore judge how you are with some prior knowledge of how you tend to behave and people to whom you are new.

You will end up with a word cluster, and this compilation of words, taken together, is a character portrait. Now let's try to separate the vital elements from those that may not be relevant. We can do this by organizing the characteristics along a few dimensions. The particular generic terms you use to group the characteristics will depend a little on the kind of words that have appeared in your portrait. So feel free to add your own generic terms if they seem more appropriate.

You will start to see a clear picture emerge of the raw material that we have to work with. Later, you have to decide which traits to emphasize in the quest to make a dominant stage character which, while not the same as you in "real" life, is nevertheless quite clearly rooted in what you are like. Then, ask the third question in the first batch, which is:

- If I were not in my current job, what kind of trade and profession would suit me?

This is where we start to find a persona for your presence on stage. What we are looking for is a profession that itself evokes a certain kind of person. So, for example, some people have a professorial air. Some people argue very forensically and ferociously, like a barrister. Some people have a nice manner, which you would like to associate with a doctor. Some people will be defined by being extremely logical and practical, which might call to mind some kind of engineer. These are, of course, blatant stereotypes and I'm not suggesting that this is telling us anything at all about what barristers and doctors are really like. We are just searching for a way of imagining yourself that corresponds with the characteristics of someone of professional standing.

For example, Margaret Thatcher had the stage persona of a headmistress, John Major came over like a regional bank manager, Tony Blair had the bearing as a speech maker of the lawyer that he actually was and Gordon Brown sounded like the preacher that he probably ought to have been. Each one had a distinctive style that can be largely captured by thinking about how they appear in these terms.

Once you have established the persona that you convey (whether you mean to or not), the second set of questions will guide you in devising a stage presence. Authenticity does need to be manufactured a little. To be natural on stage, in such an artificial setting, does require a little help. So, to add to the information that we already have, let's ask the following questions:

- Who do I remind you of, first before I speak and then after I begin?
- What do people say about me as a public speaker?

The first two questions in the second set require you to ask people who may have seen you before, or if that is hard to arrange, people who are reacting to the video footage of you performing which you are making them, against the will of both of you no doubt, sit through. You need to brace yourself for a conversation about your weaknesses. It's nice to hear that you're great but, to be frank, if you were already wonderful you wouldn't need this therapy. So, through gritted teeth, ask the following set of troubling questions.

- What is it that you do that doesn't work? Are you a bit boring? Are there moments when, as a viewer, you lose focus on what is being said?

- Do you tend to repeat yourself? Are there stock phrases that crop up again and again? Do you have favourite little lines that you weren't even aware of?

- Do you have obvious bodily mannerisms that are distracting? What do you do that you didn't know you do?

Make extensive notes as you watch. Ask your companion to do the same, without comparing notes as you take them. Then, put the notes aside and repeat the exercise. Watch the whole thing through again (I realize this has to be a good friend to put them through this). Make notes again.

There will be some aspects of the performance that you noticed first time around that you notice at once. In fact, they now seem to define the whole occasion. Anything that strikes you as important twice in a row has a very good chance of being important.

It's like the cast-iron rule for a joke, which you must never ignore. A joke that dies once might still be funny on another occasion. It needs medical attention but it may recover. If it dies twice, it is very poorly indeed and thought needs to be given to putting it out of its misery. If it dies three times in a row, it is dead. And in comedy there is no afterlife. Never use it again, even if, indeed especially if, you are still convinced it's funny. When it comes to the verdict of what is funny it's not your opinion that counts. It's the audience's and they have told you three times. So listen to their silence and work out what they are telling you.

As you watch, you will notice things that were merely intriguing on first viewing which have become irritating on second sight. There will be things that passed you by on the first occasion which now loom larger. Bear in mind that, although the audience will only watch you the once, different people will notice different things. It is not true that there are some mannerisms which will only become visible later. It is all up there for public consumption at once, and you are not in control of who notices what. Anything that might be noticed probably will be, by somebody. So make a note of it.

Then, and I promise this will be the last time, watch it again. Make a note of anything that really stands out as well as anything that strikes you for the first time. Apart from being bored of the presentation, you ought to have exhausted it by now. There's no need to look into it in any more minute detail.

Your Life in a Venn Diagram

When you have sat through the whole thing for a third time, take the notes you have made and ask your companion to do the same. Then each of you should consolidate them into a single document. Place at the top of your account anything that occurred to you on all three occasions. This will be a dominant impression that you convey. Try to place your observations in some kind of order. Remember that we are trying to add to our picture of who you are and so we need to clarify the impression you are giving. You may find that you made some observations just the once or that, on reflection, you are not sure you were right about that. Those observations remain valid. An audience only sees you the once, of course. But they are likely to be less central to the impression you are giving.

When both you and your friend have consolidated your impressions into a single side of paper, compare notes. The best way to do this, if you can stand it, is to ask him or her to read out what they have written. Then you do the same. It is remarkable how much easier it is to see if an impression is shared if it is read out loud. It is easier to hide behind the trivial similarities when you are both reading it silently and separately. When you read the impression it is a lot more brutal, which is what you need.

It is just possible that the two of you might agree entirely. Your accounts might be identical. But it's not likely. In almost all the occasions on which I have asked people to do this exercise there is an important degree of overlap. There is usually consensus on some important questions. The experiment can usually be represented visually by the classic Venn diagram that you won't have drawn since school. You probably always wondered when that would be useful and the day has arrived. Start at the top of your two accounts. Anything that occurred to both of you as important, place in the centre of the diagram. The impressions that find their way into here have been thoroughly tested and you need to take them seriously.

That will leave you no doubt with a few impressions on which you genuinely disagree. Be careful that you have not described essentially the same phenomenon in a different way. You might need to do a little translation before you start the argument. But there will be things on which you differ. So, starting at the top with the most important remaining impressions, discuss them. Tell your interlocutor why you came to the conclusion you did. Get them to do the same in return. See if you can persuade them that this is a reasonable inference to have drawn from what you saw.

If one of you persuades the other, then this can be placed in the middle of the diagram. It should be placed underneath the other observations because a conclusion you have drawn in retrospect is not as powerful as one you drew spontaneously. It is not worthless, though. People may well discuss what you had to say and they may well change their minds as they reflect on it, especially under the influence of other attendees.

There may also be some impressions that, after a discussion, the person who noticed it may be prepared to drop. Perhaps, on reflection, it didn't quite capture what you thought. But be tenacious. Don't allow yourself to drop anything lightly. You did think it at the time and that does count for something, even if you have been persuaded that your initial impression was misleading. You have to be very sure that you are prepared to give way before you drop something and it really ought not to be something that you wrote down more than once.

That will leave a few impressions on which discussion yields no consensus. One of you saw something that the other just did not see, even when prompted. That is very common. People have different reactions to the same material, delivered by the same person. One of you may have liked the message but didn't care a great deal for the messenger. The other may have thought the person on screen seemed nice enough but they were talking absolute rubbish. If you don't agree, write these impressions in the other sections of the diagram, on either side of the central part. Remember to put them in order of importance, the most vital at the top.

You now have a comprehensive pictorial representation of yourself as a speaker, which draws heavily on how you feel you have done but has some corroboration from an audience member. Clearly, if you can prevail on more than a single person to sit through this process so much the better. But you already have a lot of good information. It may not have been entirely comfortable getting there, but you now have a good sense of your character as a public speaker.

Are You Still There?

There is one question remaining that ties together everything you have discovered.

- What are the main characteristics of the person on the video? Is the description the same as how friends describe you as a person? Do you recognize the person on the video?

This is the point at which you discover whether you are still there. Let's go back to how you were described in the early sections of this chapter. Take the person who emerged from that process of self-examination. Then compare that person to the description that is contained in the Venn diagram. Do they tally or is there a significant divergence?

Take out from the initial description and from the central section of the Venn diagram anything that is common to both. You are clearly being successful in conveying that part of who you are. Now, attend to those characteristics that were important in the self-description you began with that do not feature in the account of you as a public speaker. These are the features that somehow have gone missing. Then look at what you are inadvertently replacing them with. Look at the traits that occur in the Venn diagram that, as far as you are concerned, might as well describe someone else. That is how you seem to people and it's not necessarily how you really are or how you might want to be. There is a thin chance that the public persona you are projecting is actually preferable to the person you know that you are but, in my experience, this is a very thin chance indeed.

You will now know which part of you accompanies you up to the podium. You will have considered the impression that you might want to convey and tested the extent to which you are succeeding. The very fact of being made to go through this process will have made you more self-critically aware of what you are doing wrong. Knowing yourself better than anyone else, you are the best person to decide what you need to do to put it right.

In the final analysis, that is what you are trying to do – you are trying to get the best possible version of you to mount the steps and speak. A speech is a performance by an individual. It is not a robot reading out a script prepared by a clever writer. The individual in question is you and, by now, you should have considered those aspects of your personality which are relevant to the act of speaking well. You are now ready to think about how to speak well in more general terms. You have your script and it is time to think about the final stage of preparation before the event itself. It is time to think about your delivery. That is the subject of the final chapter.

CHAPTER SIX

DELIVERY

Even though you have by now learnt how to improve your material you still face the nerve-wracking prospect of delivering the speech. You should draw confidence from the fact that your material is in good order but the performance to come will no doubt still be fraying the nerves. You ought to rehearse the speech as much as you can before you stand up to deliver it. Effective rehearsal is actually the bridge between the editing process and the moment of delivery. Poor phrasing and repetitive argument are a lot more obvious to the ear than they may appear as written text on the page. Then, when you have completed the final part of the editing process, there are ten tips you can take with you onto the podium as you speak:

1. Find out who is going to introduce you
2. Don't ditch the script
3. Learn the beginning and the end even if you insist on speaking spontaneously in the middle
4. Don't just read it out
5. If autocue is an option, take it
6. Turn your speech into notes from the full text
7. Use the cards well by looking down, taking in the information and speaking only when you look up
8. Stand tall and speak up
9. Ask yourself if you really are funny and
10. Try, if you possibly can, not to use slides. Really, try not to

Making these tips become second nature to you as a speaker will take some time but it will come, and that will complete your transformation into an effective public speaker, something you probably never thought was possible.

So You Don't Have to

You have come a long way. You have a speech and you have the beginnings of a style. Having begun this process by learning a lot more about your audience, you should have concluded it by learning a lot more about yourself. All that stands between you and triumph is the small matter of actually giving the speech. You still have to deliver it. This final chapter is designed to help you do that, to help you avoid some of the pitfalls and to answer the perennial questions that people have when they are confronted with the task of speaking in public.

The first point to bear in mind is that you will never have been better prepared. The process you have put yourself through thus far, to ensure the quality of your material, ought to give you confidence. Even if your delivery is wooden and the occasion is flat, you can at least be consoled that you said what you wanted to say and it was concisely expressed.

But the reason you are still worried is that you know a good speech is more than that. A speech is, of course, spoken. In its final form it is a speech act rather than just a piece of writing. This takes us beyond the process of composition and there is a vast literature on the topic of how to deliver a speech more effectively. Most of it is hard work. Martin Amis once said of Philip Larkin that he had lived a miserable life so that you don't have to, and I feel a little like that with the literature on speech delivery. I have read a great deal more than anyone ever should. Perhaps the only benefit to be derived from that time is that you might be spared the trouble.

Rehearsing is Good Editing

You should not hear the speech for the first time at the same moment that the audience does. In other words, rehearse. Read it out loud, properly, more than once. It is always astonishing to discover just how many speakers do not ever read their work out loud before they actually deliver it. What have you been doing? It is meant to be a speech. There's a clue in the name.

Reading your work out loud exposes all the sentences that are written for the page but not for the ear. There are long sections of this book which would sound rather odd if they were read out loud. It has not been written as a speech and we write longer sentences than we speak. It's easier to keep track on paper of a sentence that uses a series of subordinate clauses. If it is spoken, people have to supply their own imaginary punctuation and it can be harder to follow. People will have forgotten where you started the sentence by the time you end it and, unlike with a written script, they do not have the option of instantly going back to remind themselves. Most political speeches, for example, are littered with one-line sentences, most comprised of just a few words. It looks choppy on the page but, like the music of Wagner, it's a lot better than it sounds.

There's no way to find out what your speech sounds like (rather than what it looks like) other than to say it. You will immediately notice sentences that just feel too long. They read perfectly well as an essay. But they don't sound right. There will be sentences that some people could probably say, but not you. There will be phrases that you would just never use, which detract from the authorial personality you are trying to convey. This happens often when someone else has been the principal writer of the speech but it happens when people prepare their own draft too. It is easy to turn into a "writer" and produce a draft that is too formal. You will hear this at once when you read it out and you wince at the mock-academic tone of what you find yourself saying. You will hear, too, that the rhythm of some sentences is all wrong. A speech has its own music, to which the words have to fit. You will usually find that the solution will be to shorten the sentence, to split it into two separate thoughts. You will notice moments when it might make sense to pause and draw breath (stop and mark them on the text).

You will notice, too, the points at which your drafting has been less than perfect. Reading the script out will always expose two cardinal errors that, even with good preparation, you might still have committed.

The first cardinal error is to allow the argument to wander. Before you read, just remind yourself of the notes you made on your Topic. What was your essential sentence? What was your argument? Think about it for a moment and then start to read, with an ear for passages that depart from that central motif. You will soon notice that there are passages in the speech that are boring. You will start to speak more quickly because you want to get through. If you are bored, your audience will be too. Make a note to go back to the text and either excise this bit altogether, or shorten it. You will also notice when you veer off the Topic. Lots of public speakers change the subject in the middle of a paragraph, or even a sentence, without realizing they have done so. As soon as you read it out loud, the sentence will sound odd and it will be obvious. You will feel, as you read, a sense of whether the argument is coming through or not.

Devise a system for marking your text as you go. It can be something very simple, like traffic lights. On each page mark the text with Green if the material is clearly striking off your Topic and taking your argument forward. Mark it with Amber if the passage is referring to the Topic, albeit a little obliquely. It might be a passage which is a bridge back to the central argument. But think whether any of the Amber sections might not benefit from some tightening and more explicit linkages to the main argument. Then mark as Red any sections where the Topic is so buried that it is missing. Mark as Red any sections where you simply change the subject and begin, in effect, the outline of a different speech entirely.

Then be brutal with these Red sections. Either redraft them so that they do contribute to the argument, or cut them. Getting rid of whole sections like this will involve quite a lot of work. You will have to go back and rewrite all your linking sentences, all the paragraph beginnings and endings that tie the script together. But it will be worth it because the surgery will leave you with a speech that is shorter, more concise and more expertly trained on the objective in view, namely the argument you want to put across.

The second cardinal error that this rehearsal may reveal is involuntary repetition. Conscious repetition of the main argument, controlled and deliberately placed, is a good habit. But many speakers repeat themselves without meaning to. They just haven't done their editing properly. The odd thing about editing is that it is more easily done aurally. It is easy, especially when you have got close to a text, to miss the fact that you have essentially repeated a point. It is common for speech writers to make a point on page 3 and then make essentially the same point again on page 7.

The first question is why the same point is made twice, four pages apart. It would be better to bring them together and then choose the best, most eloquent version of the point. When you are combing your script as you edit, it is easy to miss this. It is almost impossible to miss it when you read the script out loud. If you talk to a friend in a pub and you make the same point three times in a matter of minutes, he will wonder what is wrong with you. Yet people do this in speeches all the time and they do it because they haven't taken the trouble to complete the editing process by reading the script out loud.

How to Speak

So let's assume that you have completed the editing of your text by reading it out loud a number of times. The day of the speech will, thankfully, not be the first time you have heard it. I cannot reiterate too often that this level of preparation really is the best way of allaying the anxiety you may feel as the day approaches. Once you have been through the process a few times you may even start to believe this for yourself. Most poor presentations are poor because the content is not good enough. It is usually a mistake to attribute a disaster to a poor performance. The rot usually sets in long before you stand up to speak. The disaster on the day is the culmination of what has gone wrong, not its sole cause.

All the same, it does not follow that good material will automatically translate into a great speech. It does still need to be delivered and many a well-written speech has been ruined by a speaker who stumbles over every second word.

So it is important that you become the best speaker you can be, as well as the best writer you can be.

This chapter introduces ten top tips on how to speak well. These are ten lines to take to ensure that you do not waste all the hard work that you have put in so far.

First Tip: Find Out Who Will Introduce You

You ought to know before you arrive at what point in proceedings you will be speaking. It may therefore be appropriate to refer to the speeches that have gone before you. It will always be courteous to thank the organizers for inviting you. But be careful not to spend too long on a litany of thanks. You don't want to turn this into Kate Winslet doing one of her interminable Oscar acceptance speeches. If there are housekeeping issues that need to be dealt with, try to get whoever introduces you to do them. It will delay the moment at which you actually get going on the prepared script.

You do therefore need to talk to the person who will introduce you, to ensure that they set you up properly. You need to be sure that they will refer to the parts of your working life and biography which are relevant to that day's event. The person who introduces you establishes your authority as someone who is worth listening to on this topic, on this day. So they need to get it right, but you have more interest in their getting it right than they do so don't be shy to suggest an appropriate introduction. It might also be charming to say something complimentary back. The person who introduced you is likely to be your host for the day and, if you are getting paid, they are paying the bills too.

Once you are up on your feet, be gracious about your presence there and, if something occurs to you that refers to the event at which you are speaking, then say it. You may even find that you can raise a laugh at this point. The reason for this is that an audience will give you a lot more leeway with remarks which they know have not been prepared. The standard of a joke which is spontaneous need not be anything like as high as it must if it is a story that you have prepared. But make sure this little preamble is short. When you have finished your short preamble, make sure you pause for an exaggerated period. You need to separate this introduction from the speech proper and you need to allow time for the room to settle before you begin. If you do this, it will then be obvious that you have begun in earnest.

Second Tip: Don't Ditch the Script

Many would-be speakers believe that the pinnacle of good presentation is to be able to speak without a note in sight. It's not. As ever, there is far more artifice involved than that. It does look impressive when someone is speaking seemingly without referring to anything at all. But there is almost always a trick involved. It is a real rabbit that they are pulling out but it's not a real hat.

Besides, speaking without notes is something that should come much later in your career as a public speaker, if it ever comes at all. So, at this stage you should ditch the quixotic notion that you might do the speech entirely from memory. You don't have time to learn it. And, make no mistake, that is what politicians who speak seemingly with no script have done. When David Cameron spoke at the Conservative Party conference in 2005 without a note in sight he had committed large chunks of the speech to memory. It had been a long time in the preparation. This was, in fact, a revival of a practice that was common in the political speeches of the late nineteenth century. Gladstone and Disraeli would work for months on a speech which they would then learn in its entirety. Some of these speeches lasted for a number of hours but every word was considered.

You don't have time to do this. Even if you do your time can be better spent doing something else, like making sure the speech is good enough.

Third Tip: Beginning, Muddle and End

The second tip on how to speak was not to ditch the script. There is no doubt that some people will disregard this advice. There are many speakers who are just a little more confident than they ought to be. Some people will say that a formal script hampers and constrains them and that the reason their personality is not fully showing through is that they need to be liberated by talking off the cuff.

Unless you really are a superb speaker this will not be true. The more probable reason that your personality is not showing through is that you are ill-prepared, not that you are overprepared. The best cure for the belief that you are better off speaking without preparation is to watch yourself.

You will notice how ragged and unformed your sentences are. You will see that your argument starts to meander as you wander off the main point. Subsidiary arguments come and go, seemingly without order or logic, and it becomes hard to see where you are going. A story occurs to you and you tell it at length, not quite connecting it to the main body of the speech. The address certainly gains in spontaneity but it loses more in cogency.

All that said, there is always a danger that reading from a script empties the address of spontaneity. The danger with being well prepared is that it can look like it. Some speeches are like buildings that have been cleaned. The improvement was impossible without erecting the scaffolding but, having made the building resplendent, the cleaners forgot to take the scaffolding down. Winston Churchill used this metaphor for the process of constructing a speech. When he was a young subaltern in the Indian Army he wrote a study which he called "The Scaffolding of Rhetoric". It is possible to deliver a speech in which the hours of toil are somehow too visible. The best response to this is to prepare better rather than to prepare less.

But, if you do want to include a section which is spoken off the cuff, there is a way of doing it which maximizes the benefit of spontaneity while minimizing the risk of the speech turning into a random walk. Speaking *ex tempore* well is not the same as just making it up as you go along. All rhetoric involves a form of duplicity, just like stand-up comedy. You haven't really just thought of it all, standing there, but you are pretending you have and you hope to draw the audience into complicity on that point. So even your off-the-cuff remarks need to be considered and prepared.

The difference is not that one is prepared and the other is not. It is that one is written in more formal language and the other is more obviously everyday and conversational.

The idea of the speech I am describing is best captured by Philip Larkin's brilliant remark that the typical English novel had a beginning, a muddle and an end. If you really insist on a section of the speech which is less formally prepared, this is the way to do it. Prepare the beginning and prepare the end and either read them or learn them verbatim. Then allow yourself to wander about a bit in the middle.

The beginning and the end of a speech are crucial for anchoring your main argument and then concluding it in the right place. If you start well you can be certain that the bridge you build to your middle section will be the correct bridge. You need to learn your link into the spontaneous middle section because it is the linking work that goes missing when we speak off the cuff. You will find yourself saying "oh yes and there's another thing". When you prepare properly all that verbal waste gets removed in the editing process. If you learn your opening and know precisely how you intend to enter the spontaneous part, the sense of aimlessness will be dismissed.

Then make sure that you know exactly, to the word, how you are going to end the speech. It is awful, and sadly too common, that people end on a damp note. A speech that ends with "well, thanks for listening, err, it's been nice to talk to you" or "and yes, well, that's it. Any questions?" leaves a really poor impression. It is likely, too, that as you talk freely you will go over your allotted time. Not many people can judge time well when they are speaking and one of the virtues of preparation is that you can rehearse and make sure that you speak for the time you have been given, or less.

The reason you will be talking too much is contained in something that John Major once said about Neil Kinnock: "as he never knows what he's talking about he doesn't know when he's finished". Most people speaking without a script find it very difficult to land the speech in the right place. Even when they do know roughly where they are heading it can be hard to script a perfectly judged and paced peroration when you are making it up as you go along. That is why it is essential to know how you are going to end the speech. Write a proper finish and have a notion of how you are going to lead out of your middle section into your peroration. From then on, once you start in the scripted section, just do it in full. You will then at least end with a bang rather than a whimper.

Now that you have agreed to these bookends in your speech you can, if you insist, go off-script in the middle. But there is off-script and there is no script. Even a section in which you do not speak from a formal text, you ought to have scripted pretty tightly in your head. It can be effective, for example, to depart from the text to tell a story but it absolutely must be a relevant anecdote. It has to add to the argument you are making. It's not good enough that it just occurred to you. It didn't occur to anyone else in the audience and they will need a little help to understand why this particular story really matters. A good editor would excise an irrelevant story, no matter if it does raise a laugh.

You need a good sense of the points you will make in this middle section and you should practise it. It can look effective to speak apparently without notes and as if you have just thought up your words on the spot. In a sense, the whole illusion of rhetoric is to try to appear as if the words have formed spontaneously when they have, in fact, been sweated over. But be clear where you are heading and limit yourself to a few minutes.

Fourth Tip: Don't Just Read it Out

Just because speaking with no script is inadvisable, there is no need to go to the other extreme. It takes a very convincing actor to bring a text to life when you are reading it. The occasion of a speech is supposed to resemble a conversation. It is an odd conversation, to be sure, in which you talk to a lot of people simultaneously for quite a long time and they say nothing back. But it's more like a conversation than it is, say, like reading a bedtime story. So you need to hide the fact that you are reading the script.

That's not to say that you should not have a full text in front of you for comfort. Indeed, you really must have a copy there somewhere, no matter how you end up speaking, just in case of disaster. You might forget a vital passage, even if you are an experienced speaker, and having a full text on hand is a safety net that there is no virtue in doing without. The text you bring must be in very large print, laid out in a different way from ordinary writing. You need to place space between each line so that you don't get lost as your eye scans down the page.

However, this is for use just in case of disaster. The speech will almost certainly sound stilted if you read material direct from a page. We need to find a way of delivering the speech that does not encourage you to be flat.

Fifth Tip: If Autocue is an Option, Take it

The one exception to the rule of trying not to read your script verbatim is if you are using autocue. If an autocue is available do take up the option. An autocue is actually quite easy to use. Words are projected onto a glass plate in front of you, or sometimes two plates, one on each side, and they scroll across as you speak. The autocue allows you to do what you really need to do, which is to look up and engage the audience. You will give the impression of speaking without notes because nothing is visible to the audience.

A number of venues will have an autocue and somebody there who knows how to use it. This person will ensure that the script rolls across in front of you at the speed at which you speak. You will not need to worry about varying your pace. It is an easy matter for the autocue operator to stay with you. Make sure that you bring a script which is written up properly. You need to start each sentence on a different line. If the text is too bunched it is much less legible. Mark up any pauses you want to make. Underline words you intend to emphasize.

For all my reassurance that autocue is relatively easy to use, there are people who never get used to it. Some people just never get used to their words appearing in front of them, as if suspended in air. The only way to discover if you are one of those people is to try it out. But if you have never used autocue before you will need to practise. Get to the venue a little earlier than you need to and seek out the autocue operator. It may be possible to go up on stage and try it out. If the stage is in use then ask if you can set up in an adjoining room just so you can get used to the technique of reading as you look at the audience. Even if you are an experienced user of an autocue it still makes sense to do this, just to check that everything is in working order.

Sixth Tip: Turn Your Speech into Notes

However, not all venues have the option of autocue and you may well be reliant on the text you have brought with you. So, you will find it helpful if you get into the habit of turning your text into extensive and usable notes. That is the best middle way between learning the speech at one extreme and reading it at the other.

The way to do this is to start with your full text and gradually reduce it to its base elements. As you go through this process, in conjunction with rehearsing your performance, you will find that you really become acquainted with the structure and shape of the speech. There will be whole sections that you know more or less completely.

Start by writing lots of paragraph headings. Those words ought to trigger a few sentences in your mind. Practise giving the speech from these headings, referring back to the original script whenever you need to. When you are comfortable with this, when you can do the speech well from these headings, reduce them further. Each change in the argument should be triggered by a word which then reminds you of the text which follows. You will be surprised at how much comes back to you as a result of these reminder words.

An example of the cards that you might use, drawn from the worked example of a speech that we saw in Chapter Four, is written out below. Each section should be on a separate card. The actual words I have used are those that would remind me of the text. They might not be exactly the same words that remind you of the text. Go through the speech yourself and break it up into words that suggest what comes next. After a few rehearsals and some time spent writing, this reduction becomes relatively easy to do and you may be surprised at just how much of the speech comes flooding back to you with the prompt of a single word.

CARD ONE: OPENING
GOOD COMPANY
MORALS AND MONEY
CANNOT GO ON LIKE THIS

CARD TWO: ARGUMENT
MILTON FRIEDMAN
SOURCE OF VALUE NOT GUIDED
BY VALUE
PROFITS DOWN 8%
FAMOUS BRANDS GONE
LIVING STANDARDS DOWN

CARD THREE: RIPOSTE
WEBER, QUAKERS, HISTORY OF COMPANY
FORD, HEWLETT-PACKARD

CARD FOUR: TOPIC
HIGH WINDOWS
LITTLE REPUBLICS
REPUTATION MANAGEMENT
ENVIRONMENT
EMPLOYEES
EVIDENCE FOR ETHICAL BUSINESS

CARD FIVE: CLOSING
TWO SENSES OF GOOD
AMNESIA CONSEQUENCES
KEY TO GOOD BUSINESS

The layout of the card is not an accident. Your notes need to be written in large block capitals, quite widely spaced, so you can see them easily at a glance. The cards must be numbered so that there is no chance that you will get lost and be unable to find your way.

Seventh Tip: How to Use the Cards

The great virtue of the card system is that it allows you to spend most of the time you are on your feet looking out into the hall rather than looking down at your notes. Make sure as you speak that you take the trouble to glance across at each section of the auditorium in turn. Don't get fixed on one side. Try to position yourself to look directly out into the middle and then slightly pivot to either side occasionally. This will be enough to give an audience the illusion that you are making eye contact. In a smaller venue you may actually be able to do so but most speech settings do not allow for that.

The best use of your cards is very simple. Don't start speaking while you are reading. That is not because it is impossible to do the two things at the same time. It's not, it's rather easy. But the reason not to do the two things simultaneously is entirely about engaging the audience. It just makes no sense to speak with your head down in your notes. Wait that extra beat and do not say a word until your eyes fix on a human face. You might feel that this is slowing you down but it is a fraction of a second. It will actually give your speech a good, assured pace. So, that's it. You will be amazed at what a difference it makes. Look down, absorb the word that triggers your thoughts, look up, make contact with the audience and speak.

Eighth Tip: Stand Tall and Speak Up

Your delivery on stage should be just a little bit exaggerated. You need to display just that extra bit of energy and just that bit more intensity and emotion than you would if you were saying exactly the same words to a single person. The distance between you and the audience flattens out the act. If you speak normally you will seem diminished and not especially interested. The exaggeration required will feel odd and uncomfortable to you but it doesn't look that way to the audience. On the contrary, you will appear diffident even though you feel you are speaking completely normally. The audience will get the sensation of you lacking confidence if you speak in your usual way. So turn the volume up a bit and make your gestures a little more decisive.

Then, as you speak, be sure to vary your pace. A speech travels through different moods and registers and a flat monotone is not appropriate, as well as being boring. Your rehearsal process should have alerted you to the point where you need to slow down and dwell on the content.

Ninth Tip: Ask Yourself if You Really are Funny

Speakers always want to be funny. Everyone wants to be funny. Unfortunately, the ability to be funny is a gift denied to most people. The best advice, if you are at all worried about your ability to be funny, is not to try. Some people are funny. Some people are so unfunny that their very unfunniness becomes funny. And some people's unfunniness is just unfunny.

A joke which falls flat is a horrible moment. A speaker has asked the audience to appreciate what he has said by making a distinctive sound and the audience has declined. It is embarrassing and the confidence will drain from the speaker.

But if you are not deterred by the pitfalls of comedy that fails, there are a few guidelines that will help. Don't add in jokes just for the sake of it, unless you are doing an after dinner speech, in which case the jokes, rather than the argument, are the point. The same standard should apply to the gag that applies to the rest of your material. If it contributes it's in and if it doesn't then it's out.

Keep a note of anything that occurs to you that makes you laugh. That is a rule you cannot flout. It has to make you laugh and laughter is a sound, not a feeling. If a story makes you smile, it doesn't pass the test. If you find it wryly amusing, that is not enough. You have to laugh out loud as soon as you hear it. Comedy is one of the few disciplines in public speaking which approximate to a scientific measurement. If the audience laughs, it's funny.

Then, select your stories carefully and edit them ruthlessly. A good joke relies very heavily on its precise elements. If you flunk the set-up of a joke you will dampen the punch line. Every line has to be polished and then you need to learn them all. You can kill off even a good joke with halting delivery. The telling of a joke is actually best done a little bit quicker than ordinary speech, so you need to know it perfectly to make it work.

Tenth Tip: Would Anyone Like More Slides?

No they wouldn't. Nobody ever asked a speaker for more slides or more information on the slides they had. In the literature on speech delivery, the use of visual aids is often said to be controversial. If only it were. In fact, their use is ubiquitous. It is rare, and therefore refreshing, to come across a corporate speaker who has the courage and imagination to turn up without the working equivalent of his holiday snaps playing behind him.

The use of slides has become so extensive that it has become a staple expectation. You may not be senior enough in your company to withstand the peer pressure to use slides. There's no point getting into trouble for the sake of the principle. But if you do have the option of speaking without any visual aids, take it. It's hardly ever true that the visual aid enhances the content. That is because the slides tend to take over. People think the slides are telling the story so they make less effort on the story they are telling. Too many speakers spend half their time with their back to the audience, pointing to the pictures. Too many speakers patronize the audience by reading out the information that is clearly visible up on the screen.

For many speakers, especially on corporate occasions, the content on the slides feels like a blanket to cling to. The speech is up there and the speaker therefore feels that the act of making the speech is simply the act of explaining what is written on the slides. It is therefore tempting to suppose that it is possible to skimp on the preparation. This is always a mistake. You are not released from the obligation to write a proper speech just because you want to transcribe some of it and place it on a screen behind you.

If you are intent on having pictures as well as words, there are a few obvious precepts that should be followed. Use as few as possible; don't put too much information on any one slide; try not to use bullet points or numbered lists; use pictures and graphs rather than text.

But if you can, don't use anything. If you speak well, nobody will ever grab you afterwards and angrily ask where the slides were.

Conclusion

The ten tips contained in this chapter should help you to get the best out of your delivery of the speech. But there is no short cut that will ever be better than practice. You need to rehearse until the precepts above become second nature to you. Good speakers will do all the right things without even thinking about them. For a while, as you are getting accustomed to the manner of speaking, you might seem a little artificial. But persist. In time, the style will click into place and you will find yourself adopting the manner of a public speaker without the thought having to travel through the conscious mind first.

There will come a day when you are standing up to speak and you will suddenly look at yourself, as if from the outside, and you will realize that you have become a competent speaker. It will be in large part because the material you have is a lot better than it used to be. But it will also be on account of the improved way you hold yourself at the podium. You will be a good speaker. The act of public speaking will no longer hold the terrors for you that once it did. It will be quite a moment.

CONCLUSION

You have gone all the way through the process and, it is to be hoped, your initial anxiety about writing and performing will have diminished. The skills of writing and speaking well are important ones to master and not just for reasons of professional advancement. We all contribute to the conduct of public discourse and the good health of the language depends on its use. It is harder these days than it used to be to make really fine speeches. Some of the great issues have disappeared, the mass audience means that language has become more demotic and politics and business are more mediated and choreographed than they once were. But it is still possible to write well, rather than badly, and the speech writer is an important person to have in the organization. Treat them well. If you don't you will be missing the opportunity to make the best case that you can make for yourself.

Attention to Detail

So, by now you have gone all the way to delivery. It probably feels like the process has had more in common with the process of having a child. But, really, it's just a speech. It won't often be the making of you and it will still less often be the breaking of you. Part of the point of this book has been to demystify the process of writing a speech, the better to allow you to be tranquil about it. Anxiety is almost always the enemy of accomplishment. It is common for people to believe that a speech writer has to have the gift of a poet. Although that would never go amiss, I hope that by now you are convinced that you can construct a good speech, even with your more prosaic talent.

You can split every speech into three acts. The first act is the thinking. In the chapters on Audience, Expectations and Topic, I encouraged you to do most of the work of your speech before you begin the actual drafting. The bit in the middle is the writing (a much smaller component part of the whole than you might suppose). This was covered in the chapters on Topic and Language. Then, the third act is the extensive process of editing, rehearsing, reading and rewriting that comes after the draft has been completed. These aspects of the process were covered in the chapters on Individual and Delivery.

Very good writers do get to the point where they can deliver a script that is extensively edited at first draft. As you get better as a writer you edit naturally as you go. As you become accustomed to sticking hard by the Topic that you have selected you begin to experience almost a physical shudder as you start to stray from the central argument. The first draft of an experienced professional speech writer should usually be good enough to deliver. But even the best writer will benefit from rigorous editing, rehearsal and rethinking.

There is a lot to remember but the advice all comes together in the maxim that good writing always pays attention to detail. Delivery, Expectations, Topic, Audience, Individual and Language will ensure you never write a poor speech.

You can now take your place in the panoply of orators down the ages. It may seem strange to place you in that tradition but, as I said at the beginning, the art of oratory is essentially what it was when the first person got up onto the stage to make a case. You won't be seeking to have your speech memorialized. Nobody has yet made a speech of historic importance about the new organogram of the office organization and they never will. People do regularly make competent speeches on topics like that, although you still can't help wishing that they wouldn't.

The Difficulty of Speaking Well

But it is important for everyone who speaks in public to speak as well as they can because that is the way that public speech is transmitted. Good public argument is not just about the politicians and the celebrities. We are all speaking the same language and we all owe it a duty of care. This is especially true in an era in which profound public speech has become more difficult than ever before. There are three reasons for this: the relative lack of pathos, the more educated audience and the ubiquity of speech.

Lack of Pathos

The first and most important reason why great speech is so much harder now is that there are fewer causes that demand greatness. The verdict that a speech should enter the pantheon is not in your hands as a writer. Anthologies of great speeches are actually collections of good speeches that were made to commemorate momentous events. The elusive element is an injustice that demands to be put right.

Consider Nelson Mandela's plea to the court which had been appointed to try him:

> during my lifetime I have dedicated my life to this struggle of the African people. I have fought against white domination and I have fought against black domination. I have cherished the ideal of a democratic and free society in which all persons live together in harmony with equal opportunities. It is an ideal which I hope to live for, and to see realised. But, my Lord, if needs be, it is an ideal for which I am prepared to die.

Read that out loud, if you haven't done so already. Even now, many years later, read by you in your living room or study or office, surrounded by your belongings rather than a court of peers standing in judgement, even now that still works. But, tightly written as it is, it's not the words that make us shiver. It's the facts. It's perfectly fine as a piece of writing although quite spare and unadorned. But that transparent quality allows us to see the facts and it's the depth of the facts rather than the surface of the rhetoric that is so alarming. It's the willingness to die that shocks us, the fact that such volition is necessary. It's a terrible offer to have to make in the knowledge that it might be taken up. In any other circumstances, this speech would be melodramatic but the pathos of the occasion makes it work. Mercifully, such occasions are rare.

In other words, the real enemy of grand rhetoric is the wonderful twentieth century. The extraordinary advances in medicine and in life expectancy, the unprecedented prosperity, the unexpected interlude of late century peace – all of these things, in the Western democracies, make rhetorical posture seem out of proportion to the facts. It's easy to be outraged when it's really uncomfortable and there will never be a great speech without a sense of outrage.

Pathos cannot be manufactured and if we don't have the same sense of occasion that we used to, that is a mercy for which we should give thanks. The big arguments either happen elsewhere or they are periodic crises. And even then, the questions are complex and technical. They translate poorly into effective rhetoric. Global problems also mean that the speaker rarely has executive authority to turn his words into action. That is why there was no great credit crunch speech. The topic is too technical, too inhabited by unlovely language.

The Educated Audience

The second reason why great speeches are now rare is that the audience has grown and changed shape. Universal suffrage and mass education have changed rhetoric. Suddenly the audience, which was once evenly and similarly educated, became broader and more diverse. References that once had a universal reach – such as biblical allusions or classical citations – stopped working. It is no longer a safe assumption that the audience will know the same body of work which is why Shakespeare, Dickens and the great English authors, once a treasure trove for writers, do not appear so often.

Speeches have ceased to be as historically literate as once they were, for the same reason. To invoke a national story was once a way of ingratiating oneself with an audience. Now it would risk a sea of blank faces. The audience is so much more heterogeneous than it was. It is not multiculturalism that is the principal cause of a fragmenting audience. It is mass education. Democracy fragments the culture far more than ethnic diversity. An overlapping language between cultures is easy. A common tongue for the reader and the non-reader is much harder.

The other countervailing force is freedom. The sheer range of available lifestyles in modern societies means that people are doing other things. The necessarily shared realm – and hence the shared compendium of references and cultural wisdom – is much less monochrome than it was. This is nothing to lament – it is a good thing. But it does make speech writing harder because there are very few things that cross over a wide audience.

Language changes over time. Words that are commonplace in one era are ornate in another. Different times have different styles and vocabularies shift. The prevailing orthodoxy of any given time is also influenced by the industries that come to prominence within it. Public speech can be dominated by metaphors drawn from the church, from science, from the military, from politics or from business. In developed societies our public speech is the combination of those influences and, like the streets of an old city, we can see influences from many times past. But still the architecture of the day looms very large. In our time, the language of business has taken over a great deal of public speech.

Speech writers now confront a very diverse nation in which they are seeking the highest common denominator. The inevitable consequence is that language becomes more demotic. The long journey from courtly to colloquial language is now almost complete. David Lloyd George once referred in a speech to "the great pinnacle of sacrifice, pointing like a rugged finger to heaven". He was admonished for being too low-brow. If anyone said that today, the commentators would think they were the poet laureate.

Channels of Speech

The third reason is television. The televised speech has two distinct audiences, of which by far the larger is the one watching at home. Some speakers – Ted Kennedy and Gordon Brown spring instantly to mind – do not translate well to television. Their tub-thumping, barnstorming style creates a lively atmosphere in the conference hall but it looks contrived and odd on television. Ronald Reagan, as a former film actor, always understood the intimacy of television. He was able to communicate as if he were in your living room, which, he understood, he was.

Television changes more than the delivery of a speech. It also adjudicates on what is seen. Editing splits a speech into tiny fragments. Speeches are now available in full online and, glacially, they are finding a space in the infinite vastness of the internet for those with enough prior interest to seek them out. But for most people, the speech will be seen, if it is seen at all, as an excerpt on the evening news.

This puts a lot of pressure on the writer to crystallize the speech in a phrase. The "sound-bite" has become a term of abuse, supposedly the symbol of an inglorious political age. This is both unfair and unrealistic. To define a speech in a choice phrase is a rare skill, one that ought to be cultivated rather than denigrated. If editing is going to leave you with a few seconds of exposure, better that those few seconds define the central message rather than say something peripheral and misleading.

Of course, there are nefarious techniques that can be employed. During the presidential campaign in 1976, Jimmy Carter started to pause unnaturally in the middle of sentences. That makes an uncomfortable edit on television and he knew it. As he approached the full stop he sped up and talked over it, ignoring the rules of oral punctuation and going straight into his next sentence. He made himself difficult to edit and got a lot more time on the news as a result.

This process, of cutting and editing, is inevitable in an age when speeches are struggling for attention. When Gladstone and Disraeli did their great speech tours in the latter part of the nineteenth century, the text, which was months in the preparation and then learnt by heart, would have been reproduced verbatim in *The Times* the following morning. Today, politics is more mediated and choreographed than it has ever been. When a politician speaks today, a search party is sent out to look for the way his words might differ from those of his colleagues. In these circumstances the incentive to be dull is high. And there are some politicians, of course, for whom no incentive is needed.

A Word in Favour of the Speech Writer

But although it is getting harder to be grand, there is still a discernible difference between good and bad writing. The speech writer is one of the people protecting the standards of the words we use in public. It is an important task. Indeed, it is a more important task than most companies and organizations appear to realize. I want to end by entering a plea on behalf of the speech writer.

The major acts of communication, even in an electronic age, remain personal and spoken. The work that should go into the preparation of these events contains, or at least should contain, the strategic wisdom of the company up to that point. Running a business well is a continuous act of persuasion, the audience in question being the present and possible future customers of the company. At those moments of high persuasion, with a captive audience and the opportunity to sharpen your central proposition, it needs to be taken seriously.

A good speech needs intensive time. It does not need small fragments of time stretched over three months. That is hopeless. But you do need to invest time in it as the day approaches and you need to invest properly in someone good, at the appropriate level of seniority, to fashion that argument and sharpen those words.

It is a matter of amazement to me quite how many corporate leaders are so dull and so unclear. Granted the space to make a pitch, they say nothing. They do not even say nothing elegantly, which is an art form, albeit a low one. They just bore their audience into submission with a torrent of weary platitudes and standard issue business-speak. It is as if they do not care.

They should care. They should care because to speak poorly in public is a bad thing to do in itself. And they should care because to speak badly in public is an opportunity missed to display your wares well and an opportunity taken to make the world think poorly of you.

It really is not that hard to be clear. It's not too ambitious. Listen as you go about your everyday life. People are making themselves clear wherever you go. Get to the point quickly, illustrate the point, stick to it and then emphasize it. The only thing you might need help with is working out what the point should be. For that you will need either to be, or to buy, a speech writer. It's more than just a detail. And you really should pay attention.

FREQUENTLY ASKED
QUESTIONS

I have done very many events when I have discussed the process of writing speeches, how I do it and how it is best done (those two things may not be the same, of course). I have gathered here the most common questions and given a version of the answer I usually offer.

When you are writing a speech, what is the process?

The speech process can vary a great deal. It depends on your preference as a writer and it depends crucially on how the speaker likes to work. The usual process with Prime Minister Tony Blair was that we would have a meeting a week before the event and discuss the basic thesis of the speech. We would always be sure to have the main argument, at least in a bare form. Without that it's not really possible to do anything at all. But that would suffice to let me know what research I needed. I would then commission the work I needed and get to work on a thorough outline of the speech.

When writing an important speech, what is more important, facts or passion? Is emotional resonance the most important thing?

It depends on the speech. Some speeches are designed to convey information and some are meant to be persuasive. Some are meant to inspire although those are the most difficult to get right. As a general rule I would not separate the passion from the argument. If the passion does not serve a serious argument it is likely to be synthetic.

Do you actively use rhetorical tools? Or is it more about gut instinct, talent and what sounds really good?

We hear rhetorical tricks so often that it is hard to avoid using them. I never actively decided to use a trick because it was a trick but rhetoric has tools of the trade for a good reason. The repetition of a resonant phrase often does work, so you find yourself drawn to common rhetorical tricks even though, by doing so, you risk cliché.

How many edits did you usually go through?

Again, this varies according to the speaker. Anything more than six or seven and it is likely that the speech is getting worse rather than better. As you get better at writing you find that you write to fourth draft standard at once. The big variable is the number of people that are involved. The smaller the number the better. One of the big tasks that the speech writer has is to keep people out of the way. A speech needs a clear voice and a clear point of view. This gets harder to maintain with every new person who is involved.

What is the ideal length for a speech?

As short as possible. The Gettysburg Address was just over two minutes long. The objective of a good speech is the same as poetry – to get a lot said as quickly as possible. If you are still talking after half an hour you have probably gone on too long. It is a good discipline, as you write, to aim for 20 minutes. That will ensure that nothing unnecessary slips through.

Is short, concise and powerful better than long and impressive?

Long is not impressive. Try short and impressive. At the last minute, a few hours before the speech is to be delivered, go through the speech and edit 10 per cent away. It will always get better. You can usually make a speech much better by losing a small amount. You will begin to enjoy the process of discarding superfluous material. It's important to learn how not to be precious about what you have written. Learn to kill off your own work. In fact, learn to enjoy doing it.

What made men like Churchill, JFK and latterly Obama and Blair such good orators?

Churchill and JFK spoke beautiful language. Their speeches actually read better than they sound. Churchill was himself a writer of the highest class. His war-time speeches are models of economic writing. JFK employed great writers who gave him an eloquence that he might have struggled to attain without them. With Obama it is all in the voice. He sings his words. His delivery comes out of the black churches and it rings out in a way the speech hardly does when you read it on the page. A Churchill speech delivered by you, in your living room, will still be magnificent. Not many Obama speeches will. Blair was very comfortable up on the podium and he made the audience feel comfortable as a result. But don't try to emulate what they did. Their task was not your task.

What were Tony Blair's key skills?

The best attributes in a speaker are courage and judgement. An effective speaker needs the courage to want to make a tough argument. Most corporate speakers fall down because they are too bland. They worry that they ought not to say anything controversial and, as a result, their speeches will never really inspire much interest. An effective speaker also needs good judgement because they need to know what they think. Speeches that don't quite define an argument are always a failure even if they are elegantly written.

Should speeches have beginnings, middles and endings?

They have them whether you know it or not. The beginning is at the start. The end is where you finish. And the middle is the bit in between. It is advisable to link them well so that the listener knows where he is. The main argument also needs to be visible in all three sections. Introduce the argument at the beginning, cement it in the middle and tie it up at the end. The middle is the seat of the argument, where all the serious work is done. If you cannot say what that argument is in a single pithy sentence, then you probably don't know. And you're in trouble.

Are three-part lists useful tools? How much of speech writing and delivery is about performance?

All ways of organizing material can be helpful as long as they are not overused. Delivery is, of course, vital but no amount of theatrical performance can redeem a poorly constructed speech. Equally, a terrible speaker can fail to do justice to excellent writing.

Finally, what are your favourite fictional speeches from film, television or literature?

The anthologies of great speeches contain all the finest moments. I don't think it gets better than the speeches that Churchill gave to the House of Commons in the dark days of 1940. But, apart from the canon of great rhetoric, I actually love Robin Williams's speeches from *Dead Poets' Society*. You can hear the violins playing but they still work. I love the speech that Hector makes at the end of Alan Bennett's wonderful *The History Boys*.

But the best piece of rhetorical writing I have seen for years was in the streets of Belfast, at George Best's funeral. Some street poet was carrying a banner on which they had written: "Maradona Good, Pele Better, George Best". Six words and everything said, beautifully. That's what you're aiming at.

GLOSSARY – THE MAIN RHETORICAL TERMS

Alliteration – the repetition of consonants

Anadiplosis – taking the last words from one clause and starting the next clause with it

Anaphora – regularly repeating the first word of a sentence

Antithesis – weighing an argument by considering its opposite

Apodioxis – the immediate and sweeping rejection of an opposing idea

Aporia – fake indecision when you are pretending to take an opponent seriously

Apostrophe – when you come out of the speech as if to address someone who is absent

Assonance – the repetition of vowel sounds

Chiasmus – swaps a sentence round ("ask not what your country can do for you ...")

Climax – building your language up to a point where it explodes

Concession – giving way on a small point in order to win a larger point

Decorum – fitting your speech to the manner that is appropriate to the setting

Dialogismus – the use of repetition

Dialysis – opposition of two points: you are either with us or against us

Epiplexis – the use of repeated rhetorical questions

Ethos – argument by character, appealing to personal trustworthiness

Exordium – the first part of a speech

Hypophora – a self-answering question, e.g. what do you want? No changes

Kairos – the moment in your speech at which the audience is ripe for persuasion

Litotes – deliberate understatement, the opposite of hyperbole

Logos – argument by logic and rationality, appealing to technical merit

Metaphor – the use of an image to stand for an idea

Metonymy – referring to something by associating it with one of its parts

Narration – the second part of a speech which usually sets out the main argument

Paralipsis – mentioning something by pretending you are not going to mention it

Paronomasia – wordplay

Pathos – argument by emotion, appealing to the heart

Periphrasis – using a description as a name, e.g. the man himself

Philippic – an attack speech

Phronesis – displaying practical wisdom and common sense

Prolepsis – when you concede a point in advance so as to win that point later

Tricolon – the familiar rule of three

BIBLIOGRAPHY

The library on rhetoric runs to many hundreds of volumes and I have limited this selection to its most recent additions and the indispensable classics.

Aristotle, *The Art of Rhetoric*, Penguin, 2004

Cannadine, David (ed.), *Winston Churchill: Blood, Toil, Tears and Sweat: The Great Speeches*, Penguin, 2007

Cicero, *The Republic, The Laws*, Oxford University Press, 1998

Clark, Tom (ed.), *Great Speeches of the 20th Century*, Preface, 2008

Cockcroft, Robert and Cockcroft, Susan, *Persuading People, An Introduction to Rhetoric*, Palgrave, 2005

Davies, Graham, *The Presentation Coach, Bare Knuckle Brilliance for Every Presenter*, Capstone, 2010

Empson, William, *Seven Types of Ambiguity*, Chatto and Windus, 1930

Heffer, Simon (ed.), *Great British Speeches*, Quercus, 2009

Heinrichs, Jay, *Thank You for Arguing: What Aristotle, Eminem and Homer (Simpson) Can Teach Us About the Art of Persuasion*, Allen Lane, 2008

Heller, Richard, *High Impact Speeches*, Pearson, 2003

Humes, James C., *Confessions of a White House Ghost Writer*, Regnery, 1977

Lancaster, Simon, *Speech Writing: The Expert Guide*, Robert Hale Ltd, 2010

Leith, Sam, *You Talkin' to Me?: Rhetoric from Aristotle to Obama*, Profile, 2011

MacArthur, Brian (ed.), *The Penguin Book of Twentieth Century Speeches*, Penguin, 1999

MacArthur, Brian (ed.), *The Penguin Book of Historic Speeches*, Penguin, 2005

Orwell, George, *The Collected Essays, Journalism and Letters, Volume 2, My Country Right or Left, 1940–1943*, Martin Secker and Warburg, 1968

Orwell, George, *The Collected Essays, Journalism and Letters, Volume 3, As I Please, 1943–1945*, Penguin, 1968

Orwell, George, *Why I Write*, Penguin, 2004

Safire, William, *Lend Me Your Ears, Great Speeches in History*, The Cobbet Corporation, 2004

Saunders, A.N.W. (ed.), *Greek Political Oratory*, Penguin, 1985

Schlesinger, Robert, *White House Ghosts*, Simon and Schuster, 2008

Sebag Montefiore, Simon, *Speeches that Changed the World*, Quercus, 2007

INDEX

Index compiled by Annette Musker

THE KILLING OF LORD GEORGE

THE KILLING OF LORD GEORGE

OF

LORD GEORGE

A Tale of MURDER and DECEIT
in EDWARDIAN England

KARL SHAW

ICON

In loving memory of Charles Leonard Shaw
8 May 1931–24 December 2021

Published in the UK in 2022
by Icon Books Ltd, Omnibus Business Centre,
39–41 North Road, London N7 9DP
email: info@iconbooks.com
www.iconbooks.com

Sold in the UK, Europe and Asia
by Faber & Faber Ltd, Bloomsbury House,
74–77 Great Russell Street,
London WC1B 3DA or their agents

Distributed in the UK, Europe and Asia
by Grantham Book Services,
Trent Road, Grantham NG31 7XQ

Distributed in Australia and New Zealand
by Allen & Unwin Pty Ltd,
PO Box 8500, 83 Alexander Street,
Crows Nest, NSW 2065

Distributed in South Africa
by Jonathan Ball, Office B4, The District,
41 Sir Lowry Road, Woodstock 7925

Distributed in India by Penguin Books India,
7th Floor, Infinity Tower – C, DLF Cyber City,
Gurgaon 122002, Haryana

ISBN: 978-178578-846-8

Text copyright © 2022 Karl Shaw

Typeset in Stempel Garamond by Marie Doherty

Printed and bound in Great Britain
by Clays Ltd, Elcograf S.p.A.

ABOUT THE AUTHOR

Karl Shaw is an author and journalist. His previous books include *Mad, Bad and Dangerous to Know*, *Abject Quizzery* and *The First Showman*. He lives in North Staffordshire.

'To Herbert Cooper I leave the sum of fifty pounds.'
The last will and testament
of George Sanger (1825–1911)

Contents

Introduction

ON 28 NOVEMBER 1911 an elderly retired showman died
violently at his home in North London. A coroner
ruled that he was battered to death with a hatchet by an
insane employee. The victim was a celebrity known to the
world as Lord George Sanger. His name was once the biggest
brand in show business and for more than half a century he
was Britain's most popular and most successful entertainer,
venerated as a national institution.

His death a few weeks short of his 86th birthday was
considered one of the most callous murders in English criminal history and it was one of the news sensations of the
age. The story read like a popular crime thriller: a crazed,
merciless killer, a famous victim, a desperate manhunt and
a dramatic denouement few could have anticipated. But for
all its dark drama, this was no work of fiction.

The details of the events leading to George Sanger's death
were widely reported but never properly tested in a criminal court. Most people including the police accepted the
coroner's verdict that he was murdered by a young man he
thought of as a son, but some, even within the victim's own
family, struggled to make sense of it all. The story hinted
uncomfortably at the possibility that there was something
rotten at the core. For more than a century, questions have
persisted about the murder.

Using previously unpublished archive material including original evidence, witness statements and police documents, this book will reconstruct the events leading up to the evening of 28 November 1911 and reveal the true story behind the brutal crime that shocked and mystified Edwardian England.

All of the words enclosed in quotation marks are reproduced directly from coroner's court files, police interviews, correspondence between detectives or newspaper reports.

A note about money. Values are difficult to compare across time, but one pound in 1911 had the purchasing power of about £120 in 2021. The Edwardian pound was divided into twenty shillings (worth 5p each of today's money and abbreviated as 's') and each shilling was made up of twelve pence (thus 2.4 to each 1p and abbreviated as 'd'). A sum of money expressed as, for example, £5 5s 6d, was five pounds, five shillings and six pence. A guinea was worth 21 shillings.

I

Park Farm

T UESDAY 28 NOVEMBER 1911, East Finchley, north London. The long, summer heatwave in the year of King George V's coronation had given way to the coldest, wettest autumn anyone cared to remember. In East End Road, several days of unrelenting rainfall formed pools of water in the ruts made by the wheel tracks of funeral cortèges servicing the nearby St Marylebone Cemetery. The temperature had not nudged above three degrees Celsius all day.

5.40pm. William Venables, a twenty-year-old butcher's assistant, was on his bicycle delivering parcels of meat for his employers Pulham & Sons. Battling the evening chill, his collar was pulled high and his chin tucked into his scarf as he pedalled through the dimly lit thoroughfares. His long day began at six in the morning and he was looking forward to being at home. William lived with his parents in a small, terraced house in Brackenbury Road, a poor but respectable part of East Finchley. His 50-year-old father Alfred worked as a gardener in the local cemetery.

Finchley was an ancient village on the Great North Road, the historic highway running out of London to York,

Edinburgh and all points in-between. It was once notoriously associated with armed robbery, the place where 18th-century highwaymen such as Jack Shepherd and Dick Turpin waylaid carriages as they made the slow journey north. At the junction of Bedford Road and High Road stood the gibbets where the corpses of executed outlaws were hung in chains and left to rot as a discouragement to others. When William Venables' father Alfred was born, Finchley was a community of small cottages and home to a modest 2,500 souls, some clustered around the mediaeval parish church of St Mary-at-Finchley, others living in the newer settlement of East Finchley. Much of the local work was to service the needs of travellers and of London, with soot and manure out of the city swapped for hay and coal, but the area was also known for its hog markets and dairy farms and the underlying clay was perfect for brickmaking. Although only five miles from the centre of London, it was a world away from the incessant bustle and noxious industries of the city.

Londoners had been attracted to Finchley for centuries, to avoid the plague or more recently for the country air and the pleasing views, but with the arrival of the Great Northern Railway in 1867 the village was transformed into an expanding town for the upwardly mobile. The old horse-drawn coach that ran every fifteen minutes from the Bald Faced Stag to London's West End took an hour and a half to reach its destination, but the steam train cut the journey to half an hour for 4d a return ticket. The railway brought a decline in the hog markets and the coach trade, but there were new opportunities. The city had a pressing need

for new burial space. The building of the St Marylebone Cemetery on 57 acres of Newmarket Farm in 1854 brought 10,000 new corpses a year, the dead pumping new life into the local economy with fresh trade for local publicans catering for mourners, a windfall for ornamental stonemasons and steady work for Alfred Venables.

5.45pm. The butcher's assistant made a left turn onto East End Road. This was once the poorest part of town, crammed with tenements and terraced houses. Like its London namesake, the neighbourhood had a low reputation and contained a largely impoverished and reputedly truculent community. A local vicar who had worked in both said he'd 'rarely seen the Finchley boy equalled for profanity and rudeness'. But the area was more recently attracting the well-to-do. East End Road's south-facing slopes were much admired by builders and developers and the thoroughfare was now fringed by several elegant villas set in impressive grounds, suitably distanced from the working-class homes and far enough away from the dirt and smells of the hog markets. One of the biggest residences, Avenue House, was the home of East Finchley's second-most-notable local, Henry Charles 'Inky' Stephens. His father, a doctor who had shared a room at medical school with John Keats, invented an indelible 'Blue-Black Writing Fluid' which became famous as Stephens' Ink and made the family's fortune. Some of the bigger houses in East End Road had been converted to convents or penitentiaries. One was a Magdalene asylum where 'fallen women' laboured in silence all year round in a laundry, their breasts bound and their heads shaved, symbolically washing away their sins. Many of those locked

away were little more than children, some as young as thirteen. Further eastward on the East End Road, where the houses were smaller and closer together, was the Venables' local watering hole, The Five Bells. It was favoured by East Finchley's working classes and was once a venue for bare-knuckle boxing. The champion pugilist William Springall, 'a barn door in boots', once fought here before he retired to East Finchley and became a landlord and boxing promoter. He is buried in the nearby cemetery beneath a small headstone bearing the legend 'Gone but not forgotten'.

5.47pm. The black clouds that had threatened rain all evening were finally releasing a deluge. William Venables put his head down and pushed harder on the pedals, hoping to escape from his errands before the worst of it came. His route would presently take him past Park Farm, one of the best addresses in the neighbourhood and home of East Finchley's most famous resident. Until a few years ago it had been one of the few surviving dairy farms in the district, before it became the winter quarters of Sanger's Circus. It was now the retirement home of its celebrity owner 'Lord' George. Ahead, by the yellow light of a gas lamp, the cyclist could make out a figure standing by the gate leading into Park Farm, their shadow indistinctly reflected on a roadside puddle of water. As he drew closer he heard a sort of choking yell, then the figure staggered into the road and called out clearly: 'Will no one help us? Herbert is murdering us!'

Venables slowed. He recognised the figure as Arthur Jackson, a customer at the butcher's shop and lately an employee at Park Farm. The cyclist came to a halt alongside and saw by the lamplight that there was blood on Jackson's

face and shirt collar. Almost directly across the road was a cottage, Park Farm View. Venables abandoned his bike and hammered on the cottage door to summon help.

It was presently opened by a familiar face. His friend, 24-year-old Tom Cooper, worked at Park Farm with his brother Herbert and their father, Thomas senior, the farm bailiff. Tom looked across the road and saw two men illuminated by the flickering street lamp. As he approached he saw that one of the men was reeling and holding his head in his hands. Then he noticed the blood on the man's face and clothing. Venables urged: 'Tom, something bad has happened at the farm. You'd better go over there.'

Park Farm stood silent, cloistered by fir trees. Venables watched as his friend Tom entered the premises by the farm gate then disappeared into the shadows. Light spilled from the sash windows of the farmhouse but there was no sign of movement from within. Finding the front door unlocked, Tom Cooper stepped inside. At the end of a passage a heavy oak door to the drawing room was ajar. He pushed on the door and opened it wider. On the floor, near a hearthrug between the fireplace and the dining table, he could see the body of an elderly man lying spread-eagled on his back. He recognised him as George Sanger, the farm owner. Beneath his head a dark trickle of blood was visible. Kneeling, he gently raised the old man's head and spoke his name but there was no response. He called out to see if anyone else was home. Silence.

Less than a minute later, Venables and Jackson watched as Tom Cooper emerged running from the farmhouse towards them.

'It's the Guvnor, he needs a doctor quick. Billy, give me your bike.'

The butcher's assistant surrendered his bicycle and watched his friend pedal off into the darkness.

5.50pm. PC Frederick Nicholls was cold and wet. He was on fixed point duty at Fortis Green Road about a mile and a half from Park Farm. The Metropolitan Police district extended to a radius of about fifteen miles from Charing Cross and covered more than 700 square miles. The force was divided into twenty divisions. In each, as well as local police stations, there were fixed points at which a constable could be found, normally from 9am to 1am, the hours varying depending on local circumstances. They were scattered widely and their locations advertised in newspapers and on police station notice boards. Fixed point duty was the curse of the beat bobby because it was neither challenging nor rewarding police work. PC Nicholls was not allowed to leave his post unless ordered to do so by a superior, even to give assistance if it was needed, to the frustration of the public. In an emergency, a constable thus engaged could only direct someone to the nearest police station or raise an alarm by blowing his whistle so the nearest bobby could respond.

Nicholls swung his bullseye lantern in the direction of a young man approaching on a bicycle. He knew him as one of Thomas Cooper's sons, Tom junior. The cyclist shouted: 'Go round to Sanger's farm at once.'

'What's the matter?'

'I don't know, but I'm going for a doctor.'

Ignoring his brief, PC Nicholls abandoned his post and set off in double-time towards Park Farm.

The St Martin's Church clock was striking six o'clock as the constable entered by the farm gate. There was no response at the front but finding the back door of the farm-house unlocked he went inside. The door opened onto a long passage with various rooms off it. On the left at the end was a kitchen. Nicholls recognised the man now standing inside the kitchen doorway as Arthur Jackson and noted the blood on his face and collar.

Jackson spoke: 'Herbert Cooper did it, and he did the Guv'nor as well.'

Thomas Cooper senior entered the kitchen. He was in his mid-fifties, a little shorter and stockier than his son Tom. Indicating Jackson's injuries, PC Nicholls asked Cooper: 'Where is the man that did this?'

Without replying, Thomas Cooper ushered the constable down the passage leading into the drawing room. There Nicholls found the farm owner George Sanger sitting in a chair, bleeding from an ugly wound to his head. He was being attended to by his house servant, Jane Beesley. Nicholls asked Sanger if he could tell him what had happened, but he could see that the old man was barely conscious and in no fit condition to answer. Nicholls went back to the kitchen. On the floor, under the table, he found a broken razor blade with the handle and blade in two parts.

Tom Cooper junior returned to the farmhouse and informed Nicholls that a doctor was on his way. Nicholls instructed Cooper to get a bowl of water to bathe Jackson, then the constable went outside and flagged down a passing cyclist. He asked the man if he knew his way to the local police station. The man confirmed that he did.

'Go there and tell the officer on duty to send someone, a sergeant if possible, round to Sanger's farm at once. There's been an attempted murder.'

Ten minutes later Dr William Orr arrived from High Road in East Finchley and he dressed Sanger's and Jackson's wounds. A few minutes after that they were joined by the first of several visitors. James Holloway was married to the farm owner's sister Amelia. He arrived to find his brother-in-law sitting on a chair in the living room with his eyes closed. Holloway, Dr Orr and the Coopers carried the injured man into his ground-floor bedroom and laid him on his bed.

News of the disturbance at Park Farm spread quickly. At 6pm, 31-year-old PC Albert White was mid-way through his shift, proceeding as he was obliged to do at a steady walking pace of two-and-a-half miles an hour, patrolling the area between East Finchley and Church End. The average beat length all over the Metropolitan district was seven-and-a-half miles for day duty and two miles for night duty.[1]

As the constable turned onto East End Road at the junction of Brackenbury Road he was approached by a woman whose name he couldn't recall, but he knew she worked at the local off-licence. The woman had a question for White. Did he know if anything had happened at Sanger's Farm?

'No, what have you heard?'

'I hear there is a policeman gone there.'

White thanked her and headed towards the farm. He'd made his first circuit of East End Road past Park Farm not long since and all was quiet, but he decided he'd better take another look. From the road outside the farm, White gave the premises a cursory once-over but could see nothing

suspicious. Satisfied that his detour was a wasted effort he went on his way, but when he got as far as Church Lane he thought better of it and turned back. He knocked at the front door of the farm and it was opened by a familiar face, that of the farm bailiff Thomas Cooper senior.

'Has anything unusual happened here tonight, Mr Cooper?' The constable could already see from the man's expression that something had.

Cooper replied quietly. 'One of your comrades is here, you'd better come in.'

In the kitchen, the constable found PC Nicholls and two men with their heads heavily bandaged. One of the injured men PC White already knew as Arthur Jackson, the other he learned was Harry Austin, an equestrian who worked for George Sanger's circus. Austin, they learned, had also been injured during the incident and had returned having fled to seek help. PC Nicholls took his colleague to one side.

'There's a big assault job gone on here.'

'What have you done about it?'

Nicholls explained that there were no telephones at Park Farm, so he had sent a passing cyclist to relay a message to the police station.

'Can you trust him?' Without waiting for a reply, PC White instructed Nicholls not to allow anyone else to enter the house and hurried off to find the nearest phone.

7.50pm. At Finchley station, 45-year-old Sub-Divisional Inspector John Cundell took a phone call from PC White at the Five Bells public house. White informed him that 'something serious' had happened at Sanger's and a senior officer was needed there immediately. Cundell made a note of the

time, then took his bicycle and made haste to Park Farm, arriving at about 8.20pm. He found White standing sentinel at the door. The constable's job was to preserve the integrity of any evidence that existed, but Cundell found the crime scene already busy with anxious members of the extended Sanger household, including James Holloway, the house-maid Jane Beesley, the farm owner's grand-daughter Ellen Austin and her sister-in-law Agnes Austin. Soon they were joined by the police divisional surgeon Dr Baker.

Cundell debriefed the two constables who were first at the scene, then took statements from the two injured men, Jackson and Austin. He then went to check on the farm owner, who was lying limp and insensible on his bed. The police inspector thought it likely he was already beyond any medical help that could be offered. All the doctors could do was make their patient as comfortable as possible.

In the drawing room, Cundell noted signs of a struggle. Opposite the door stood a grand stone fireplace. On the mantlepiece there was a broken glass-fronted clock. On the floor on the opposite side of the room, a large, heavy, bronze diamond-shaped candelabra lay broken in two pieces. On the base of the candelabra there was a blood stain. The fire irons had been knocked into the grate. On the floor there was a black, hard felt hat, badly damaged with a chunk of it lying adrift nearby and some shards of glass, presum-ably from the clock. There was a bloodstain on the floor near the hearth and a second blood stain on the end of the table nearest the door.

Cundell returned to the injured man in the bedroom. He was comatose and dying – Doctors Orr and Baker were quite

certain they could do nothing to prevent that – but there was at least a small hope that he might recover consciousness long enough to confirm the identity of his attacker. Cundell made arrangements for the attendance of a justice and a justice's clerk to take the old man's dying deposition, just in case.

By 8.30pm the police presence at Park Farm had grown to include the two men who would be taking charge of the case, Detective Inspectors George Wallace and Henry Brooks of the Metropolitan Police S (Hampstead) Division. Wallace and Brooks were annoyed, having arrived at the crime scene to find it swarming with people. Because of the delay in reporting the incident, before any pursuit could commence in earnest, the perpetrator would have a head start of more than three hours. In this chaotic situation the investigation continued. Taking charge, Wallace made his displeasure known to Cundell and issued a sharp instruction to organise a thorough search of the farm outbuildings.

Park Farm was once the hub of a thriving dairy business covering hundreds of acres. Set in large gardens, the farmhouse and courtyard were flanked by outbuildings, easily visible beyond the low stone wall fronting the premises. It was little altered since George Sanger bought it in the mid 1890s, although of the original 200 acres of grazing land, sloping away towards Hampstead Heath and Golders Green, about half had been sold off to the new Hampstead Garden Suburb development for the building of residential homes. The old farm property was a long, straggling building built at right-angles to the East End Road, comprising two large yellow sandstone cottages knocked into one. Over the porch of the front door of the cottage nearest the roadside there

was a royal coat of arms, a relic of Astley's Amphitheatre on Westminster Road and a reminder of the times when the famous owner performed for the late Queen Victoria and her son the Prince of Wales. Inside, to the left was a large drawing room containing a fireplace, two chairs, a table and a sideboard. Wallace and Brooks noted the signs of a struggle, including the splashes of blood on the floor and the edge of the table. They made notes, but no photographs were taken. Cameras had been used to capture images of convicts for more than 40 years but no one in the Metropolitan Police thought them useful to routinely record crime scenes.

In the drawing room and throughout the house, on sideboards, mantlepieces and in corners, there were mementos of the owner's former life and travels, including several large statues of famous circus horses. He had a particular fondness for silver plate and there was a considerable quantity of it lying around, including silver soup tureens, candelabra and a large, eye-catching silver cup, labelled 'Presented by the Prince and Princess of Wales'. From the drawing room, there was a long corridor with ground floor rooms off it, including the kitchen, pantry and scullery and a downstairs bedroom. Park Farm was a substantial property with several upstairs bedrooms, but after more than 80 years of living in a caravan, the owner had never got into the habit of climbing stairs to go to sleep. In the kitchen, on a mantlepiece, the senior detectives noted a bloodied cut-throat razor with the blade tied open with a piece of string.

In addition to the main house there were various outbuildings, including four stables and two fowl houses forming three sides to the square cobbled courtyard. To the

left rose a curious-looking building, a high barn with huge glass doors. This was Sanger's former elephant house. In front of the building there was a bench on which was placed an elephant's skull. According to local legend, it belonged to a beast that broke loose at Crystal Palace and killed his keeper. There were also a few ducks, geese and pigeons. A parrot on a pergola screeched *George! George! George!* while a large dog forlornly wandered the courtyard.

At the front of the premises nearest to the road there were two small garden enclosures and a path between them to the right sloped away to a large circular duck pond. In the gardens there were large fir trees and chrysanthemums growing wild among the borders of the lawns. Until their owner's retirement six years ago, a great menagerie had wintered at the farm, but now the only survivors from the circus days were four small ponies and two black piebald horses in an outbuilding. George Sanger had occasionally used them to drive up to the town, but the horses, like their master, were now old and worn.

In a space between one of the two fowl houses and a stable, the police found signs that someone had fixed up a makeshift bedroom. In this den, one of the many officers milling around the scene had found an old unloaded six chamber Enfield revolver. It was recorded in the evidence book, but no one was particularly excited by the discovery. It was an obsolete standard-issue firearm of the armed forces and there were plenty of them in circulation. There were no clues as to the owner's whereabouts or his state of mind.

More police officers were arriving by the minute from nearby S Division stations. By 9pm Wallace and Brooks had

about a hundred uniformed men at their disposal, scouring the surrounding district by lantern light. An officer was sent by cab to contact all the fixed pointsmen on the route between Swiss Cottage and East Finchley and supply them with a description of Cooper. Meanwhile the two senior detectives were trying to piece together Herbert Cooper's movements earlier in the day and were taking statements from his father and his brother.

By 10pm Wallace and Brooks had marshalled the basic facts of what they believed had taken place at Park Farm earlier that evening. From testimonies given earlier, they learned that until five weeks ago, Herbert Cooper, 26-year-old son of the farm bailiff Thomas Cooper and older brother of Thomas John Cooper, had served at the farm as personal attendant to George Sanger. Herbert Cooper had worked for Sanger in this capacity for about six years and he had the run of the house. He slept in Sanger's room, read newspapers to him, accompanied him on trips into town and generally acted as his confidential helper. For reasons yet to be determined, Herbert Cooper had fallen out of favour and his job had been taken by Arthur Jackson. Cooper was still working on the farm as a general labourer but was no longer allowed in the house and was thought to have been sleeping rough in one of the farm outbuildings.

It appeared that Herbert Cooper had taken the loss of his status badly. At around 5.45pm that evening he entered the farmhouse and went into the kitchen where Jackson was sitting alone at the table, reading. Cooper told Jackson he had come to retrieve his gramophone from the pantry, but then Cooper attacked him from behind, slashing at his throat

with a cut-throat razor. There was a furious struggle and Jackson was left bleeding and semi-conscious on the kitchen floor.

Harry Austin meanwhile was sitting with George Sanger in the drawing room when they were interrupted by a noise from the kitchen. Austin went to the door and saw Cooper charging towards him wielding a large, heavy axe above his head. Austin tried to block his entry by closing the door, but Cooper was too powerful for him. In a wild, frenzied attack, Cooper first set about Austin, then the defenceless Sanger, battering them with his weapon. Leaving both men for dead, Cooper fled the scene and disappeared into the night. Neither Jackson nor Austin had any doubts about the identity of their assailant.

Two police officers had waited by the stricken man's bedside in the hope that he would rally sufficiently to give them a statement, but George Sanger did not recover consciousness. Doctors Orr and Baker jointly pronounced life extinct at precisely 11pm. The manhunt for his murderer was on.

2

Press gang

I'T'S NOT ALTOGETHER CLEAR exactly when George Sanger was born. When it came to details of his past he had a complicated relationship with the truth, or you could say he had a showman's flair for telling tales. It was most likely in 1825 but he always claimed that he was a couple of years younger.[2] We only know for certain that the happy event took place in the market town of Newbury in Berkshire. His father James was a travelling showman, one of many itinerant performers who tramped the roads from March to October working the country fair circuit. Some of his fellow travellers did it for the love of the trade and some married into it. Many found the nomadic life a convenient hiding place from a problem left behind, perhaps a broken marriage or something much worse. Others drifted into it for want of anything better to do. For James Sanger, the showman's life was the choice between the devil and the deep blue sea.

The Sangers were Wiltshire people. According to a romantic family lore, they were once mediaeval wandering minstrels who came to England in the early 13th century. Another version holds that a Sanger was a jester in the

court of King John. It's more likely they were strolling Yiddish performers from Germany. Sanger was a common German-Jewish surname and since the early 1700s Jews provided two-thirds of the travelling showfolk of England. When he was an old man, George would refer to the Hebrew market traders of north London with affection as 'my people', to the bafflement of younger members of his family who had never before considered that any Jewish blood may run through their veins.

For many generations the Sangers were tenant farmers, tilling the fields around the village of Tisbury on the edge of Salisbury Plain. As soon as he was old enough, James Sanger was apprenticed to a toolmaker in town. On his day off, his father put him to work around the farm. When he was not quite eighteen, James said goodbye to his mother and father and set off with his elder brother John to visit some friends in London. It was the last time James ever saw his parents.

It was December 1798 and Britain was at war with France. The beat of the recruiting drum was sounding in town squares and on village greens all over the country. Britain's strength lay in its navy, as it had for a hundred years and more. In London, James and his brother were making their way across London Bridge when they heard the cry 'Press! Press!' Impressment was the age-old right of the Crown to the labour of seafarers in time of war and press gangers roamed the towns and cities, taking men against their will to serve, making sons and husbands disappear for months, even years on end. The Sanger brothers fled in opposite directions. John ducked into a druggist's warehouse where the proprietor's pretty daughter allowed him to hide.[3] James

spent the night in a barrel under the bridge, but when he emerged the next morning another group of gangers was waiting. He fought back with fists and feet but was heavily outnumbered and battered into submission. An hour later, bloodied and bruised, he found himself on a ship near Deptford with about 150 fellow victims, scooped up to fight Britannia's battles on the high seas. A few days later, James Sanger was transferred to HMS *Agincourt* and he and his fellow recruits were mustered on deck to hear the harsh rules that would govern their daily life. Some of those on board would have already showed the livid cross-hatching of scars where their backs had been subjected to the lash. It was used liberally to tame reluctant sailors, every stroke biting into their flesh. Below deck, James was packed with hundreds of men into a cramped, fetid space stinking of unwashed bodies, tobacco, tar and sewage. Sickness spread easily and typhus, cholera and dysentery posed a greater threat to sailors than battles at sea. On deck they were at the mercy of the weather and novice sailors were often blown overboard and drowned. From the deck of HMS *Agincourt* James witnessed a terrible storm and saw two warships go down.

After a couple of years he was transferred to HMS *Pompee*. It was captured from the French at Toulon and was now a 74-gun Royal Navy ship of the line, a brute killer of the deep. In the Caribbean, James saw his first action. HMS *Pompee* was designated flagship of a British invasion force to capture the French West Indies. It was equipped with carronades, lightweight guns known as 'smashers' because of the destruction they wreaked at close range. For three days and nights James's ship was engaged

in a 500-mile running battle with the French flagship *Hautpoult*. On 17 April 1809 the *Hautpoult*'s mizzen mast was brought down and the *Pompee* drew alongside to use her carronades to deadly effect. Below deck it was hot and airless and every surface shook from the thunderous recoil of guns. Men wrapped scarves around their heads to protect their ears from the pounding of the cannon. Competing with the stench of blood and burning flesh were the screams and moans of the wounded and dying from every corner. After a terrifying 75-minute exchange of fire, the crippled *Hautpoult* surrendered having sustained heavy casualties, and was taken as a prize. Back at Dartmouth, there was an outbreak of typhus on the *Pompee*. Two men went down with symptoms of 'vomiting, a foul tongue, quick pulse and pain in the head, back and loins'.[4] One died the next day and within a week many more were taken ill.

Between the risk of disease, the lash and the thunder of cannon, James's most regular enemy was boredom. Routine was important for discipline because if it broke down there was the risk of mutiny. Time passed slowly, every day a ritual of scrubbing, cleaning, painting and sewing, but then one day there was an exciting arrival that would change the course of James Sanger's life. While the *Pompee* was moored at Deal, the ship was visited by bumboats ferrying supplies and trafficking with the sailors. One of the boats carried the brothers Israel and Benjamin Hart. They were strolling conjurers seeking to earn some money by performing for the crew. Their enterprise was cut cruelly short when the ship's captain found out the Harts had naval experience and he seized them for the service of the King. But it was

James's good fortune. He enjoyed the company of the Hart brothers and in-between duties his new friends taught him some simple conjuring tricks.

Family legend has it that James Sanger was transferred to Nelson's flagship HMS *Victory* and served on her at Trafalgar. In the thick of the battle, he and 25 others boarded an enemy vessel. Eleven of his shipmates were killed in action while James sustained a severe head wound, smashed four ribs and lost several fingers. He was back on the deck of the *Victory* in time to see Horatio Nelson fall. In 1815, ten years and eight months after he joined, James Sanger left the Royal Navy.[5]

Britain's naval triumphs were followed by thousands of personal tragedies among the people who had made them possible. Almost a third of those who fought died from wounds or fever and the bulk of the rest faced redundancy. The King and his government cared little for the welfare of the laid-off seaman. Officers retired on half-pay, but for those among the lower ranks the return to civilian life was cruel. Dismissed from the services without pension or acknowledgment, James Sanger and his fellow return-ing sailors found themselves adrift in an economy that was shrinking fast and a labour market that was already over-crowded. After nearly eleven years away, James went home to find his parents long dead and little sympathy from his siblings. Perhaps they reminded him that he had abandoned his family for a reckless adventure at sea while they bore the brunt of the worst economic hardship anyone could remember. Now he was back, not a returning war hero, but a nuisance and a burden. Harsh words were exchanged and James left never to return.

The Wiltshire country roads were full of people on the move, some like James Sanger recently returned from the war, others habitual vagabonds, thrown out of parishes because they could prove no right to poor relief. The French wars had been running endlessly and a series of bad harvests had savagely driven up the price of bread. There was hunger everywhere. On the roadside, nettles sold for twopence a pound, to be eaten with salt and pepper as a substitute for potatoes. In every town and village there were discharged soldiers and sailors, many badly injured or mutilated by amputations, destitute men with no alternative future but crime or beggary and an early death in the workhouse.

Remembering the conjuring tricks he'd learned from the Hart brothers, James Sanger decided to try his luck as a showman. Even in the worst of times, there were fairs and fetes in Regency England everywhere from south to north. They were the perennial climaxes of the holiday calendar, part of the seasonal rhythms of rural life. Most fairs had ancient origins as places for traders to show their wares. They attracted saddlers and harness makers, cloth traders from Yorkshire, earthenware sellers from the Potteries and dairymen bringing their cheeses from Derbyshire and Cheshire. There were also statute fairs or 'mops' held for the autumn hiring of agricultural labour. Entertainers followed close on their heels. Amid the ribbon sellers, trouser salesmen and 'scrapers of cat gut' there were swing boats and merry-go-rounds and stalls selling sugar plums, lollipops and gingerbread. Over time, the business side of the fairs faded away and they became places of pleasure and entertainment.

The variety of ways that men, women and children found to turn a penny was infinite. Rope and wire dancers competed with conjurers, tumblers, clowns and trick-riders, hurdy-gurdy players, dancing booths, glassblowers and Chinese sewing-needle swallowers. There were freak shows, human and animal. At Bartholomew's fair in London you could see 'a Mare with Seven feet,' a misshapen sheep, a young Oronatu Savage, a 120-stone hog, 'the smallest woman in the world, Maria Teresa the Amazing Corsican Fairy', a giantess from Norfolk and 'a man who performed the disgusting feat of eating a fowl alive'.[6]

At Bristol Haymarket James Sanger tried to prise a few pennies from reluctant pockets, inviting passers-by to judge his sleight of hand: *Step up for a little hanky-panky. One, two, three – presto – begone! I'll show your ludship as pretty a trick of putting a piece of money in your eye and taking it out of your elbow, as you ever beheld!*

He invested his earnings in a portable peep show. It was the most basic of entertainments, the staple of fairs, wakes and market days. There were hundreds of peep-show operators working the big cities, many of them military veterans like James. His humble show was contained within a large box on a folding trestle which he carried on his back. The box had six peep holes fitted with lenses through which customers were invited to peer. A penny or a halfpenny bought a performance comprising a series of crudely painted scenes attached to strings, lowered into view as the spectator kept his eyes glued to the hole. These scenes illustrated a story narrated by the operator, the whole made more plausible by very dim illumination from tallow candles. The perennial

favourite subjects of the peep show were notorious murders and famous military victories. They were exhibited over and over until they fell apart and it was often only through the showman's expert patter that anyone could guess which conflict the scene represented. Charles Dickens saw a worn-out peep show that had 'originally started with the Battle of Waterloo and had since made it every other battle of later date by altering the Duke of Wellington's nose'.[7]

James's first show was the Battle of Trafalgar. He was a natural storyteller and he quickly picked up the spieler's art. As his customers craned their necks, straining to make sense of the dimly lit images within, he seduced them with dramatic tales about the famous battle he claimed he had actually fought in. Daily he tramped the thoroughfares carrying his simple peep show on his back, setting up a pitch wherever pedestrian traffic was heaviest. There were many times when he was sodden, frozen and there were no customers in sight, but at least he kept starvation at bay.

At Bristol Haymarket he met Sarah Elliott, a lady's maid. After a brief courtship they were married at Bedminster where Sarah's mother kept the Black Horse inn. The couple settled at Newbury where James had relatives in the fruit and vegetable trade. Newbury was a small market town on the River Kennet, straddling the roads to London and Bath. Through the winter the couple earned a living shuttling back and forth to London, dealing in fish and fruit, which they sold from a stall every Thursday in the marketplace. For the rest of the year they were travelling show people, James carrying the peep show on his back while Sarah sold toffee apples from a tray for a halfpenny each.

When Sarah gave birth to their first child, the small family was able to live cheaply lodging with relatives. The need for larger accommodation became a pressing concern with the swift arrival of a second. James rented a small house on Wharf Road near to the market square where the stocks still stood. Tramping the country roads on foot with small children in tow was no longer an option, so James got together the materials to build his first caravan. It was a primitive affair, the roof and sides made from thin sheets of iron. In the summer it was suffocatingly hot inside and so bitterly cold in winter that they preferred to sleep in a tent, but on the whole it made travelling more tolerable.

James's show was evolving too, with a new source of income, a makeshift children's roundabout. He made some wooden horses, crudely fashioned from sticks and half-inch deal boards covered with rabbit skin, painted up in white with red and blue spots. Horsepower was supplied from local boys at the fairs, happy to push the contraption around for the reward of a ride later. Travelling in a caravan also meant that James could carry a bigger and better peep show. His new deluxe version had 26 apertures and new painted scenes supplied by a drunken Irishman who charged three-shillings-and-sixpence for battle scenes, seven-shillings-and-sixpence for extra corpses. James's convincing patter did the rest.

While touring the West Country, he added some daring new attractions to his mobile show to sate the Victorian public's appetite for 'human curiosities' – Madame Gomez 'the tallest woman in the world' and two 'savage cannibal pigmies of the Dark Continent'. The acts relied heavily on

James's ingenuity and powers of persuasion. The exotic Madame Gomez was neither foreign nor very tall, but where nature fell short, a raised platform and long skirts provided. Similarly, the 'savage cannibal pigmies' were not as advertised. Trumpeted as 'fully grown, being, in fact, each over thirty years of age' they were supposedly captured by Portuguese traders in the African wilds: 'incapable of ordinary human speech … their food consists of raw meat, and if they can capture a small animal, they tear it to pieces alive with their teeth, eagerly devouring its flesh and drinking its blood'.[8]

In reality the pygmies were talkative brothers aged nine and ten years, borrowed from their Irish father and black mother who lived in Bristol. Feathers, beads and greasepaint gave them the requisite verisimilitude. The credulous folk of the West Country were hugely impressed, but the authorities were not. James Sanger was forced to abandon his display of living cannibals when he was reported for operating at Plymouth fair without a licence. He fled the district to avoid arrest and his wife and family caught up with him later at Newbury. His performing 'cannibals' were removed to the Bristol workhouse. It was James Sanger's very last experiment with freak-show acts.

The country fair circuit started in Wrexham in early March and finished with the Sheffield wakes in late November. In-between, the Sangers in their tiny wagon, Sarah sitting up front with the latest addition to the growing family in her lap, travelled from town to town and fair to fair, stopping occasionally at a friendly inn along the way or setting up their show wherever else they found a few folks gathered and so hoped to earn a few pennies by

passing round a hat. Often the weather was cruel and a few days of rain could wash away the hopes of the most resilient peep showman, but when spring gave way to summer and the days lengthened and the temperature climbed, they had cash to spare and life was good. The open road had many pleasures and in the cool of a summer morning as their little wagon rattled along the country lanes it was a joy to pass pleasing fields of green and yellow under a bright blue sky, with the scent of wet grass and hawthorn blossoms. At the end of the day they pitched up on a wayside strip of grass, the horses were released from the shafts and there was nearly always a rabbit or grouse for the pot. When the leaves turned red, the Sangers went home to Newbury and their winter work, carrying goods around Berkshire.

But much of the familiar landscape was changing. The wide-spreading hedgerows were being grubbed up to make room for more crops and the commons that had been open to all for centuries were fast disappearing, parcelled up and handed out for private ownership. The new landlords enforced the game laws with zeal and the penalties were high. The law made no distinction between the unemployed and those who chose the nomadic lifestyle, leaving James and his family at the mercy of ruthless statutes designed to punish beggars. Even when they found some haven to present their simple entertainments free from official harassment, at the end of the day there was always the possibility that local hooligans would beat up the defenceless showman and trash his belongings for sport.

But these pressures and hostilities bred solidarity among the wayfaring showfolk. Suspicious and fearful of outsiders,

they kept the world at a distance and spoke a language that only other travellers understood. They lived by their wits and developed a hair-trigger readiness to defend their own against any odds. This was the world into which George Sanger was born on 23 December 1825, the sixth child of ten.

3
Manhunt

Twenty-ninth of November 1911. The search for George Sanger's killer continued through the Tuesday night and into the following morning. Groups of police officers carrying lanterns were despatched to scour the poplar-lined pathways and fields surrounding Park Farm. Meanwhile 40 officers armed with beating sticks and pitchforks probed Grange Wood, a square mile of thick plantation at the back of the farmhouse providing plenty of cover for a man anxious to hide. At Marylebone Cemetery, less than half a mile away, policemen stepped over graves and shone their lamps into newly dug trenches and corners to make sure the fugitive wasn't lurking among the headstones and mausoleums.

When the chilly grey of dawn broke at 7.38am, a low fog hung over Park Farm and the surrounding fields and there was still no trace of the suspect. The farm outbuildings were searched again in case anything had been missed in the mayhem of the night before. Neighbours watched from the adjacent buildings as officers emerged from the skylights of barns and stables and clambered over the rooftops. Herbert Cooper's makeshift bedroom was the focus

of intense police scrutiny, the contents sifted for evidence, but it yielded nothing more of note. Detective Inspector Wallace considered the possibility that Cooper might have killed himself. Four officers were sent to drag the large duck pond behind the outhouse buildings. Another posse of constables walked East End Road, scouring the hedgerows for a body or anything else that might offer a clue. The usually quiet thoroughfare was now swarming with local bobbies and nosy bystanders.

At 9am the exhausted search team was relieved, replaced by hundreds more policemen and volunteers from surrounding neighbourhoods. The search was extended as far as Hampstead Garden Suburb a couple of miles away and to outlying areas of Hampstead Heath. On Wednesday afternoon, attention switched to Finchley Power Station, whose tall brick chimney could be seen from miles around. The station stood in Squires Lane, about half a mile to the north of the farmhouse, and it had a large cooling pond with water up to eighteen-feet deep. An enterprising employee had introduced carp into the pool hoping to breed and sell them for profit but hadn't reckoned on local poachers. Officers spent the morning dragging the pond, but their efforts revealed nothing, least of all carp. By teatime every available man in S Division, extending from Euston Road to the borders of Hertfordshire, was searching for Herbert Charles Cooper.

On Wednesday evening, exhausted by 30 sleepless hours on the case, detectives Wallace and Brooks checked in at Finchley station to consider their next move. Superintendent John Williams had already typed duplicate copies of the first police report to Scotland Yard outlining the crimes

committed at Park Farm the previous day. In summary, Herbert Cooper, 'well-known to several of the police at Finchley and also at Whetstone and Hendon', was the only suspect for the murder of George Sanger and the attempted murders of Arthur Jackson and Harry Austin. Williams concluded: 'It appears that the motive for the crime is one of jealousy.'

Unlike the great sleuths of popular Edwardian fiction, detectives in the Metropolitan Police weren't born to the job, they were promoted into it. Most came from the rank and file and after two or three years any officer who showed promise was given the opportunity to become a detective. A conspicuous act of bravery was often enough to advance a bobby's chances of promotion. James Berrett, who rose to the rank of detective chief inspector, got his break by saving a man from drowning. Detectives were better paid but rarely better educated than the average uniformed bobby. No formal training for the job yet existed. The rough and tumble of life as a working copper in a large or busy town, plus a little theoretical study on the basics of criminal law, was considered more than adequate. Drawn from the uniformed ranks, detectives were invariably well built, strong and above average height. Metropolitan bobbies on the beat were often targets for local thugs and it made good sense for lone patrolling police officers to be tough. It's reasonable to assume that Wallace and Brooks could both be relied upon to acquit themselves nobly in a rough-house. So long as an officer could also handle the paperwork he was a suitable candidate, although the Met was not unduly concerned if some of their detectives struggled to write a report. Wallace

and Brooks had both enjoyed long careers in law enforcement and were near to completing the 25 years' service that would automatically give them a full pension. The pension and free health care were what made the police force attractive to most recruits in the first place. Wallace joined the force in 1888, the year of the Ripper. Looking back, he considered himself fortunate not to have had a senior role in the investigation. The press and public used the police's failure to catch anyone as a stick with which to beat them and reputations had died in the Whitechapel slum where Jack did his killing.

Wallace and Brooks had established an effective working partnership as a murder investigation team and had made a name for themselves with one of the headline-grabbing cases of the day. In April that year they worked together on a landmark case of which they were justifiably proud. Alice Linford, a 22-year-old parlour maid, had the misfortune to become engaged to George Pateman, a 33-year-old gardener with a violent temper. When she broke it off, her ex-fiancée fatally attacked her in the street outside her home in North Finchley, slashing her throat with a razor. The detectives apprehended the sleeping killer in his lodgings in High Barnet, still wearing his bloodstained clothes. When aroused from his slumber, Pateman was 'peculiar in his manner, with a glaring look in his eyes'.[9] For the very first time, human blood found on clothing was used as evidence. Alice Linford suffered from anaemia. The Home Office team, featuring the rising star of forensics, a young Dr Bernard Spilsbury, determined that the bloodstains found on Pateman matched those of an anaemic person. Pateman's defence team pleaded

insanity, but he was convicted of wilful murder and sentenced to death, later commuted to imprisonment for life.

Wallace had already made arrangements for a description of Herbert Cooper to be circulated via Scotland Yard to police stations in the Metropolitan district and to the press.

Wanted for murder on 28th, Herbert Cooper (26), six feet; complexion, hair and moustache dark. Recently worked as a farm labourer. Dress – blue suit and light cap; clothing probably bloodstained. He has money and may endeavour to leave the country.

Now the police also had a good photograph of Cooper supplied by his father Thomas, but when Wallace saw the image he began to have doubts about the accuracy of the description that had already gone out. The picture showed a neatly groomed young man with thick, dark, wavy hair parted in the centre, good looks and a modish moustache, smartly dressed in a dark suit with a bold polka-dot tie. He looked nothing at all like an agricultural worker, more like a movie star. Wallace was anxious that the words 'farm labourer' should be removed from the description circulated by Scotland Yard. The young man in the photo didn't look like one and the description could be misleading. He instructed Superintendent Williams to add a note to the bottom of his police report: 'early steps should be taken to correct the impression that he [Cooper] looks like a farm labourer'.

Next, Wallace and Brooks considered motive. Had the violent attacks been planned, or were they the spontaneous act of a madman? A couple of weeks earlier, Herbert Cooper had told Sanger's coachman Harry Grierson that he

was thinking about going to Australia. The detectives contemplated the possibility that the crimes were the unhappy result of an attempted robbery to raise money for his passage. Perhaps Cooper hoped to find the old man alone or asleep. He could have easily overpowered him and made his escape with cash he knew was often left casually lying around or haphazardly heaped in drawers. Did it go wrong when he was unexpectedly disturbed by two members of the household, Jackson and Austin? It was also conceivable that Cooper had planned only to murder Arthur Jackson because he was resentful about losing the job he valued so highly. There was only one certainty: there was a dangerous fugitive on the loose and they had to find him as quickly as possible.

All through Wednesday, Park Farm exerted a voyeuristic magnetism as the sympathetic and the curious came to stand and stare, hoping to savour some of the drama. In East End Road, reporters circled with pencils sharpened and press photographers struggled with heavy cameras, trying to light their magnesium flares in the drizzle, while groups of men, women and children loitered outside the farm gates, jostling for advantage. A single police guard was posted at the farm gate under orders to deter curiosity seekers from straying onto the farm premises for a better look. Much of the population of Finchley wandered by the murder scene and perhaps hundreds more from further afield jumped on the train to join in the excitement.

Murder tourism was all the rage. It had even accelerated the growth of nearby Muswell Hill. In 1896 an elderly resident was beaten to death in one of the area's smart detached houses. Seventy-eight-year-old retired engineer Henry

Smith lived alone. Local rumour had it he was a wealthy miser keeping large sums of money in the house. Fearful of intruders, he devised his own alarm system, a series of trip wires connected to a detonator, but professional burglars Albert Milsom and Henry Fowler coolly dismantled it and forced their way through a window at night and murdered Mr Smith. His body was discovered bound in shreds of blanket by his gardener. The police found the murderers hiding in a travelling waxwork show called The Chamber of Horrors. The pair turned on each other almost immediately, each blaming the other for the crime and in custody Fowler tried to strangle Milsom. At their hanging, they had to be forcibly separated to prevent from them attacking each other. According to the *Hornsey Journal*, after the murder, 15,000 to 20,000 people went to Muswell Hill to see the scene of the crime and many of the visitors liked the area so much that they bought houses there.

It was the second time in recent memory that an East Finchley murder had attracted nationwide attention. Just a mile away from Park Farm there was one of a growing number of private establishments known as baby farms. They catered mostly for desperate young girls who had left it too late to avail themselves of illegal abortion. Claymore House, a semi-detached, red-brick villa in Hertford Road, Finchley, was run by Amelia Sach, who announced herself as a certified nurse and midwife. She assured her clients that their babies would be put up for adoption with wealthy families. The babies were then poisoned and their bodies dumped on rubbish tips or thrown into the Thames. As a high infant mortality rate was a part of daily life, it was thought that the

deaths of a few illegitimate children were unlikely to raise many eyebrows. The murders were performed by an associate, Annie Walters. On her arrest, Walters was described as 'feeble' and is thought to have had a mental age of about ten. She had changed address frequently to avoid difficult questions, but the suspicions of a policeman landlord were aroused when she asked fellow lodgers to buy her chlorodyne and carbolic acid. She was apprehended with a dead baby boy in her arms, killed by a few drops of poison in his feed bottle. Sach and Walters were tried at the Old Bailey in January 1903 and it took the jury just 40 minutes to find them guilty. They were hanged the following month, both women carried screaming to the scaffold, the last double female hanging in Britain.

As Wednesday wore on and the hullaballoo mounted, so did the pressure on Inspectors Wallace and Brooks. Their experience encouraged them to believe that sooner or later someone would come forward with solid news of Herbert Cooper's whereabouts. Across London, police divisions followed up sightings and tip-offs. An East Finchley greengrocer, Charles Norton, told police that at 6.40pm the previous evening he was in his horse and trap outside the Wellington public house on the Great North Road when he saw Cooper wearing a blue suit and cap riding a bicycle towards London. Norton got such a close-up view that the suspect had almost collided with his horse. He told police: 'it is impossible for me to have made a mistake'.

The greengrocer's story was repeated in *The Evening News*, who went with the headline: 'IS THE HUNTED MAN IN LONDON?'

Norton said he had known Herbert Cooper for four years and was positive he saw him cycling down Highgate Hill just under an hour after the murder. *The News* noted that Cooper was 'clever as an acrobat'; acquaintances had seen him turning a succession of somersaults and he was able to ride a bicycle in the saddle. *The News* speculated that these skills would have attracted the attention of the former circus owner Lord George Sanger and led him to single out Cooper as a personal assistant. Norton said he was returning from the market with a load of produce when Cooper passed almost under his horse's head. 'He didn't say anything to me ... I was rather surprised because we often used to have a chat together about horse racing.' Norton explained that it was hard to mistake Cooper because he was 'a very tall fellow ... he was riding quite calmly and did not seem to be in a particular hurry so far as I could judge'.[10]

Wallace had already figured out what had happened at Park Farm, but the big question was still unanswered: where was the murderer now? London was the largest city on earth with a population of 7 million people. If Cooper was hiding there the police were going to need a large slice of luck to flush him out. Very soon it seemed they had one.

4

Peep show

GEORGE WENT TO SCHOOL for a day, but it didn't suit him. He received a caning from his teacher and went home in tears. His mother promised, 'Don't mind, Georgie, you shan't go back anymore.' The classroom was never a concern for him after that.

For the children of travelling showmen responsibility came prematurely. No one was too young to earn their keep or turn a penny. From the day George was able to take his first unsteady steps down the short ladder from his parents' carriage, he was immersed in the sights, sounds and smells of the fairground and initiated into its routines. He couldn't read or write, but at seven years old he knew how to feed and water a horse and conduct a dozen different operations of his father's trade. He already had his own showman's patter. In his clean pinafore and tiny well-greased boots, he summoned passers-by to sample the attractions of his father's latest peep show.

Walk up! Walk up and see the only correct views of the terrible murder of Maria Marten. They are historically

accurate and true to life, depicting the death of Maria at
the hands of the villain Corder in the famous Red Barn.

The Red Barn Murder was a grisly crime that had Georgian England spellbound and the details were as fresh in people's minds as the day it first made the newspapers. No one lost money by overestimating the British public's preoccupation with murder. From Madame Tussaud's touring waxworks show exhibiting the faces of France's decapitated victims of public executions to the humble peep show, violent death and all of its details was the perennial fascination of the age. George's father had done well from the Red Barn Murder, but he was always on the lookout for new material for his peep show. In the summer of 1833, it seems he got lucky. According to the story James Sanger retold many times over, one early evening he was nursing a solitary glass of ale in a Wantage public house when a young farm labourer entered. From the large sickle he carried on his shoulder James guessed he came directly from his work in the fields. The young man got into a row with the landlady, voices were raised and he flung his beer money on the floor. As the landlady bent to pick it up, the visitor raised his cutter high and brought it down across the back of the neck, slicing her head clean off her shoulders. The woman's decapitated body lay in a crimson pool of blood, her head lying some four feet away, staring sightlessly toward the doorway through which the perpetrator had now fled.

That night, James went to work on his new peep show. Scenes from the Red Barn Murder were repurposed to portray 'the terrible murder at the Red Lion as described by an

eyewitness of the dreadful deed'. The paper Maria Marten was cut in two, her body pasted onto a background scene, her head onto the floor, 'and with a plentiful supply of carmine for gore the trick was done'.[11] James's show, full of lurid detail and drama designed to beguile the listener and disguise its shortcomings, was a huge hit. The next day the crowds came to drank ale under the hot sun and eat handfuls of gingerbread while watching the Wantage pub landlady die and die again. For many years afterwards, George and his brothers and sisters would sit around the campfire and their eyes grew wide as their father retold the tale of his encounter with the savage sickle man, the 'Red Lion Murderer'.[12]

The nation's fairgrounds were hotly contested territories. From March to November, showmen large and small, from Wombwell's mighty menagerie to the old soldier carrying the Battle of Waterloo on his back, travelled the highways and byways praying for good weather and decent business. The bigger rival attractions in their massive wagons raced through the countryside to grab the best pitches at the next country fair. Occasionally the tensions boiled over into violence. Wombwell's and Hilton's were the largest travelling menageries of the day and fierce competitors. One early May morning they clashed on the road from Reading to Henley. A Wombwell driver blocked a Hilton wagon trying to pass. Hilton's driver retaliated, knocking Wombwell's man from his seat with a tent pole. It turned into a pitched battle as grooms, drivers and animal trainers laid into each other with crowbars, poles and whips. Even the 'freaks' joined in: 'the Fat Man made for the Living Skeleton with a door hook; the Living Skeleton battered at the Fat Man with a peg mallet'.[13]

The mêlée blocked the road and as other fair vehicles behind were held up, their owners ran to join the fray. The fighting was ferocious and men lay bleeding and senseless in the road. Wombwell's terrified elephants ran amok, smashing wagons to splinters, overturning everything in their path. George and his brother William were alone in their wagon when their horse took fright and bolted, leaving their home overturned in a ditch. Inside, a lighted stove was thrown across the floor. Flames took hold of the woodwork and wagon went down blazing. The young boys' cries were heard by bystanders watching the ruckus. They drew buckets of water from the ditch and doused the fire through the broken wagon window. George and William were rescued, wet and terrified but otherwise unscathed.

Their father made enough money to buy a couple of horses and a new wagon. It was typical of showmen's vans at the time, made from rough oak boards held together with copper nails, the roof boarded then covered with layers of linen or canvas. For eight months of the year, George shared this space, no more than twelve-foot long, seven-foot-six-inches wide and seven-foot tall, with his mother, father and his nine brothers and sisters. Life on the road for a small child was fraught with hazards. George and his siblings were encouraged by their father to learn a useful performing skill as soon as they could walk. George was already showing promise as an acrobat, but for now he just made himself useful however he could. At a fair in the Romney Marshes in Kent, he was left in charge of his father's roundabout, standing in the centre while it whizzed around him. There was a moment's inattention, a careless movement and he slipped

and lost his footing. He was caught by a flying metal bolt, almost ripping the calf muscle away from his right leg. George watched as dark red blood welled out of the gash and ran thick down his ankle and foot. His father ran towards the howls of pain, bound the boy's leg with strips of tent canvas, threw him across the front of his horse's saddle and galloped three miles to the nearest physician. The medic inspected the damaged leg and advised immediate amputation. The wound was severe and potentially gangrenous. Removal of the injured limb wouldn't guarantee George's survival and with no anaesthesia stronger than a shot of whisky he might die of shock under the surgeon's knife, but it was his best chance.

George's father demanded a second opinion. Another doctor was called in, but he concurred; the leg had to go. Angry words were exchanged. George lay on the medic's table listening to the adults arguing back and forth, then he heard his father say finally: 'whether the boy lives or dies it shall be with all his limbs on him'. With that, James dressed his son's wound, bundled him back on their horse and dashed across the fields back to their wagon. George may have watched his short life flash before his eyes as his father carried him home.

Back in their caravan, James produced a long needle and a length of catgut and by the dim light of a tallow lamp he stitched the torn calf back together, his hands slippery with blood, all the while urging his son: 'Don't holler Georgie, be a man.' The next four days were unbearable for George's parents. During this time there was a chance of infection and amputation would be inevitable. All George could do was lie in bed and pray; the options for a wooden-legged

acrobat were limited. But his father's reckless gamble paid off. Miraculously, six weeks later, the boy was back on his feet, his condemned leg fully restored.

In 1833, smallpox came to Newbury. It arrived as flat spots on the skin which soon became fluid-filled blisters. The disease spread rapidly, killing a third of those who contracted it. Generations of parents had watched helplessly as their children succumbed to the dreaded minister of death, or else had seen them disfigured or blinded by infection. Inoculation was new and risky and most people preferred to take their chances with the disease rather than risk death from the cure. George's parents counted the dead carts as they came and went and prayed nightly that 'the scourge' wouldn't visit them, but then one of his younger sisters began to show signs of infection. James gathered his children together, drove his trusty long darning needle into each of their right arms then rubbed into each wound with discharge taken from the pustules of his daughter's face. To each child he also administered a foul draught of his own creation, 'unpleasant to think of, let alone to swallow'.[14] George's sister survived, although her face and legs were pitted with smallpox scars, worsened by her endless scratching. Her siblings caught the disease but only mildly.

⌐

In June 1837, two days after Waterloo Day, the Sangers were on the road to Somersham in Huntingdonshire when news reached them that the dropsical old King William IV had died and his eighteen-year-old niece Victoria was now Queen. James Sanger set to work commissioning pictures of

the deathbed, the lying-in-state and the funeral of Britain's former monarch as attractions for his portable peep show.

Fairgrounds provided employment for many jobbing artists. In Leather Lane in High Holborn, James tracked down the current artist-in-chief to the travelling entertainer, the Irishman Jack Kelly, but first James had to coax him out of the local tavern. Kelly's genius for knocking out painted tableaux of topographical scenes and national events both historical and contemporary was much appreciated by the fairground community. It was generally understood that if not for his insobriety, the Irishman could have made a big name for himself. For pictures of King William's death and funeral, Kelly demanded the same price as his battle-pieces, seven-shillings-and-sixpence. George's father winced, but the Irishman stood firm. 'Sure, it isn't every day that kings die. It would be a scandalous thing if a monarch's deathbed didn't equal in cost the killing of a lot of ignorant soldiers.'[15] But Kelly did a sterling job and James Sanger was more than pleased with his investment. For the next few weeks the family ate well at the expense of the dead Sailor King.

The following year, on 28 June and for the next four days, a great fair was held in Hyde Park between the Serpentine and Park Lane to celebrate the coronation of the new young Queen Victoria. There was a riot of entertainment on offer from hot-air-balloon rides to Shakespearean dramas. The heavyweights in the fairground world, Wombwell, Hilton, Scoughton, Baker, Smith, Webster and Atkinson took up their positions on the most prestigious pitches in the park. Lower down the ladder of amusements there was Fred Randall the Giant, Fat Tom the Heaviest Man on Earth, Skinny Jack the

Living Skeleton, armless Bob who painted with his feet, fair Circassians and Hottentot Venusians, Irish giants and Welsh dwarfs, children with two heads and animals with none, learned pigs and fortune-telling horses galore. Squeezed in-between the large exhibits amid an army of hopeful minor showmen, was James Sanger and his morbidly inappropriate royal death show and small wooden roundabout.

George was transfixed by the collection of human odd-ities, especially the giantesses, represented by the American Cockayne twins, tall, gorgeous girls, unrelated and born in Whitechapel, and Madame Stevens, 'the Pig-faced Lady', who turned out to be a shaved brown bear clothed in a dress, shawl and bonnet. As George wandered through the painted booths and caught glimpses of these curious people plying their extraordinary trades, he dared dream of a day when he would run his own show and of the array of entertainments it might bring.

George's career as an acrobat crash-landed shortly after take-off. He was keen to try out a few of his moves, so his father loaned him to Malabar the juggler to patter outside his show and assist in the performance for four shillings a day. Malabar, born Patrick Feeney, was an Irish colossus, six-feet-four-inches tall and a much-beloved character at horse races and fairs throughout the British Isles. He juggled balls, rings, bottles and daggers, balanced a heavy coach-wheel on his chin, turned somersaults and swallowed swords. Malabar was chiefly known for two signature tricks. He could toss a heavy brass ball high in the air and catch it in a metal cup strapped to his forehead, but on account of Malabar's fondness for whisky he often misjudged the flight of the

missile. His broken nose and scarred face were as familiar to fairgoers as his exotic Chinese show costume. For his grand finale he strapped a donkey to the top of a sixteen-rung ladder, then passed a plate around to the audience. Only when the platter was full of money was he persuaded to balance the ladder and donkey on his chin. On the second day of the fair, someone stole Malabar's four-legged assistant and it was agreed that George would deputise. His impersonation of the pilfered ass was completed a couple of times successfully, the boy balancing in mid-air at the top of the ladder, on the chin, forehead, shoulder and arm of the great juggler. But Malabar was drinking heavily that day, a complication unknown to his apprentice until it was too late. George was at the top of the ladder when Malabar lost his balance and small boy, ladder and all, came crashing down on the heads of spectators. Malabar was inebriated for the rest of the fair and despite risking his neck, George's professional debut as an acrobat went unsalaried. That evening, as his mother applied cold vinegar dressings to his sore limbs, George was already plotting his next career move.

The Hyde Park coronation festivities were brought to a close on 9 July and the police declared it the biggest gathering ever seen in London. It was a triumph for George's father and made him more money than he could have hoped for. When the fair broke up, the Sanger family took to the road again in high spirits. During a break from the great London fair, James took George and his older brother John to the famous Astley's Amphitheatre in Lambeth. Sitting in the sixpenny gallery they marvelled at the horsemanship of Andrew Ducrow, 'the Colossus of equestrians'. This was the

Astley's loved by Charles Dickens and praised in *The Old Curiosity Shop*. George was wonderstruck and the idea of a career formed in his young mind. On that day he found a star to follow.

Travelling performers worked to a seasonal schedule and their prospects for the winter months were generally bleak. The Sangers were luckier than most because they had their off-season business, buying fish, fruit and vegetables from London and selling it in Newbury and the surrounding Berkshire villages, but navigating the rural highways was dangerous, especially during the long winter nights. Gangs of footpads were an ever-present menace in Berkshire, where the infamous 'Blacks', a band of black-face robbers who hid in the woods next to the main roads, preyed on night travellers. There were more Gothic horrors lurking in the shadows. One January evening, father and son were returning from London and rested up at a roadside inn a few miles from Reading. James was approached by three strangers begging for a ride into town. He agreed to accommodate them and they set off in their wagon. As they travelled, George was curious about a large, heavy parcel their passengers had placed on the back rail of the wagon. He loosened the neck of the sack and in the moonlight he glimpsed first a bare arm, then the chalk-white face and blue lips of an obviously dead woman.

It was a time when body snatchers were ransacking graves to supply the unstoppable demand for corpses for anatomical instruction. Medical schools were allowed to use the corpses of executed criminals for dissection, but demand far outstripped supply. The business was at its most brisk in

the winter months when medical schools were in session and cadavers were more easily preserved by the cold weather. The plunder and desecration of graveyards in England's towns and cities was a cause of much dread. As well as tales of so-called 'Resurrection Men' unearthing human remains for the dissecting tables of scientists, rumours abounded of corpses dug up for their hair, teeth and fat to provide the wigs, dentures and wax candles demanded by the wealthy. Increasingly, the vaults of the rich were being protected by iron bars to keep out the grave robbers. The body in the back of James Sanger's wagon was rifled from a local churchyard and destined for a college in Oxford. George whispered his hair-raising discovery to his father, but James had already figured it out. When the passengers dozed off, James was able to get word to a passing traveller and a warning was sent ahead to Reading. Further down the road, their wagon was intercepted by an angry mob armed with cudgels and pitchforks intent on delivering summary justice to the three graverobbers. They were saved from a lynching by the arrival of the local constabulary, who hauled them away. The terrifying image of the dead woman was seared into George's brain and would revisit him in his nightmares for many years to come. Did the grave robbers know who had ratted them out? The thought haunted him.

～

On 4 November 1839 the Sangers were in Newport in Monmouthshire for the annual cattle fair.[16] It was one of the biggest events in the country and everyone was anticipating good business. After several poorly attended shows

they were insolvent and desperate to reverse a run of bad luck. On the Sunday night before the fair, Newport was anxious and buzzing with rumour. Word got around that a large number of Chartist demonstrators, perhaps as many as 30,000, was heading their way intent on destruction. The Chartism movement was terrifying the authorities. It started out as a peaceful protest for universal voting rights for men and better working conditions among the poor, but when the government turned a deaf ear, the campaign turned towards violence. At Newport, several Chartists were held under arrest at the Westgate Hotel. A group of militants led by a linen draper named John Frost planned to march on Newport, free the prisoners and take control of the town. The insurrectionists would enter under cover of darkness in the early hours of Monday. On Sunday the streets of Newport were deserted and local shops and businesses shuttered in anticipation of a bloody confrontation. Most of the showmen who had travelled for the fair prepared to flee, but James Sanger pitched up by the roadside just outside town and hunkered down, hoping for the best. For thirteen-year-old George the next few hours were among the most terrifying of his life. As his mother and brothers and sisters lay in their beds sick with fear, his father sat up all night with his shotgun loaded, prepared to defend his family with his life. The next morning, just before 9am, the men from the mining and ironworking valleys marched into town four or five abreast, wielding mandrels, pitchforks and sticks, breaking the windows with stones as they went. 'On they came, many of them half drunk, yelling, swearing, and waving great cudgels, a terrifying mass of men.'[17] It wasn't

until the main body had passed the caravan that the Sanger family dared draw breath again.

The Newport Rising, as it became known, was bound to fail. The Westgate Hotel held an attachment of 32 soldiers from the 45th Infantry. The showdown between troops and Chartists was predictably brief, the men gathered outside the Westgate Hotel easy targets for the musket-firing troops within. The next George and his family saw of the routed mob was when they were fleeing in the direction they came into the countryside beyond, leaving the streets of Newport littered with bodies and abandoned weapons. Around 50 of their number were seriously wounded and upwards of 22 killed. There was a silver lining for the Sangers. The Rising and the courtroom trials of the Chartist leaders Frost, Williams and Jones was fodder for the family peep show, although, as George cheerfully admitted, his father's interest was purely financial; radical politics was not and never would be his concern. The daily needs and concerns of a fairground traveller were a million miles from that of the average Victorian working man.

Travelling showmen generally turned a deaf ear to insults and they didn't go looking for trouble; they had enough problems without courting it. But when trouble came, they knew how to take care of themselves. Every August, the Sangers went to Bath for the Lansdown fair. Bath was a fashionable spa resort, but beyond the beautiful Georgian townhouses there were parts of the city where no tourist dared venture, streets that even policemen feared to tread. One was home to the most notorious criminal gang in the west country, the Bull Paunch Alley gang.

Lansdown fair started at around ten in the morning and continued until midnight. It was a tradition for the poor of Bath to make the most of Lansdown fair and the revelry would go on late into the evening. In 1840 the crowd was in a particularly lively mood and fights broke out during the afternoon. With darkness came chaos. As the Sangers were packing their stall away, the Bath mob stormed the showground. They were led by a flame-haired woman known as Carroty Kate, said to be 'strong as a navvy, a big, brute animal' variously known as 'mistress of Bull Paunch Alley', and 'Queen of the slum'.[18] Already worse for drink and inexplicably half-naked, she gave the order: 'Wreck the fair!' The gang looted the show booths, overturned wagons and beat up their owners. Anything they couldn't carry or drink they vandalised, smashing and burning the stalls in their wake. Outnumbered and helpless, James and his family could only watch, but as dawn approached and Carroty Kate and her gang tramped back to the city, the showmen regrouped. Mounting their show horses, they set off in pursuit and captured the gang leader and twelve of her followers. The showmen gave no mercy. The gang members were yoked to tent poles and dragged roughly through a pond, then their limp, half-drowned bodies were horse-whipped. Finally, their red-headed leader was stripped to the waist and tied to a table where 'two lusty young women administered the thrashing of a lifetime' with penny canes from the fair.[19]

The law did not impress George, then or ever. It was an article of faith among travelling showmen that the authorities could never be relied on to give them justice when it was due.

He knew this to be fact after the incident at Uphaven. The Wiltshire town was famous for its October fair, traditionally an ancient market for pig farmers but now mostly attended by pleasure seekers. Like Lansdown fair, it was targeted by street gangs who wrecked the showmen's property when the fair was over. At three in the morning, Sanger's wagon was besieged and overturned by local bullies. George's mother and his sisters screamed as the contents of the vehicle flew around them. The girls were badly cut by glass from the broken windows. Luckily the wagon was thrown over with the side-door uppermost and James and his family were able to clamber out. As the gang ran laughing down the road, James vented his fury. He put a marble in his blunderbuss and took aim. From the resulting shriek he knew the missile had found its mark. It cost several pounds to make good the damage to the caravan and James was determined that someone should pay.

When he heard that a youth had visited the village doctor to have a marble removed from his back, James laid his complaint with a local constable. The local squire-magistrate, who also turned out to be the injured youth's employer, denounced James Sanger as a lying vagabond and offered to have him locked up for trespass. George's father left the town a bitter man. From that day on, any mention of Uphaven brought his blood to the boil.

⌒

Most of the time George's family lived on a knife edge. There was no insurance against prolonged bad weather or a hostile crowd. A single misfortune – illness, accident, a lame horse,

a child's funeral – wiped out any margin between comfort and poverty, but by the standards of their fellow travellers they were not so badly off and there was never room for self-pity. The 'hungry forties' were a calamitous time for all but the rich, a decade of unemployment and cholera, harvest failure and economic depression. Daily survival was difficult enough, but the Sangers were also vulnerable to 'smashers' – customers who paid with counterfeit coins. Fairgrounds were awash with fake currency and some showfolk were known to be dealers. Counterfeiting carried a high penalty and smashers could be hanged, but the police made little effort to catch the culprits at fairgrounds and few were ever prosecuted. George's parents were always vigilant for bad money, but he never forgot their anguish when they counted the day's takings and found their meagre rewards useless. All the same, his father always destroyed any bad coin that came his way lest it caused more misery to others worse off than themselves. George, who would see many more counterfeit coins over his long career, always followed his father's example.

In those years of terrible privation, the family's winter business of transporting fish and vegetables from their home in Newbury also suffered badly. James had always managed to stay one step ahead of the debt collectors, but then his luck ran out. The tax-collector issued him with a summons for a disputed unpaid bill. In a rage, James disgorged the contents of the family home into the street and sold them off for anything they would fetch. He locked the door of the house, hitched his wagon to the horses and the family left Newbury never to return.

They made their way to London. There were no winter fairs, but the metropolis at least offered some hope of turning a penny on the street with the peep show or perhaps some casual work for James as a carpenter.* Migrant tinkers and professional showmen alike often wintered on the fringes of the city before taking their shows and wares on the summer circuit of provincial fairs. The Sangers pitched on some waste ground on Kennington Road, a sort of rent-free shanty town for showmen. Most fairground folk struggled to make a living in the summer months and in winter some literally starved to death. One of their neighbours in this slum was a towering Scot named Thompson who travelled the fairs as 'the Scotch Giant, the tallest man in the world'. He was a quiet man and he generally kept his own company, but he was liked and respected by all. Unusually for a fairground 'freak' he was literate, and he could earn a few pennies by writing letters or reading business documents for his fellow travellers, but these opportunities were few. One freezing January morning a neighbour called on Thompson's wagon with a letter for him to read but there was no answer. At length someone kicked in the door and found the owner's emaciated corpse on the floor of the tiny, bare home. He had long since traded everything that was saleable and hadn't eaten for days, but he was too proud to ask for help. With no heating and rotted by malnutrition, the giant had lain down and passed quietly away.

---

* For a man who supposedly lost several fingers at Trafalgar, James Sanger was surprisingly handy.

It was the bitterest of winters for the Sanger family. With no income, all they had to live on was their pitifully inadequate savings. With the return of spring, the wandering tribes of Kennington Road began to stir. The showmen put their caravans in harness and set off on the roads that ran out from London like the lines of a spider's web to meet the country lanes and on to the first of the season's fairs.

George struck a new line of winter business. On Hackney Marshes he saw large numbers of people skating on the frozen ponds. He found children carning odd pennies by sweeping ice for the skaters and people hiring out skating equipment, but he was puzzled by the absence of street food hawkers despite the large crowds. He knew how to make rock and toffee, the staple of the fairground. George bought ten pounds of sugar at seven-pence-a-pound and some oil of peppermint, borrowed his mother's pans to boil it up and very soon had a large stock of peppermint rock. Back at Hackney Marshes he sold out within the hour. Pressing his brothers William and John into service, they upscaled their business, bought as much sugar and oil of peppermint as they could lay their hands on from a grocer on Whitechapel Road, boiled it into rock and cut it into penny lumps. That evening they returned to their caravan with their pockets loaded with coppers amounting to over two pounds profit. The problem of winter survival in London without blowing all of their summer savings was solved. Life had never been sweeter.

5

Vine Street

WEDNESDAY EVENING, 29 NOVEMBER 1911. It had been 24 hours since the death of Lord George Sanger and the nation waited to see if his assassin would be caught. Detective George Wallace knew that they would be expected to move swiftly to make an arrest or S Division would face the censure of the press and public, but as each hour passed there was a diminishing chance that they would successfully track Cooper down. Wallace still had nothing new to offer the reporters hovering around the entrance to Finchley police station. Then from out of the blue there was some promising news.

At about 6pm a breathless young man presented himself at Vine Street police station, just around the corner from Piccadilly Circus in the heart of London's West End. The young man introduced himself to desk sergeant John Prothero as Harry Wright, a correspondence clerk in Thomas Cook & Son tourist agent office at the north-east end of Piccadilly, less than a hundred yards away. He told Prothero that at that very moment, a person answering to the description of Herbert Cooper was sitting in his works

office, attempting to arrange a passage on a ship leaving Liverpool the following day bound for South America.

Prothero alerted Detective Inspector Fowler and within a couple of minutes the two policemen were dodging the crowds of pedestrians on the busy Piccadilly thoroughfare on their way to Cook & Son to take a look for themselves.

When they arrived they found a dark-haired young man, smartly dressed in a blue suit. He was a very good match for the written description circulated by Scotland Yard. There was also a strong resemblance to the wanted man's photograph as shown in that evening's edition of *The Star*. When questioned, the suspect identified himself as Leonard Dixon, age 30. He said that he had been working in South America for the past thirteen years as a farm labourer. He returned home to England in June to visit his family, but now he was heading back to his job.

Fowler was more than suspicious. The softly-spoken, blue-suited young man sat across the table from him looked like anything but a farm labourer. His appearance, the detective surmised in his report, was 'decidedly superior to the ordinary person of that class'. Could 'Dixon' confirm his identity? He offered the names of two sisters, Elfreda and Marian, the first a live-in servant at 82 Regent's Park Road, the second living in Hornsey, who could. The suspect was placed under arrest and taken to Vine Street station while Prothero was despatched to track down and interview the two sisters.

At 6.30pm, word reached Inspector Wallace at Finchley that a man answering the description given for Cooper was being held in the West End. Within a few minutes Wallace

had procured a cab and was on his way. At last, there was a solid lead from a trusted source, and maybe, he mused as he headed towards central London, it was the only one they would need.

It was shortly before 7pm when Wallace pulled up outside Vine Street police station and alighted from his cab. Tucked away in a tiny side street branching off Swallow Street in the apex formed by Piccadilly and Regent Street, Vine Street was London's busiest police station despite its modest location. It served the densely populated byways and alleys of Soho and it policed the delinquents, drunks, thieves, pickpockets and fraudsters who operated in the bohemian underbelly of the city. At one time so many arrests were made that the Vine Street cells were packed like sardine tins. It was to this station that P.G. Wodehouse's fictional delinquent toffs were hauled. It was to Vine Street that the Marquess of Queensberry was taken and detained when he libelled Oscar Wilde, setting in motion the series of events that eventually led to Wilde's imprisonment.

Inspector Wallace's hopes were immediately raised. The man in the police station basement cell indeed bore a striking resemblance to Herbert Cooper. On the identification of suspects, however, the police were especially wary. Wallace's Metropolitan Police colleagues were still smarting from the infamous example of Adolph Beck, a Norwegian engineer who over the preceding fifteen years had languished in prison having been wrongfully convicted for fraud on the basis of eyewitness testimony, while the lookalike criminal remained scot-free. The lesson of this 'lamentable business', wrote police chief Sir Melville Macnaghten,

'was unquestionably the extreme unreliability of personal identification'.[20]

At Vine Street, Wallace interviewed the suspect again, but learned nothing new. The man was calm, courteous and repeated his story again. He had worked in South America for thirteen years and after a long overdue visit home it was time for him to go back to his work. There was one way to find out for certain if he was lying. Wallace gave instructions to send for someone who knew the fugitive well: Herbert Cooper's friend, Frederick White of Cleveland House, Finchley.

While they were waiting for White, Sergeant Prothero phoned in to Vine Street with disappointing news. Dixon's sisters had fully corroborated their suspect's story. Around half an hour later at 9pm, Frederick White arrived at the station. It took him just one look to confirm that the man being held was not his friend Cooper, although he agreed that there was some similarity. Cooper's doppelganger was released with an apology, graciously accepted. Wallace returned to his waiting taxi and rode it back to Finchley on the home leg of his wild goose chase.

London was now awash with rumours that the 'madman' Cooper had already fled to France. Detective Inspector Wallace was also unsettled by the growing certainty that Cooper would attempt to escape overseas, if he hadn't already done so. He had enough of a head start to easily put himself out of reach. Wallace widened the net. Telegraphic messages were sent to the Thames docks with instructions for departing vessels to keep a vigilant eye for the wanted man and police at Folkestone, Dover, Southampton, Harwich,

Hull and Liverpool were ordered to stop and search any young men seeking passage on boats leaving England. Before the day was out there was another sighting to contend with. Late on Wednesday evening the police acted on information that someone fitting the description of the suspect had also been spotted in Tottenham, but by the time uniformed policemen arrived to search the district, the trail had already gone cold.

Then there was a fresh lead. Police in Chelmsford phoned Scotland Yard to report that a man seen hanging around the local railway station closely resembling Herbert Cooper 'with the exception that his moustache is trimmed up' had boarded a train bound for London. Half-a-dozen officers from Chelmsford, the Metropolitan and City police pounced on the suspect as he alighted from the train at Liverpool Street station and challenged him to produce some identity. He revealed himself as Sidney Lewis, a 40-year-old tailor's assistant from Cambridge. The London police quickly agreed that this was not the man wanted and let him go. A flustered Inspector Burch later explained to his superiors that 'the suspect looked very much younger with his hat on'.

By the following day, the challenge confronting Inspector Wallace had become exponentially more daunting. Somehow Cooper had evaded detection despite a manhunt of an intensity rarely seen in S Division. The lack of forward motion in the investigation was more than discouraging.

Late that morning, Scotland Yard received a letter from an Alec Brown who identified himself as an acquaintance of Herbert Charles Cooper. Brown alerted them to the

likelihood that their suspect would try to escape across the Channel. 'He [Cooper] knows the Kentish coast quite well as he was often with Mr Sanger at Margate and he knows the road well so no doubt he will make for Dover or Folkestone.' Having dobbed in his former pal, the informant added, 'I always regarded him as a good chum and he always spoke well of Mr Sanger.'

Perhaps Brown's speculations were no better, nor any worse, than those of the detectives leading the manhunt. It no longer mattered, because Herbert Cooper was already beyond the law.

6

Lion Queen

Stepney Fair, Easter Monday 1848. George Sanger is making his professional debut as a travelling magician.

George was a boy when he first saw his muse Bill Bright, 'the professor of magic'. He was a fairground veteran, travelling the West Country with his wife and daughter, scratching a living with a type of variety show that was almost out of fashion. Bill's daughter danced a quickstep while blindfolded on a carpet of eggs to the sound of pan pipes without breaking a shell. As the 'cackler dance' grew quicker and quicker, Mrs Bright, providing the patter, racked up the tension by placing a gentleman's watch borrowed from the audience among the eggs. When her daughter's capering was done, she returned the intact timepiece to the anxious owner. This was the preamble to the main event, her husband's display of 'fine wizardry'. Bill Bright was one of the oldest performers on the circuit and of no particularly great repute in the world of fairground magic, but to the impressionable young George he was miraculous. Whenever the magician asked for an audience member to step up to the platform to assist, George's hand was first up. He'd seen the show so many times that

he knew the routines inside out, including the fairground classic, cutting off the head of a chicken and then restoring it. George spent his days trying to puzzle out how the tricks were done, then practising alone he taught himself the rudiments of conjuring. He mastered a few basic card tricks and tried them out on his family. Eventually he had a small repertoire of tricks with coins, cards and handkerchiefs and felt confident enough to try them on a stage.

His family had spent the winter on a yard attached to a tavern on Mile End Road, amid the overcrowded Dickensian rookeries of east London, where the dwellings were little more than hovels and a great number of the population lived on the fringes of crime. For his stage debut, George took on an empty furniture warehouse in nearby Bethnal Green and worked some tricks with apparatus made for him by a Petticoat Lane tinsmith. For his finale, he hired a dozen local teenagers to stage some fashionable *poses plastiques*.[21] George's little unlicensed show attracted so much attention that he had to bribe the local beat bobby to look the other way. He persuaded his brothers William and John to join him in a regular travelling exhibition; George was the talent, his brothers would take the money and work as road crew. Although he was the youngest of the three it was always understood that George was the brains in the family, and William and John were more than happy to take their little brother's lead.

There was a swagger about George. He'd already acquired a local reputation as a show-off and a dandy. He wore his hair long and curled with tongs, and was dressing up for his performances, cutting a dash in his 'Hamlet'

costume – a white shirt with linen cuffs, a black velvet tunic and a hat with ostrich feathers. The fairground folk christened him Gentleman George. His father, whose basic working uniform of beaver hat, white smock-frock, knee-breeches, worsted stockings and buckled shoes never varied through his entire career, wasn't sure what to make of it and mocked him as 'his lordship'. The girls had noticed George too. At five-foot-four-inches he was short, but athletic and handsome. His costume-maker Anne Hartley and fairground food hawker 'Watercress Betty' had a stand-up fight over him outside his caravan, earning George a stern rebuke from his parents. When a much older widow started to show an interest in him, threats were issued by her two large grown-up sons; one offered to beat George up if he didn't marry her, the other offered to do the same if he did. George's parents decided it was time to leave the district.

Stepney fair was a three-day event and the biggest gathering of its kind in Middlesex, drawing market sellers, showmen, musicians, cheapjacks, dealers, street beggars, pickpockets and hustlers of every stripe from all over the south-east of England. Londoners flocked there in their tens of thousands to eat, drink, gamble, fight and have fun. Stepney fair was held across two large fields and the range of the performances on offer was extraordinary. Shakespearean actors competed with puppets, peep shows, wild beasts, rope dancers and sausage salesmen. There were booths for boxing, sagacious dogs, waxworks, contortionists, mice, armless violinists and limbless painters. There was the usual diet of giants and dwarfs and anything else out of its due size and proportion. One humongous booth, 350-feet long and

50-feet deep, belonged to 'Gipsy Stevens the Essex higgler' and served as a dance hall where the polka was performed 'in a manner worthy of Almack's'.[22]

The Sanger brothers presented their show from their modest travelling wagon, or 'The Hall of Mystery'.[23] It had a door in the middle of one side that formed a show front and a hinged timber deck that folded out to create a stage. Behind this, a painted cloth announced the 'Wizard of the West'. On the first day of the fair an agreeably sizeable crowd formed up front, curious to see the skills of the newbie Jacobean dandy. One of the Sanger brothers banged on a Chinese gong to attract attention as George began his trickery. Business was brisk all day. Most of the established magicians on the circuit – Anderson, Jacobs, Robert-Houdin and Herr Dobler – had luckily decided to give Stepney a miss, and George's only direct competition was the celebrated but ageing George Bernardo Eagle, making his very last appearance as 'The Wizard of the South'.[24]

The crowd that year was estimated over 300,000 and most were in holiday spirits, the air thick with drunken song. The Irish community were there in numbers, living up to their reputation for hard drinking, and there were dozens of arrests for drunken and disorderly behaviour and assaults on the constabulary. The last day of the fair was disrupted by a huge fire in an adjoining ropeworks. Ropemaking for ships was Stepney's biggest industry, and the linseed used in the process was notoriously combustible, as several local ropeworks owners had discovered at great cost. George and many of his fellow showmen dashed into the flames in a mad, surreal effort to save the building.

Amid the flying sparks, and in and about the burning buildings, could be seen clowns, knights in armour, Indian chiefs, jugglers in tights and spangles, rope-walkers in fleshings – in fact, all the characters of the fair in full dress, striving with might and main to combat the flames.[25]

At least part of the ropeworks was salvaged and for the fire-fighters there was an unexpected bonus. Word of the inferno had spread and even bigger crowds turned up to see the damage and the performers who had helped fight the blaze.

At Stepney, George renewed an acquaintance with a childhood friend. Ellen 'Nellie' Chapman was six years his junior, born in Liverpool the eldest daughter of Harry Chapman, an itinerant peep showman. George and Nellie's families had travelled the fairs together when she was a little girl, but she was now a very attractive, petite, dark-haired seventeen year old. With beauty came bankability. George was astonished to learn that she was now one of the star attractions at Wombwell's menagerie – a female lion tamer, earning her employer a staggering 100 pounds a day. By the time Stepney fair ended, the rookie magician had worked his spell on Nellie, and when she and George went their separate ways they agreed to keep in touch.

❧

George and his brothers continued to learn their trade in the exotic and mysterious world of the Victorian showground. The young magician was growing in confidence with every performance. From Stepney the Sanger brothers took their little conjuring show to King's Cross in north London,

hoping to catch a crowd at one of the new fairs springing up alongside the established holiday events. The fair was on a piece of wasteland on Euston Road, soon to become the London hub of the Great Northern Railway, but now being used as a vast rubbish tip. It was dominated by an evil-smelling mountain of human and industrial filth, mostly cinders, ashes and other contents from dust-holes and bins, generously laced with rotting vegetable matter and whole animal carcasses. The pile was popular with feral pigs, and an army of human foragers, who regularly pillaged it for everything from lumps of coal, broken pottery and oyster shells to dead cats, recycled to make fur trims for ladies' hats. This teetering heap of foul-smelling detritus posed a health risk to everyone, but three times a year the show-men and their public held their noses and made merry in its shadow. At King's Cross the Sangers learned the secrets of fortune-telling ponies and learned pigs.* George found out that these porcine performances that amazed the public, such as picking out cards in answer to simple mathematical and logic questions, were the fruits of a very tedious, week-long routine of drilling a pig into learning a series of finger-clicks. The Sanger brothers resolved never again to work under the stinking Great Dust Heap of King's Cross and to stick to touring the rural fairgrounds in future.[26]

---

* At the time there was a small army of card-sharping, mind-reading domesticated animals doing the rounds, including a celebrity porker called Toby, said to be 'a far greater object of admiration to the English than ever was Sir Isaac Newton' (*Leisure in Britain*, John K. Walton & James Walvin).

There were changes to the Sanger company. In May John was married at St Mary's in Whitechapel to Elizabeth, daughter of the menagerie owner Samuel Atkins. With his brother Thomas, Sam had opened Liverpool's first zoo in 1833. There was also a departure from their small troupe. William Sanger was going to set up his own waxworks exhibition. Madame Tussaud had stopped travelling with her famous show and settled in Baker Street, leaving the field open for rival booths exhibiting waxwork celebrities, items of anatomical interest and the odd violent murder. Fortunately, George and John's energy and organisational powers were such that William wasn't missed, and the new Mrs John Sanger more than compensated, bringing to the show her popular mind-reading act.

In 1848, England was in the grip of cholera. It took hold in the new industrial northern towns of Hull, Leeds, Liverpool and Manchester, and by July it was laying waste to London. Anyone who had seen the Victorian era's greatest killer at work knew the effect on victims was truly terrifying. Skin shrivelled, eye sockets collapsed and skin turned blue; in the final throes, victims screamed and thrashed with muscle spasms before they collapsed, exhausted. They often died within hours of the first symptoms. There was ignorance and confusion about cholera's causes, treatment and prevention. The wealthy, whose fashionable flushing water closets sent sewage flowing freely into the very rivers from where people drew their tap water, blamed the poor for bringing the disease upon themselves by their ungodly habits. The church attributed it to divine punishment and declared a day of fasting and prayer to ward off the disease.

Labour organisations pointed out that the poor had already fasted enough. Everyone agreed that cholera seemed to strike places that were heavily populated, so people stopped going to fairs. It was calamitous for business. By September, London deaths from the pandemic were up to 3,000 a week. The Sanger brothers fled the city and headed for Liverpool, where the worst had already passed. George and John considered themselves lucky to have survived the winter and there was huge relief when the northern spring fairs came around again.

For many workers in the North and Midlands the most eagerly anticipated time of the year was the annual Wakes Week. It began as a celebration of a saint's feast day but had outgrown its original purpose and was now an occasion when men and women could celebrate a brief escape from the shackles of the field or factory in the wildest possible fashion. George was shocked by the casual violence he encountered at these events. At the Stalybridge Wakes he claimed he saw a gingerbread salesman viciously kicked to a pulp by a mob of drunken miners wearing iron-tipped clogs. George was haunted by the sight of the battered, shapeless victim lying in the sunlight and the colour of his blood, curiously purple on the ground, and was sickened by the indifference of the police: 'Some little time after the brutal deed had been done one or two constables made a leisurely appearance, looked at the body as though such sights were common to their ordinary day's work, and the corpse was removed.'[27]

George had another reason to remember the event with clarity. It was on the same day he and his brother John

learned that their father had died. Although London was officially cholera-free, James Sanger caught it while working his peep show at Rotherhithe. The letter bringing news of his death had a distressing postscript. Business had been so bad that their mother had to pawn everything she had to pay for her husband's burial. The days when a travelling peep show could support a family were long gone, and some showmen were so desperate that their entertainment could be seen for rags, bones or old bottles. James Sanger's summer trade had been in steady decline for years and he was doing whatever work he could to survive.

There wasn't time for George and John to get back for their father's funeral. The best they could do was stay on at the fair and earn some money to send to their mother. It was a bittersweet year for George. On 1 December at St Peter's Church, Sheffield, he married his Lion Queen, Nellie Chapman. He was 25, she was nineteen. Neither bride nor groom could sign their names in the register.

George was marrying into fairground aristocracy. Nellie's mother Harriet was a principal dancer with John Richardson, doyen of the travelling theatrical booth and one of the wealthiest and most successful in his business. Her older sister married into the travelling Manders family, and when Nellie was a youngster they employed her as their carriage girl.[28] When she about sixteen she went to work for George Wombwell, the greatest of all the Victorian travelling menagerists. By the late 1840s just about every self-respecting menagerie owner had a female lion tamer on his books. Nellie Chapman was about fifteen when she began working for Wombwell's menagerie, billed as Madame

Pauline de Vere, Queen of the Lions.[29] She was selling herself short because she also performed with tigers, leopards and even boa constrictors. While the great American lion tamer Van Amburgh beat his beasts into submission with the ferocious use of a crowbar, Nellie had a more subtle approach, manipulating the animals around the cage simply by pointing her whip. She brought her performance to a breath-taking climax by placing her head inside the mouth of Wombwell's celebrated lion Wallace. Her temples passed between the lion's fangs and the fit was said to be so tight that Nellie's forehead bore the permanent scars of repeated insertion and withdrawal. There were multiple reports of injuries sustained during Nellie's lion-taming days. The *Liverpool Mercury* described an attack on her by a lion at King's Lynn during which she was bitten twice, the reporter adding: 'the foolish woman entered the den again in the evening!'[30]

Circus and menagerie owners loved to concoct stories and feed them to the press to sell tickets, and the public liked nothing better than to visit the site of a good mauling. The celebrated Van Amburgh was killed on paper several times, had his back broken at least twice and his head was once swallowed by a Bengal tiger (in fact he died quietly in his own bed). But Nellie's injuries were real enough. At Stamford one of the lions seized her by the thighs with both paws and as she tried to beat it off it clawed her on the head. She collapsed unconscious while the keepers beat the lion off with iron bars. The next day she went through her performance with her head bandaged. Her employer charged double, and many more people were turned away. At the time Nellie

made light of the serious injuries to her back and head, and always wore her scars with pride.

Nellie became a national celebrity after she appeared with Wombwell's menagerie by command for Queen Victoria at Windsor Castle in October 1847. The Queen had a weakness for lion-taming acts. They were the sort of spectacle, she wrote in her journal, 'one can never see too often'. As good as her word, she saw Van Amburgh perform half a dozen times in just over a month. Legend has it that the Queen and her household watched Nellie's performance from a castle window overlooking a courtyard. According to George's memoir, his wife spent half an hour in the cage, entertaining the royal family with various stunts including her head-in-lion's-mouth act. Afterwards she received a pat on the back from the Prince Consort and a gold watch and chain from the Queen.[31] Nellie's exalted patronage was trumpeted far and wide and adverts were placed in the provincial press in advance of her appearances all over the country. Charles Dickens was among those who found the prospect of seeing a woman sharing a cage with lion and tigers irresistible. He was on holiday in Broadstairs that year and was caught up in a 'whirl of dissipation' after discovering Nellie's lion-taming act, and he dashed off a letter to his friend: 'Seriously, she beats Van Amburgh. And I think the Duke of Wellington must have her painted by Landseer.'

One way or another, the royal visit cemented Nellie's status as a *bona fide* celebrity. In 1847, as Madame Pauline de Vere, she was clearly doing exceptionally well for herself and was being advertised 'as presented before Her Majesty'. Nellie was a superstar in her own right and it was a testament

to her devotion to George that she was willing to give it all up to become a humble assistant to a minor fairground conjuror.

George Wombwell was not best pleased at forfeiting his star attraction, but lost no time replacing her with his relatively inexperienced, but apparently fearless, seventeen-year-old niece, Ellen Blight.[32] She too was no stranger to wild animals, having travelled with her uncle's menagerie since she was a small girl, but she was perhaps a little too eager to prove herself a worthy successor to Nellie. Ellen's first few months as a lion tamer passed without incident but her beginner's luck ran out. After a public performance at Chatham, while trying to impress a couple of flirty young naval officers, she rashly clipped a dozing tiger on the nose with her whip. The big cat launched at her, fatally sinking its fangs into her face and throat.

According to George's memoir, Nellie was so shocked by the death of her young successor that she gave up all thought of ever again working with big cats. It hardly mattered. The persuasive young magician and his very capable young wife were going places.

7

Three persons
butchered

TWENTY-NINTH OF NOVEMBER 1911. London was the world's most populous city, with 7 million people, but cold-blooded murders were rare. The death of the internationally famous showman Lord George Sanger made the Wednesday morning newspapers and was received with horror and disbelief. The brutal slaying of a defenceless old man was one thing. The idea that it was done in his own home in a frenzied axe attack by a trusted employee was quite another.

Newspapers as a popular, sensational medium were a fairly recent innovation. The repeal of the newspaper tax made them cheap, and rising literary rates created a rapidly growing demand. Since 1870 all children had to attend school until they were thirteen, and readers who had cut their teeth on the much-maligned Victorian penny dreadfuls could now savour reports of real-life violent crime in the newly expanded Edwardian popular press. The pre-eminent press baron of the era, Alfred Harmsworth, shaped

the emergence of a new style of popular newspaper in which sensational content was the order of the day.[33] The assaults at Park Farm in East Finchley had all the hallmarks of a 'classic' crime – unusual violence, the mutilation of the victim, a fleeing perpetrator and a widely publicised manhunt. Fleet Street duly pulled out all the stops.

The early reports lingered on lurid descriptions of the attacks and the injuries suffered by all three members of the Sanger household. The *Daily Mirror* reported that Herbert Cooper had rushed into the parlour armed with a razor in one hand and an axe in the other 'and without warning aimed a smashing blow at his [Sanger's] head'.[34] Detectives from Scotland Yard arriving at the scene had found the scene 'drenched with blood'. The *Daily Telegraph* described how 'the prince of showmen' was 'brutally murdered' with a hatchet by Herbert Cooper, leaving the victim 'lying in a pool of blood in the dining room ... he had evidently been attacked while sitting in his chair, his head was covered with deep and ugly gashes caused by a heavy instrument'.[35]

The newspapers agreed that it could have been a double or even triple murder. Arthur Jackson and Harry Austin's 'lucky escape from death', it was reported, left them 'discovered bleeding and helpless' while Sanger was 'lying in a pool of blood in the front room and terribly cut about the head'.[36]

On Wednesday evening the provincial press dedicated many more column inches to the crime, containing a mixture of speculation, indignation and graphic descriptions of the injuries. The *Aberdeen Journal* described at length the 'savage attack' and described how Cooper had slashed Jackson's

throat, then laid into Austin, opening up his head with a chopper, before turning his attention to the old man, striking him 'several terrific blows to the head'. The victim 'with his scalp laid open' and covered in blood had somehow managed to crawl from the room and was joined by the two injured men.[37] The *Leicester Post* reported that Cooper, 'a man of great strength', rained 'several blows with his formidable weapon', and 'watched as Lord George Sanger sank helpless to the ground'.[38]

The newspapers printed irreconcilable accounts of what happened next. Several followed the lead of the *Birmingham Daily Mail* in misreporting that the elderly showman had temporarily rallied from his beating with the axe. Under the headline: LORD GEORGE SANGER MURDERED – KILLED BY AN EMPLOYEE WITH A HATCHET, the *Mail* revealed that Sanger had recovered sufficiently from the murderous attack to escape from the house with the two injured men.[39] The *Daily Mirror* noted that the police had found Sanger 'insensible by the gate, to which he had crawled terribly wounded'.[40]

There was disagreement about the possible cause of the attack. The *Daily Mirror* interviewed George Sanger's nephew James Crockett junior, son of the circus owner's late lion tamer, who told them he and the rest of the family were 'completely mystified' by the crime. The *Mirror* concluded that 'no motive so far can be assigned for the crime, and it is supposed that the assailant suddenly went mad'.[41] The *Birmingham Daily Mail* agreed: 'the only explanation is that the assailant's mind may have suddenly become unhinged'. A few lines later the *Mail* correspondent changed

tack: 'A possible motive for the tragedy is suggested in the fact that recently Jackson has been taking the place in which Cooper formerly occupied in his employer's confidential affairs.'[42]

One newspaper described Herbert Cooper as 'a handsome, headstrong youth' who 'appears to have given both his family and his employer some anxiety'.[43] It was one of several press reports linking the attack with a previous incident on the farm. It transpired that a couple of years earlier Cooper had confronted a couple of trespassers on Sanger's land and had warned them off. There had been some sort of tussle and Cooper allegedly hit one of them with a stick. There was confusion in the press about the outcome. The *Birmingham Daily Mail* claimed that Cooper embarked on a 'furious attack' on the two interlopers without provocation. The *London Evening News* confirmed that Cooper was 'a man of violent temper' as he had been 'fined for a serious assault on some trespassers' on Sanger's farm.[44] A contemporaneous account in *The Hendon & Finchley Times* provides what we assume is an accurate record of proceedings at Hendon court two years earlier, when Herbert Cooper was charged with affray. Cooper had challenged Dr William Cowper, Cowper's brother and 'other gentlemen' who he found walking across Sanger's fields. Cooper told them that they were trespassing and asked them to go back by the way they came. 'The gentlemen resented the manner in which they were spoken to', then Cooper, it was alleged, set his dog on them. There followed a struggle, Cooper hit Cowper over the head with his stick and the doctor fell to the ground unconscious. Dr Godfrey, a

witness for the prosecution, said the wounded Cowper was too seriously injured to attend court. Cooper testified that Cowper attacked him first and he acted in self-defence. His employer George Sanger spoke as a character witness for the defendant, and Cooper was fined ten pounds. The imputation remained however that Herbert Cooper had a terrible temper and was potentially a violent man.

Cooper was broadly painted as intimidating and volatile, and almost every news story about the Tuesday night attacks at Park Farm emphasised his great size and strength. The *Birmingham Daily Mail* described him as 'a man of extraordinary strength and of passionate temperament'.[45] The *Birmingham Daily Gazette* reported that he was 'a big powerful fellow, six feet high and one of the strongest men in the neighbourhood'. One of the men Cooper overpowered, Harry Austin, the newspaper noted, 'was also a very strong man, but had been weakened by a recent operation on his varicose veins'.[46] It was explained that George Sanger had invited the Austins to stay with him for a couple of months while Harry was recuperating from the procedure.

Reporters were knocking on doors looking for any juicy titbits they could dig up on Herbert Cooper. A *Daily Mirror* reporter was able to uncover a handful of people who claimed they knew him, including a mysterious German, referred to as 'an inventor', called Herr Klauk. He described Cooper as 'extremely powerful' with the strength of four men … 'he [Cooper] was fond of spending money, and asked me to drink with him sometime, *but I did not care to accept!*' The *Mirror* reported that Cooper had boasted to friends he had earned twelve pounds a week as George Sanger's valet,

adding that this was doubtful because Cooper was 'vain and very fond of showing off in all sorts of ways'.

Herbert Cooper's relationship with George Sanger was the subject of great press interest. The *Daily Telegraph* described the assailant as 'a kind of companion and also assisted in the farm buildings'.[47] *The London Evening News* reported that 'besides doing work around the farm, Cooper also acted as companion to his employer, reading to him and attending his personal wants ... It was also his daily practice that this man should read his letters and the newspapers to him and in this way he became intimate with Mr Sanger.' Several newspapers agreed that Cooper was taking revenge for losing his job as Sanger's personal attendant. A commentator for the *Birmingham Daily Gazette* noted: 'the motive for the crime is stated to have been a morbid jealousy aroused by the supposed favouritism among the servants'. The *London Evening News* alone introduced a note of caution; Cooper's redundancy 'does not sufficiently explain an attack on a man of eighty-four, enjoying in retirement the fruits of his famous career'.[48]

Following Wallace's request that Scotland Yard play down the description of Cooper's job as a farm labourer, the press published an amended description of the fugitive:

Wanted for murder on 28th, Herbert Cooper (26), six feet; complexion, hair and moustache dark; smart military appearance and may be taken for an actor or city clerk. Recently worked as a labourer. Dress – blue suit and light cap; clothing probably bloodstained. He has money and may endeavour to leave the country.

The next day, newspaper headlines around the world from New York to Auckland broadcast Sanger's murder. The callous nature of the attack excited general expressions of horror and disgust, and there was even less restraint in the reporting. The *West Australian* reported: AN ENGLISH TRAGEDY – THREE PERSONS BUTCHERED: 'The servant Cooper split Mr. Sanger's head open with a hatchet and Austin and Jackson, although badly injured, are likely to recover.'[49] The *New Zealand Post* noted that Cooper, 'a powerful young man of 25, must have gone suddenly mad ... before the old man could defend himself [Cooper] struck him several blows on the head, laying open the scalp and causing him to drop helpless to the floor'. In South Africa, George Sanger's grandson picked up a newspaper he found in a Johannesburg tea shop and was profoundly shocked to learn that his grandfather had died, 'brutally murdered under a welter of axe blows'.[50]

There was more loose conjecture about the mental health of Sanger's assailant. The *Melbourne Argus* described how Cooper launched his attack on Sanger as the elderly victim sat in his chair: 'the maniac split open the head of the old man with the axe and cracked the skull of Austin, who was so horrified by the attack on his master that he was powerless to protect himself'.[51] In North America, more newspapers followed the lead of the *New York Times*, reporting that Sanger had been slain by an 'insane employee'.[52]

As details of the murder and attempted murders emerged, editors around the world took the opportunity to reprise highlights of the flamboyant showman's long career, although the information they provided was less

than reliable. The *Melbourne Argus* reported that: 'the circus, as it exists today, was largely the conception of Lord George Sanger', adding 'he had many friends including Queen Victoria'. The *Daily Mirror* commented that Sanger had 'probably appeared before more crowned heads than any other performer of recent years, theatrical or otherwise'. Syndicated news reports in the US noted that one of the peculiarities of the deceased showman was that he never removed his hat: 'He lived in his hat and died in it'. The *New York Times* helpfully informed its readers that 'the English Barnum ... lived in an imitation mediaeval castle'.[53]

Nearer home, the outrage at Park Farm competed for attention with the other big news story of the week: suffragettes had stormed parliament. Armed with hammers and bricks, they broke windows in government buildings, gentleman's clubs and newspaper offices. Two-hundred-and-twenty women and three men were arrested. The Thursday morning papers lamented that no arrest had yet been made for the 'savage attack' in East Finchley, and for the first time displayed a photo of the suspect. Confusingly, the supposed villain was far from the criminal type of popular post-Edwardian imagination. The face looking back at breakfast-time readers was that of a young, well-groomed, handsome young man with dark hair and dark eyes, wearing a suit, collar and tie. The broadsheets were again picking over the details of the previous day's police activity. In the absence of anything new to report, their correspondents ferreted for information from neighbours and associates, with no attempt made to separate uninformed gossip from fact. The *London Evening News* reported that Cooper had

secretly 'fitted up a little den' in one of the outbuildings of Park Farm, which was 'furnished with some taste'. In this space it was claimed Cooper owned a small safe in which he kept valuables, and it was where he read 'French and English novels of a very sensational class'. A solicitor who said he acted for George Sanger told the *Evening News*: 'he [Sanger] had the biggest heart of any man I've met' and offered an insight into the showman's marriage: 'He was very proud of her [his late wife Nellie], and especially of the wounds she had received in her lion-taming work.' The *Evening News* reprised Herbert Cooper's previous run-in with the police as evidence of his violent nature. The *News* quoted Henry Imhoff, a retired policeman who served on the jury when Cooper was tried for 'violent assault on a trespasser'. Imhoff was certain that Cooper 'would no doubt have been sentenced to imprisonment if Lord George Sanger had not pleaded for him ... I saw them both at Margate sometime after, and the old man seemed quite happy to think he had Cooper near him'.[54]

The press was again keen to remind their readers that Herbert Cooper was a violent, unstable character, referring to him as 'a madman' or 'insane'. Every scrap of information and rumour about the wanted man, no matter how trivial or misleading, was presented as fact. According to the *London Evening News*, a quantity of theatrical make-up had also been found in Cooper's room, although there was no mention of it in any of the police reports. The newspaper again offered sympathy for the cruel fate of 'the retired Circus King, enjoying his peace to which his crowded career and his 84 years entitled him, murdered while he was being read

to by a friend of his showman's days, in his drawing-room, the blow dealt by the hand of a young personal attendant whose benefactor he had been'.[55]

The *Daily Mirror*, the first British newspaper to dispense with the usual long columns of densely packed type and make regular and lavish use of large photographs and eye-catching headlines, splashed two pages of photos of Park Farm and its occupants. One of the images showed George Sanger in his trademark top hat and morning coat, posing outside his farm alongside his groom, his bailiff Thomas Cooper and his son Herbert Cooper. Another photo showed an employee, presumably Cooper, holding a heavy felling axe. It was captioned: 'The wanted man with an axe.'

While revelling in the most lurid aspects of the story, the *Daily Mirror* noted censoriously that a 'morbid crowd' had filled the road outside Park Farm the day after the attack, but this hadn't prevented the killer's brother and father reporting for work on the farm as usual. The *Mirror* ratcheted up the tension by misreporting that 'Cooper is believed to be armed with a revolver'. He was 'a betting man who had lost a great deal of money lately and was rumoured to have made enquiries about booking a passage to Australia … he may have made for Liverpool Street or Charing Cross to get the Continental train'.[56]

The regional papers rehashed the previous day's stories, adding some lively colour of their own. The *Leicester Post* repeated the story that about an hour after the attack, a greengrocer who knew the wanted man as a regular customer saw Cooper on Highgate Hill riding a bicycle in the direction of London. The informant had a very good view

of Cooper and was certain it was him. Hedging bets, the report added: 'the tradesman is rather short-sighted'. The *Post* said Cooper was often seen riding around the neighbourhood on a bicycle that was much too small for him and he was immediately recognisable by his 'cramped position'. The *Post* reminded readers that George Sanger was known for his philanthropy: his home was 'the last resort of many down and out showmen, clowns, lion tamers and equestrians ... even passing pedlars and gypsies were not excluded from the showman's help'.[57]

The *London Evening News* picked over the details of the previous day's police activity and had more details about Herbert Cooper's likely whereabouts: 'It leaves no doubt that he reached the heart of London last night on his bicycle.' There was more detail too about Harry Austin: 'an athletic man and at ordinary times might have been able to grapple even with a strong assailant, but a recent illness has left him very weak'.[58] Arthur Jackson meanwhile was enjoying his moment in the spotlight, and was quoted in the *Morning Post*, describing the attack to their reporter: 'While I was sitting in the kitchen reading, Cooper came in and attacked me with a hatchet, saying "Take that!"'[59]

Back in East Finchley, the local weekly *Hendon & Finchley Times* carried a lengthy, fulsome, almost reverential tribute to 'the Circus King', concluding: 'It is impossible to think of a more tragic end to an active, picturesque, and, it may be at once said, benevolent and kindly life than that which befell the world's greatest showman.'[60]

The press were all in agreement on one point. It was an extraordinarily pitiless act of killing and nothing quite like it

had ever happened before. The victim was a national treasure, loved and respected by all. Who but a madman would do such a thing?

8

Bodies

IT WAS THE SMELL PEOPLE NOTICED at first, then the rats. They were swarming from Enon Chapel, a small building in Clement's Lane just off the Strand. It was once an ordinary Baptist church ministering to the inhabitants of one of London's poorest parishes, but lately it served a more macabre purpose.

In the early years of Queen Victoria's reign, London's population had exploded to 2.5 million living souls and disposal of the dead was an increasing dilemma. Burial grounds and churchyards were filled beyond capacity, coffins stacked on top of each other in open graves. Gravediggers dumped their putrefying clients in pits and landfill to make more space or ground up their bones to be sold as fertiliser, and coffin nails and plates were scavenged and sold to second-hand shops. Clergymen whose income was dependent on burial fees turned a blind eye. Charles Dickens said the city smelled of 'rot and mildew and dead citizens'.

In 1823 Enon Chapel was taken on by an enterprising minister, Reverend W. Howse. He saw a gap in the market and offered extraordinarily cheap burials at just fifteen

shillings a time – almost half the cost of a burial at Wren's elegant St Clement Danes nearby. The upper part of Enon Chapel was dedicated to the worship of God, with the corpses buried in a narrow pit below. The dead were separated from the living by a single layer of wooden floorboards. The pit was small, 60-feet long, twelve-feet wide and six-feet deep, but it could accommodate up to 500 extra cadavers a year. Rev. Howse took a few shortcuts. After the funerals, coffins were emptied, chopped up and used for firewood. This way, the bodies could be packed together more tightly and the pit was filled with quicklime to help them decompose faster. The building was directly above an open sewer and it was speculated that Howse probably dumped at least some of the remains directly into the sewer, so the waste made its way to the Thames.

Enon Chapel's human landfill had not gone entirely unnoticed by the worshippers above. There was none of the usual lath and plaster below and the boards shrank, causing gaps to appear, through which the stink of decomposition escaped. Some of those who breathed in the noxious fumes of rotting flesh from the burial pit below fell ill. Children attending the chapel's Sunday school christened the insects they saw crawling and flying around in vast numbers during the summer months 'body bugs'. Then there were the rats, hundreds of them, running from the building and infesting nearby houses. Still, nobody yet suspected the true scale of the horror beneath Enon Chapel.

Eventually, concerns were voiced. In 1840 a House of Lords select committee heard that the chapel held the remains of 'ten or twelve thousand' dead. A few of their

lordships thought they had better take a look for themselves, but Rev. Howse denied them access to the vault with 'extreme unwillingness and violence'. The good minister settled the matter two years later by conveniently dying, and was himself buried beneath the chapel floorboards.[61] The authorities simply closed the premises and revoked the burial licence. There was no further attempt to investigate, remove or even count the bodies.

By now the charnel house in Clement's Lane was the talk of London. The building changed hands a couple of times, then it became a dance hall. The new tenants placed a layer of brick over the original wooden floor and put down some new floorboards. There was no attempt to hide the building's dark history, in fact it was the defining attraction, as the advertisement for opening night cheerfully revealed:

> *Enon Chapel – Dancing on the Dead – Admission Threepence. No lady or gentleman admitted unless wearing shoes and stockings.*

These morbid entertainments proved very popular and continued for about four years, until the philanthropist George 'Graveyard' Walker decided to put an end to the scandal by buying the property for 100 pounds, then at his own expense paid for the bodies to be removed and reburied in West Norwood. The floor of Enon Chapel was bricked and cemented over.

At the end of the 1850 summer season, the Sangers spent the winter in London again on a yard next to the King Harry's Head tavern on Mile End Road.[62] George

and John Sanger hoped to make a profit on the lowest rung of the Victorian entertainment industry ladder: the shady, cut-throat underworld of the unlicensed penny gaff business. There were hundreds of them in London, popping up in empty shops and other disused premises. At the inconsiderable cost of a penny a ticket, customers could see 'a melodrama (with three murders and a ghost), a pantomime, a comic song, an overture, and some incidental music, all done in five-and-twenty minutes'.[63]

Enon Chapel had been standing empty for several months when the Sanger brothers took up the lease in December 1850. They quickly fitted it up as a performance venue with a stage and scenery and took on some extra performers: the cornet player James Crockett; two actors, Harvey and Simpson; and a clown, Watty Hildyard. To promote their unlicensed show, they hired a twelve-piece band to play up and down the West End on the back of a wagon drawn by two horses. On Christmas Eve, the Sangers put on a pantomime. It went down well and on Boxing Day they staged five performances to full houses. Business was still booming when their show was brought to sudden and dramatic halt. The police had learned that the man engaged by 'Graveyard' Walker to remove the bodies from beneath Enon Chapel had not carried out the terms of his contract. His workmen were overheard in a pub boasting that there were over a hundred barrels of human bones and remains still hidden under the floorboards. Ironically, the former owner Rev. Howse was among them, interred directly under the very spot where the Sanger brothers' new stage was erected.

According to George, it was only when they received a tip-off from the local police that the building was about to be raided that they learned for the first time about the grim history of Enon Chapel. The Sangers and their crew scrambled to flee the building, taking with them stage props and all. They moved into a large vacant space above a public house on Mile End Road where they put on a hastily improvised New Year's Eve masquerade ball. In the early hours of the morning of 1 January 1851, the busy ballroom floor gave way under the weight of the dancers, bringing down the ceiling onto the heads of a bar full of revellers directly below, putting an end to the festivities and saddling the Sanger brothers with a hefty bill for repairs.

It's hard to imagine a more disastrous start to the year, but the horrors of Enon Chapel and the disaster of Mile End Road were swiftly put behind them. They had an appointment to look forward to that could wipe out all their debts and set them up for the rest of the year. In four months' time, London would host the Great Exhibition.

❧

George was in his mid-twenties, but he'd already lived through a time of extraordinary change. His sailor father had returned from the wars with France to a country feeling the full force of the depression that washed in their wake. There were high taxes and skyrocketing food prices, chronic unemployment and so much civil unrest that revolution seemed likely. But the 'hungry forties' gave way to a period of recovery and the economy was developing more rapidly and more creatively than ever. Britain was emerging

as the world's pre-eminent superpower and was enjoying a manufacturing boom thanks to incredible advances in science and technology. Now Britain was to show proof of her glorious present and a glimpse of a boundless future in a giant international trade show, a grand display of manufactured products featuring cutting-edge science, technology and engineering, to educate the masses and inspire British designers and manufacturers to compete in the international marketplace. Foreigners were welcome to display their own wares too, but there was no mistaking that it was primarily a celebration of British industrial might. As host, she occupied the lion's share of the display space with a vast array of exhibits from the Home Nations and the Empire. Among the display of wonders there were printing presses that could knock out an astonishing 5,000 copies of *Illustrated London News* in an hour, textile and agricultural machines and every kind of steam engine, including giant railway locomotives and a dazzling steam-hammer that could, with equal accuracy, forge the main bearing of a steamship or gently crack an egg.

Some had predicted there would be riots, that the structure housing it, Paxton's giant Crystal Palace, would collapse like a giant soufflé, that the Exhibition would be targeted by foreign terrorists and heads of state would be assassinated. None of these nightmares came to pass. By the time it closed on 11 October, over 6 million people – equivalent to a third of Britain's population – had passed peacefully through the turnstiles and, instead of the loss predicted, the Exhibition made a substantial profit. *The Times* conceded that it had been a great success: 'a sight the like of which has never

happened before, and which, in the nature of things, can never be repeated'.[64]

The Great Exhibition was the envy of the world and showed that London was the capital of world trade, but away from the glamour and excitement in Hyde Park, life went on much as usual that summer. The metropolis was still the sink of child prostitutes, of sweatshop workers, of pickpockets and beggars, of mudlarks and professional dog-shit collectors, all trying to negotiate a miserable and precarious existence. For the struggling fairground folk at least there was the prospect of a few crumbs falling their way. To accompany the main event there was to be an Exhibition Fair, held a mile or so away at Bayswater, on a piece of waste ground that had been cleared for building works.

Like most other travelling showfolk in London, the Sangers anticipated making the most of the thousands of visitors who were expected to pour into the capital every day and spent months planning for the event. Hundreds of caravans converged on the space, bringing the biggest touring exhibitions in the country. Wombwell's, Cooke's, Hilton's, Atkins's and Richardson's each took up their assigned pitches and prepared for the opening day, their spirits up. The morning of the much-anticipated bonanza dawned fine and bright.

Then it rained. And it kept on raining like never before.

For the first eighteen days of May, London experienced an almost continuous deluge. The ridge and valley roof of the 'crystal palace' was watertight and kept visitors dry, but the open fairground with its rickety caravans, flimsy wooden

booths and saggy canvas tents couldn't begin to cope. On the first day of the fair there was barely a handful of visitors and little business done. The second day was a washout. The persistent, pitiless downpour continued into the third and fourth days, and the shows remained shut. Two days of dry weather gave everyone hope. A handful of visitors braved the badly waterlogged fairground, but after the brief respite, the rain came down harder than ever. It continued into the second week and the rough ground became a black, treacly bog into which caravan wheels sank hub-high, the brightly painted fronts of the big travelling theatres mud-splattered beyond recognition. The atrocious weather refused to abate. George and his family sat in their wagon, scanning the skies, praying for a break in the clouds that never came. The big menageries were the first to throw in the towel, abandoning the sticky ground while they still could, but their heavy wagons had already sunk so deep into the sludge that no amount of horsepower could budge them. Eventually, assistance was provided by 200 workmen hired by the showmen to drag them out. Battling with ropes fastened to the sinking vehicles, they heaved them one by one from the churning quagmire to the safety of the main road. A few desperate showmen lingered in hopeless prospect of better weather, but then the godforsaken fair was finally evacuated.

The collapse of the event from which so much was expected was a cruel blow. Some of the bigger travelling shows made devastating losses and faced ruination. The Sangers were a pitiful sight as they took to the road again, soaked, mud-caked, hungry and dispirited. They prayed for better weather so they might scrape together enough money

from what was left of the season to survive another winter without severe hardship.

George gambled on turning their fortunes around by trying his hand at some of the 'magic lantern' shows that were currently in vogue. They were crude projections of a series of glass slides onto a large white sheet. Magic lanterns had previously relied on candles and oil lamps for a light source and the results were disappointing, but there was a new form of illumination generated by burning mineral lime, oxygen and hydrogen – hence the phrase 'in the limelight'. This combination of chemicals was also extremely unstable and dangerous.

On 14 September 1852 the most famous man in the land, the 83-year-old Duke of Wellington, died from a stroke. The hero of Waterloo had lately served as a deeply unpopular politician, but in death all was forgiven and a million people turned out to see his funeral cortège. From a manufacturer in Sheffield, George bought two large magic lanterns and from his old friend, the artist Jack Kelly, he commissioned sixteen scenes, each painted on glass slides, measuring fifteen inches by four inches, representing the state funeral procession of the recently deceased Iron Duke. George had figured out how to do the chemistry himself, making the gas required to produce the limelight in his living wagon. One evening he was cooking his mixture in preparation for a show at the town hall at Northwich. While the concoction was bubbling away on the caravan stove, George and Nellie got ready for the show. George was putting a wave in his hair with his curling tongs and his wife was getting into her show costume when the container caught fire and there was

a massive explosion. The walls and the roof of the caravan were blown away, leaving only the undercarriage. Nellie was knocked off her feet into the field beyond, and was badly bruised and burned about the face and arms. George's carefully groomed coiffure vanished, along with his eyebrows, beard and moustache. His face and hands were scorched black and his dress-coat hung off his body in charred tatters.

The explosion was heard a mile away and a large crowd gathered to see the damage, among them a doctor who dressed George and Nellie's burns and dosed them with laudanum. The next morning, they found they had been robbed. Under cover of darkness, everything of any value that hadn't already been destroyed in the blast was gone, including the tin box holding their life savings. All that remained was a few shillings George carried in his ragged trouser pocket.

In George's memoir it reads like a comedy sketch, a literally hair-raising, cartoonish explosion in which the protagonist is left sooty-faced, his clothes hanging off him in shreds, his wife blown sky high and left in the mud with feet in the air, but George and Nellie were hospitalised for the next nine days and were literally scarred for life. The townsfolk of Northwich rallied round and local joiners did what they could to try to patch up the demolished caravan. When George was sufficiently recovered he tried to repay their charity by putting on a couple of shows, conjuring with his left hand still heavily bandaged, and over two nights they raised twelve pounds. George's final word on the incident in his memoir is telling. He claimed the authorities agreed that the blame for the disaster lay squarely with a local chemist's

assistant, who supplied a faulty mixture of perchlorate of potash. Not George's fault at all; he was just the guy who made a bomb in his living room.

Travelling performers always kept their wagon in tip-top condition. It was their home and their livelihood, but when they took to the road again the vehicle was barely functional. It was midwinter and the rain came through gaps in the roof and the wind howled through cracks in the sides. That Christmas was the bleakest, most cheerless time they could ever remember. To add to their trials, Nellie was now heavily pregnant. It was a huge relief when George found some comfortable lodgings near Derby.

About sixteen miles west in the village of Alton, George hired a large room in a local hotel and set off to drum up some custom for his magic lantern show scheduled for the following Friday, 23 January. Wearing his patched-up Hamlet costume, he paraded the villages of the Staffordshire Moorlands announcing his arrival. On the eve of his show he heard that Nellie had just given birth to a boy. He saddled a horse and raced back to visit them, then galloped straight back to Alton just in time to perform. His magic lantern shows of the Duke of Wellington's funeral and Captain Ross's rescue mission went ahead on schedule and played to a full house, although this time without combustible gases and illuminated with old fashioned seal oil and cotton wicks.

Otherwise it was a miserable year of disaster piled upon bitter struggle. While his wife was nursing their infant son, George and his brother John arranged their first short tour north of the border with their miscellany of conjuring tricks, performing rabbits and birds and their magic lantern show.

In a few benighted pockets of Scotland, however, they found themselves up against extreme religious prejudice and local superstition. George's sleight of hand and his mastery over small animals spooked the God-fearing people of the remote towns and villages of the lowlands, and local churchmen denounced his trickery as malign and devilish. The mood turned uglier by the day. Anticipating a lynch mob, the Sangers hurried across the border and returned south. There was more bad news waiting for them when they re-joined their family at Newcastle upon Tyne. George and John's mother Sarah had travelled north to meet them and to see her new grandson for the first time, but had been suddenly taken ill. At Durham she died, aged 72. The brothers buried their mother at Houghton-le-Spring and moved on. Shortly after, the little company suffered another terrible bereavement with the sudden death of Elizabeth, the wife of their loyal clown Watty Hildyard.

A run of bad weather and poor business deepened the malaise. At York, there was a sharp reminder that they had still not risen above the legal status of 'rogues and vagabonds'. At the great hiring fair, the police served them notice to quit the town within the hour. They piled their belongings into their caravan and headed south for Lincolnshire. At Corby, one of the horses died and the cost of replacing it wiped out all of their savings. Bad weather prevented them from putting on any shows to recoup their losses. They were dead broke and stuck. A tollgate at the end of the township provided yet another obstacle. A whip-round among the little company of five failed to raise fifteen pennies to get from one side of the tollgate to the other. George offered to

pay with the only disposable item of any value they had, a Chinese gong they used to pull in a crowd, but the tollkeeper had no use for it. The pathetic company of performers was rescued by a passing clergyman, who took pity and gave them ten shillings in exchange for a private performance for his own four small children in a local tap room.

On the road to Corby, George and Nellie's unbaptised son fell ill. Soon after leaving town, the infant had a convulsive fit and died. The parents washed and laid out the small body in the back of their caravan. The troupe travelled to Stamford and, in the heavy snow, they put on their costumes, masked their grief with their best show smiles and performed until they had enough pennies to pay for a decent burial in the churchyard of St Mary.

Nellie Sanger was already pregnant again with their second child, a daughter they would name Laurina.

～

By the end of the 1853 season, the Sanger brothers had recovered sufficiently from their financial setbacks to save enough money to set up their own small circus. They wintered at Norwich in the yard of a riverside public house and put their plan into operation. George bought a Welsh pony from Croydon for seven pounds, and taught it how to count in response to the click of fingernails. A second, larger horse was acquired for eighteen pounds, and trained to gallop round a circus-sized ring. Their human performers were a scratch company of nephews and nieces, plus three experienced artists, their old friend Watty Hildyard the clown, an equestrian called John Crouste, then finally

an all-rounder, William Kite. The last recruit was the most exciting. Kite was the same age as George but already had an impressive circus pedigree. He was an equestrian, acrobat and tightrope walker and 'could do almost any ring business you could mention, [he] strutted forth before the public gaze, in tights and trunks, everybody, including even the showmen, was impressed and astonished'.[65] Kite could also play the trombone while balancing on his head on top of a pole. He's doing it on a famous vintage circus poster bought by John Lennon in 1967.[66]

Through the winter they drilled the junior members of their nascent troupe in the basic circus arts of juggling, ropewalking, trick-riding, tumbling and clowning. On the evening of 13 February 1854 George put the finishing touches to his giant, painted-canvas show front, announcing to the world that the Sangers were now circus proprietors. The next day they opened at King's Lynn, admission one penny, reserved seats threepence. The town's Charter Fair was one of the oldest events in the country, marking the start of the travelling season, and despite the occasional February cold snap it was always well attended. It was the perfect place for the Sanger brothers to launch their new venture.

The expense involved in taking even a modest travelling circus on the road was a high-wire gamble, but when they counted their takings, the Sanger brothers were relieved to find that good fortune and hard work had favoured them and they had made a tidy profit. After a couple of weeks at King's Lynn, George and John dismantled their equipment and moved on to Lincoln, Stamford, Cambridge, then the great Easter fair at Norwich. In between the fairs, if they

found a decent-sized space in a local village, they set up a few seats around the shape of a ring and charged a penny a seat to see a 'grand performance of juggling, rope-walking and trick-riding'. Midway through, John passed a hat among the spectators, then they finished the show with their fortune-telling pony.

The Sanger travelling circus was still an open-air affair and customers and performers were at the mercy of the weather. When it rained, the ring was often ankle-deep in mud. In time they were able to build themselves something resembling a proper arena, with a raised spectator gallery, but it was a ramshackle affair with everything done on a shoestring budget and the brothers had to beg, borrow or steal the materials. At Bury they were caught red-handed, pilfering from Sam Wild's Travelling Theatre. Wild owned one of the biggest and most impressive shows on the road and at the end of a performance every seat, plank, shutter, bracket nut and bolt was stored away in four huge wagons, ready for transportation to the next town. When a couple of his crew members went to see Sanger's circus, they were surprised to find that most of the hardware used to erect the gallery – portable steps, poles and brackets – looked suspiciously like their own. When confronted, the Sanger brothers offered a contrite apology but privately feared the worst. Luckily, Sam Wild adjudged their little show such a 'poor affair' that he took pity and offered to lend them anything else they might find useful.[67] Just a few years later, Wild would be astonished (and jealous) to find that the name of Sanger was known throughout the land and easily eclipsed his own.

Expansion was ambitious and fast. By the time Sanger's Circus arrived in Manchester in June for the Whit Monday fair, they had increased their stud to nine horses and two ponies. The Sangers reached Carlisle just in time for the annual August festivities, and over a week took almost a hundred pounds – about £12,000 in today's values. In Scotland they bought thirteen more horses and another pony. With a more ambitious programme came another price hike, with seats now ranging from sixpence to two shillings. At Glasgow there was a hugely successful five week run with the equestrian drama *Mazeppa* followed by Dundee, Paisley, Greenock, Aberdeen, Edinburgh and finally Inverness for the Highland Games.[68]

Although John and George were equal business partners, from very early on John gave his kid brother free rein to put his own stamp on their joint venture. George was always front and centre, the public face of Sanger's Circus. In appearance the brothers were much alike, both short in stature with John a slightly older, heavier version of George. Both lost their hair early and wore small beards, forming around their mouths a little 'O' like a sawdust ring. There the similarities ended. Where George was flamboyant, talkative and outgoing, John was shy and modest to the point of diffidence. He said little and hated attention or dealing with strangers. If anyone asked him if he was Mr Sanger, John would shake his head and jerk a thumb towards his younger brother.

George's assertiveness was growing with every show. He was also making enough money to indulge his taste for fancy tailoring. His new shiny top hat, smart dress suit and patent leather riding boots became his calling card, and he

was seen striding around in his new outfit in every town they visited, trying hard to get himself noticed. His family was growing too. That summer their tiny caravan was filled with a second child's cries, those of Harriet, a sister for two-year-old Laurina.

At the end of the summer season they usually wintered in London, but in 1854 there were another 10,000 cholera deaths in the capital. The Sangers decided it was wise to stay north. They built their first permanent circus on a piece of waste ground on Bannister Street in Liverpool, a large timber building with a canvas top that could hold up to a thousand spectators. For the next five months they gave three performances a night to full houses. Fortune favoured them here too. Under the management of William Cooke, Astley's in London was struggling, and some of the top performers left to join Sanger's Liverpool circus.

The Sanger brothers' rise over the next five years is hard to overstate. Every year their circus increased in size and turnover. As George's directorial talents blossomed, he added a greater variety to their shows and the money was ploughed back into new performers, new equipment and attractions. In 1859 he went to Europe for the first time, scouting for talent in Paris and Madrid. By the end of their sixth year their stud had grown to over 60 horses, and they had their own orchestra and a company of circus performers rated among the best in the country.

George was prompted by the spirit of competition to introduce performing lions, and bought six from Jamrach's Menagerie in London's East End. Sanger's new 'lion conqueror' was the tall, full-bearded James Crockett. He

stumbled across his profession in the way lion tamers did. He was a bandsman in Sanger's orchestra and married George and John's younger sister Sarah, but Crockett developed a respiratory problem and struggled to play his trumpet. George offered his impressively built brother-in-law the job of resident lion tamer, simply because, as George put it, he looked the part. George's wife Nellie was also persuaded to come out of retirement to take part in various lion-based entertainments, mostly sauntering among the big cats doing her 'Serpentine dance'.

The national census taken on 7 April 1861 captured George and John in their travelling carriages in Manchester, with George's wife Nellie and his daughters Laurina and Harriet, age eight and six, and John's wife Elizabeth and their seven-year-old son John and four-year-old daughter Lavinia. They had just opened a new premises in Portland Street and were playing to full houses of 3,000 people. By the end of the decade George and John would build nine more permanent circuses between Plymouth and Aberdeen. Sanger was already the biggest name in touring circuses in the British Isles, but the brothers hungered for more.

In November 1871 George Sanger realised a childhood ambition when he and his brother John bought Astley's Amphitheatre at the knock-down price of 11,000 pounds. By that time the Sangers already had permanent circuses in Manchester, Birmingham, Liverpool, Glasgow, Dundee, Aberdeen, Bath, Bristol, Exeter and Plymouth, and at the Agricultural Hall in Islington in north London. Acquiring a second venue in the city was an astonishing leap of faith and a sign of the new owners' soaring ambition.

When the Sanger brothers took over Astley's, they pulled down a large part of the old building and enlarged and modernised it, with a new ring and the biggest and best-equipped stage in the city, lit by 200,000 jets of gas. To the delight of spectacle-hungry Londoners, the lavish equestrian dramas were revived, complete with lots of pretty chorus girls and voluptuous, scantily clad pantomime artistes recruited from the West End theatres. On 21 October 1871 the venue reopened with an equestrian drama, *The Last of the Race; or The Warrior Women*, a strange set-to between Afghan generals and Georgian Amazons.[69]

Keeping two London venues afloat in the teeth of relentless competition required creative marketing. A couple of months after the re-opening of Astley's, George pulled off one of his most notorious publicity stunts. The twenty-seventh of February 1872 was designated Thanksgiving Day to mark the recovery of the Prince of Wales from typhoid fever. The government, grateful for an opportunity for a display of loyalty to the Crown in a time of surging anti-monarchism, organised one of those public spectacles that Londoners can't get enough of. A service at St Paul's Cathedral was to be preceded by a grand procession of royal carriages through the city and a rare public appearance by Queen Victoria. On the big day, tens of thousands of people, many of whom only a couple of weeks earlier had questioned if there was any point in having a monarchy at all, gathered along the route, craning their necks to get a glimpse of 'the widow of Windsor'.

As the police and military struggled to marshal the crowds of onlookers, the procession left Buckingham Palace

at noon, bound for St Paul's with the Queen's coach bringing up the rear. Six people were reported killed in the crush and hundreds more were hospitalised. George Sanger, the most ardent of royalists, demanded a piece of the action. At the appointed hour, he set off from the Agricultural Hall in Islington with his own mini parade, a rolling advertisement for his circus, featuring his wife Nellie dressed as Britannia, holding a shield and trident, sitting on top of a giant, ornate gilded wagon and with an actual lion at her feet. At the top of Park Lane, Sanger's tableau wagon found a convenient gap in the royal parade and elbowed its way in. George later claimed he gambled on the convoy being hemmed in on both sides by the crowd so the authorities would have no option but to let him continue, but it would have surprised no one if he'd greased a few palms as well. Exactly as George anticipated, the police allowed him to proceed to St Paul's. As the line of state coaches carrying princes, princesses, dukes and duchesses made their sedate progress to the cathedral, right in the middle of them there was little Nellie Sanger, perched with her lion on top of her tinsel tower, smiling gamely at the quizzical faces below. Her husband boasted later that the 7,000 pounds he reckoned he had lavished on his stunt that day was the best money he'd ever spent because his show wagon was seen by at least 100,000 Londoners.[70]

On Boxing Day 1873, customers at Astley's Amphitheatre saw the pantomime *Lady Godiva* with the lead role played by the actress 'massive' Maud Forrester, billed with a knowing wink as 'Godiva Golightly'. The show was significant because it was the last ever production under the joint management of George and John Sanger. After twenty years on

the road together, the two brothers, so very different in temperament, agreed to part company. The split was amicable. Their families were growing, and they decided that the best way forward for everyone was to run separate establishments. George bought out John's minor share in the two London venues, Astley's and the Agricultural Hall. John would concentrate on touring as the John Sanger & Sons Circus. Everything else was simply divided on the toss of a coin: the winner took the goods and paid over half their value to the loser. Thus, an estate with a net worth valued at upwards of 100,000 pounds (over a £1 million in today's values) was divided up without quarrel or disagreement.

For the next couple of years George ran the same show at both London venues. Every day at the end of each performance his crew jumped in cabs on Westminster Bridge Road and raced to North London and the Agricultural Hall. When the lease of the Islington venue ended, all of his resources were concentrated on Astley's. His brilliant, brazen showmanship restored prosperity to Astley's Amphitheatre for the next twenty years. In the refurbished, rebuilt venue, spectacle was everything and the shows became more zoological. On Boxing Day 1874, Sanger's version of *Aladdin* featured a herd of trained elephants. In 1876 his new ringmaster Henry Bertrand introduced the extravaganza *Gulliver's Travels*, which George modestly described as 'the biggest thing ever attempted by any theatrical or circus manager before or since'.[71] The hyperbole was justified. In one scene there were on the stage at the same time 500 adult performers, 200 children, thirteen elephants, nine camels, 52 horses, plus sundry lions, ostriches, emus, pelicans, deer, kangaroos, buffaloes

and bulls. The Lord Chamberlain, under whose jurisdiction all British theatre performed, asked for reassurances that the stage would not collapse under their combined weight.

Life at Astley's under Sanger's management was full of surprises front and back of house. The recovered Prince of Wales, a fan of George's famous line-up of beautiful chorus girls, Sanger's 'pretties', was among the famous who just appeared to drop by at random and make themselves at home there. George's grandson wandered into the kitchen at Astley's one evening and was surprised to find the Prince deep in conversation with Britain's chief hangman James Berry. Another frequent visitor, the great theatrical scene-painter Joseph Harker, laid bare some of the details of this strange inner world in his memoirs. Beneath the stage at Astley's there were what seemed like several miles of dark labyrinthine passages, dimly lit by burning gas jets set in cages and reverberating to the sound of roaring beasts and the clatter of hooves from stabled horses. One day Harker descended into this mysterious subterranean space and in the half-light, he could make out the shapes of several wild animals, roaming freely and looking for something or possibly someone to eat. As Harker was groping his way down a long passage, gingerly stepping over the neck of a recumbent camel, his hand touched something soft and warm. On closer inspection he discovered that he was fondling a lion. There was more apprehension when Harker was suddenly confronted by a large baboon. It was making a beeline for the door directly behind him, the ape followed by three keepers in hot pursuit. They laughed at the painter's evident panic; the baboon, they told him, was 'meek as a lamb', but

Harker couldn't help noticing that each keeper was armed with an iron bar.[72]

George Sanger's ambition had always eclipsed that of his brother John and now he was free to spread his wings. He was only halfway to becoming not just the most successful circus owner in British show business, but the owner of an empire of fame and size without parallel in Europe. In the spring of 1874, the George Sanger circus set off on its very first annual visit to the continent. Over the next eleven years, he divided his time between England and Europe, crossing the channel every April with his vast arsenal of amusements and returning at the end of October, touring France, Germany, Austria, Bohemia (the Czech Republic), Spain, Switzerland, Denmark and Holland. By the end of the decade the Sanger brand had a toehold in every European country west of Russia. George was now the richest and most famous show business impresario on this side of the Atlantic.

9

A lethal certainty

THURSDAY 30 NOVEMBER 1911 dawned bitterly cold and foggy at Highgate station. On the northbound side of the station's island platform James Boyer, a 24-year-old railway porter, shuffled his feet to try to keep warm. The busy terminus was on the Great Northern Railway (GNR) line, nestled in a deep cutting excavated from Highgate Hill. Tunnels penetrated the hillside at each end of the station, leading towards East Finchley to the north and Crouch End to the south. When the new station was built in 1867, Highgate was a sparsely populated town surrounded by open countryside, but the tide of bricks and mortar had since advanced rapidly beyond the northern perimeter of the metropolis and the open spaces of the 'Northern Heights' were now covered by a maze of terraced housing. The journey on the steam train in and out of the city centre had become overcrowded and unpleasant and the line was congested with goods traffic. The atmosphere in the small railway compartments was stuffy, but passengers tempted to open a window risked being enveloped in smut and steam from the engine. The morning commuter trains were usually

packed before they arrived at East Finchley. The doors of the carriage compartments were locked with a simple square key and some passengers were having their own keys made at local ironmongers and locking the doors from the inside. On most mornings there were bad-tempered exchanges and even blows traded between frustrated commuters.

James Boyer had been portering at Highgate station since he was a boy. He owned a suit for Sunday best and a corduroy uniform for work, his cap emblazoned with a badge denoting the company he served. He helped with luggage and offered directions and made sure carriage doors were closed and windows were up. Between train arrivals, he swept the platforms and kept the edges whitewashed and made sure the oil in the signal lamps was topped up. There were also packages to be dealt with and sorted ready for collection. He was also expected to clean out livestock carriages heading for the London abattoirs, an unpleasant job, especially if the cattle had been on the train for a few hours. His wages were low and he was more than ready to accept a tip. If he was lucky, a passenger might pay him to keep a carriage door locked so that no one else could sit there or give him threepence to carry luggage, supply a travel rug or look after a pet.

7.30am. James was now twenty minutes into his shift. A couple of yards from where he stood, a green and gold locomotive from King's Cross exhaled steam. It had just disgorged its passengers and was slowly pulling out of the station towards Barnet. As the train passed, a passenger shouted to James from an open carriage window. The man had grim news. A few minutes earlier, when the train stopped

momentarily at the fog signal box just outside Crouch End, he looked out of the window and thought he saw a body.

Since the 1840s, a wave of speculation and construction had created a vast rail network that spanned rivers and busy streets and country lanes, cutting swathes through farmland, bisecting rural communities. Anonymous death by train was depressingly common, coming swiftly and often. You only had to turn your back and you could be killed by the GNR. Hundreds of people died and tens of thousands were injured in railway accidents every year. For railway employees in particular, workaday life in close proximity to railway lines offered constant exposure to danger. Their injuries were often grotesque. The wife of the signalman at Barnes lost both her legs while rescuing her infant son when he strayed onto the line. At Stretton, stationmaster Simms saw his wife knocked down and the wheels of the carriages cut up her body into several pieces. The gangs of itinerant labourers employed in the back-breaking toil of creating a new transport infrastructure took the heaviest casualties, but people going about their daily business were also exposed to danger; coal or timber merchants sending or receiving goods; carters moving goods from the railhead to their final destination, farmers using a right of way across a railway line. Every week, lives were destroyed at rail crossings. There were widespread fears that the railway came at the considerable cost of mental health too. There were around a thousand railway suicides a year.[73] They occurred so frequently that some people believed that railway lines induced 'suicidal delirium' among those of a nervous disposition. More likely, the wheels of a train offered a lethal certainty.

James Boyer informed a ticket collector, 37-year-old Thomas Potter, what the passenger had told him. Like most railway workers, Potter lived within a short walking distance of his job at Highgate, with his wife Ada, their ten-year-old son and Thomas's elderly parents. Before he worked on the railway, Potter was an agricultural labourer. This was a step up, with better pay and regular work. The railways were one of the few workplaces in post-Edwardian Britain where someone like Thomas could improve his pay and prospects through promotion. The opportunities were small, but for the hard-working they existed.

At around 7.45am Potter went to investigate. Near Archway signal box he encountered James Roberts, a plate-layer. Potter told Roberts about the sighting and asked if he'd seen a man on the line. Roberts said he had not, but a passenger had shouted something to him from the carriage window of a passing train – he hadn't caught what was said. Potter replied: 'Well, there's maybe one here somewhere.' The two men set off down the line towards Crouch End.

For one category of railway worker the opportunities for advancement were out of reach. A platelayer like James Roberts was at the bottom of the pile with no way up. He was allocated a section of line to maintain, perhaps a mile or two. He spent his day walking the line looking for faults in the track and mending them using picks, shovels, hammers and track gauges. He also had to maintain line-side fences and keep culverts clear. These tasks were performed in all weathers for six days a week. Roberts worked a twelve-hour shift from 6am and at the end of the day he had to make sure that the line was clear and in good working order. If his work wasn't done

by 6pm he had to stay until it was. For this graft he received seventeen shillings a week, the worst pay of any male railway employee. Platelayers were alarmingly expendable. There was no sick pay and because of the hazardous nature of their work, insurance against accidents was unaffordable. They were the rats and mice of the railway industry, everywhere but rarely seen. Because of their lowly status and generally ragged appearance on account of their arduous manual work, platelayers were forbidden to go near station platforms or passengers.[74] This was the least of James Roberts's daily hardships. He was also expected to retrieve anything, or anyone, that may have fallen from or under a train.

The gravel crunched underfoot as the two men continued along the railway line southbound from Highbury station, looking for signs of the reported body. This was an ordinary duty Roberts had not yet learned to face without dread. Still, there was a thick low-lying fog, and he fancied the passenger may have been mistaken and had seen a dead dog. Half a mile from Crouch End station his optimism evaporated. About 50 yards from Stanhope Road railway bridge, as Roberts and Potter peered through the gloom, they saw a body lying to the left of the line. When they got closer a dreadful scene revealed itself. The dark-suited figure of a man, crushed and mutilated at the neck, was lying on his back with his feet pointing at right angles to the railway line. A portion of the man's head, face and brain was lying about three yards away.

Potter went to find help while Roberts remained with the body until the arrival of his foreman, Arthur Guiver. The foreman said that a gang of platelayers had walked right past

the very spot on the opposite side of the track about half an hour ago, but had not seen the body on account of the fog.

At 9.15am William Woodcock, acting stationmaster at Crouch End put a call in to Crouch End Hill police. A body had been found on the line and an officer and an ambulance were required. Constable Charles Burden met Woodcock at the railway station and together they walked the short distance to the scene. Burden took notes. The man's feet were pointed towards the embankment in the direction of Spencer's Farm. From the position of the body it appeared that he had laid down by the side of the line, placed his head on the rail and was killed by a passing train. Woodcock estimated that at least six passenger trains had used the line during that time. Unless the train's driver came forward, it was unlikely the carriage that killed him would ever be traced.

The fog had started to lift a little and so PC Burden, accompanied by the newly arrived Constables Gale and Linnott from Hornsey police station, walked the track and scoured the nearby embankment for anything else that could have been overlooked. Nearby, trains running to and from London clattered intermittently over their tracks as Burden scrambled to the top of the embankment to the place where the tracks met the nearby railway bridge at Stanhope Road. Scanning the surrounding area, he noted that the dead man could have got on the line by climbing over a wall by the side of the bridge or from the field adjoining. Dr Thomas Parry from Crouch End Hill arrived and estimated that the man had been dead for about two hours. Parry ordered the removal of the body to Hornsey mortuary. Meanwhile PC Burden searched the dead man's clothes for clues as to

his identity. He found a pocket address book, and inside the cover was written:

H. Cooper, Park Farm View.

Burden rode with the body in an ambulance litter to the mortuary at Hornsey, where he searched the dead man's pockets more thoroughly. In his notebook he made an inventory of the items recovered, including just over eleven pounds in loose change, a rolled gold watch and chain, a pen-knife, a door key and various other bits and pieces, including two small scraps of paper. On the first was a note scribbled in thick pencil:

> *Dear Dad,*
> *Something at the farm has happened, I don't remem-*
> *ber doing it I can only call to mind someone speaking I*
> *seemed to come to my senses no one knows what I have*
> *gone through the govener [sic] turned against me what for*
> *I don't know and blamed me for things I never knew any-*
> *thing about after spending six years with him and Jenny*
> *Beasley [sic] and George Austin with their lies has turned*
> *my brain she is the worst woman I have ever heard of*
> *I cant send this by post as I havnt got a stamp but all*
> *what belongs to me share out between you, you must look*
> *behind the picture over wash table you will find some*
> *money I drew from one of my old books and have not*
> *put it all away dont think of me any more I have been*
> *greatly wronged by that woman Good bye all my brains*
> *has turned hope you will forgive me for some great wrong*
> *Good bye Tom Dick Len and you Dad*
> *Your broken hearted son*
> *Herb.*

On the second piece of paper, also in pencil:

Dear Harry,
I am sorry things should have come to this, know one [sic]
knows what I have gone through, what I told you was the
truth and Mr. George turned like he did after all that time
I have been with him, I couldn't stand it, I have blamed
Jenny Beesley for all and let her think it over.
                                        Good bye.

PC Burden gathered up all of the possessions and returned them to the station at Finchley. Meanwhile Thomas John Cooper was called to the mortuary and tasked with formally identifying his brother's decapitated body.

Later that morning, Inspector Wallace, accompanied by Chief Inspector Fitt and George Sanger's brother-in-law James Holloway, went to Park Farm and searched the outbuilding Cooper had occupied to look for the money mentioned in the note. In a small hole in the wall, behind a picture about ten feet from the floor, Wallace found thirteen pounds and ten shillings. He instructed Fitt to give the money to Thomas Cooper senior as soon as possible.

Enquiries were also being made by GNR transport police among the train drivers who had used the route between Crouch End and East Finchley earlier that morning, but no one could recall seeing anything suspicious on the line. This was not particularly surprising. When London was buried under a typical November fog, thick, yellow and all-encompassing, anything more than a few feet away was reduced to a shapeless blur. It was easy to miss something very dark taking root. The newspapers often reported

bizarre fog-related incidents, including one which involved a famous Finchley resident, Dr Henry Stephens. He travelled daily by horse-drawn coach from his home in East End Road to Paddington, to catch the new Metropolitan Railway to his office in Farringdon Street. One foggy day, the 68-year-old doctor was returning home with his son and they lost contact on the crowded platform at Farringdon station. Henry Stephens junior assumed his father had boarded the train without him and took another carriage home. His father had collapsed and died on a busy, crowded platform at Farringdon station, but in the thick fog, no one noticed his body until the next day.

⤻

The ferocious attack on the elderly George Sanger and two members of his household and the manhunt for the alleged murder had created a media frenzy, but the apparent discovery of the fugitive's headless body and a suicide note pumped new blood into the story. Cooper's suicide seemed to confirm what everyone already knew. A violent, crazed assassin had taken advantage of a vulnerable old man's benevolence. Now he had cheated the gallows by taking the coward's way out. *The Times* reported under the headline 'LORD' GEORGE SANGER – SUICIDE OF THE MURDERER:[75]

> *The decapitated body of Herbert Cooper, the murderer of 'Lord' George Sanger, was found yesterday morning by some railway employees on the railway line between Crouch-end and Highgate … the man is believed to have got to the place during the heavy fog of Wednesday night*

or early that morning ... In the neighbourhood are a number of empty houses in which Cooper could have taken shelter.

Reaffirming the supposition that Cooper was unhinged, the suicide note found in his jacket pocket was widely reported in the press as 'rambling' and 'badly-written'. A colourful theory was put forward by the London *Evening News*, whose correspondent congratulated the police on identifying the body, despite a dastardly attempt to dupe them. 'Cooper, it is thought, had attempted to prevent identification by laying his head on the rail. The result was sufficiently terrible, but it could not deceive those who were called to inspect the body.'[76] The author of this story overlooked the fact that the dead man left a suicide note in his pocket with his name on it. The *Tewkesbury Register* interviewed a friend of the late Sanger, described as 'an old East Finchley resident', who told their reporter that it was 'more than likely that, when the will of the veteran showman comes to be proved, it will be seen that Cooper would have benefitted largely under it'.[77]

Fears that a lunatic killer was on the loose somewhere in Middlesex were at least now allayed. The questions about why Herbert Cooper had descended into a psychotic, murderous frenzy that cold November evening and how he had evaded detection, however, had yet to be answered.

To one newspaper correspondent it all seemed stranger than fiction. 'The whole tragedy has been played out within a space of forty hours. Balzac has conceived no story of human vagary more extraordinary.'[78]

10

Lord of the ring

THERE ARE AT LEAST half a dozen accounts of how George Sanger came to be a Lord. During his lifetime and for many years afterwards, most of the people who came to see his shows assumed that his title was genuine. Everyone had a theory about how he acquired it. There was a popular story doing the rounds that Queen Victoria had made him a peer in return for services rendered to the Lord Mayor's Show, including the loan of carriages and elephants. Another yarn that entered the realm of urban mythology held that the Queen raised him to the peerage because he'd allowed her to put her head inside the jaws of one of his lions. George was too astute a showman to have any of these rumours contradicted, but the likely truth was more prosaic.

In the summer of 1887 Britain was looking forward to a party. Victoria, Queen of Great Britain and Ireland and Empress of India had been on the throne for half a century. There would be a summer of celebration, with street parties, grand balls, sporting and artistic events. The highlight was to be an extended holiday weekend, climaxing in a glorious parade through London attended by 50 foreign kings and princes,

along with the governing heads of Britain's overseas colonies and dominions, with Victoria herself as its magnificent centre-piece, in open landau escorted by Indian cavalry. But by far the biggest draw in England that summer, upstaging all the pomp and ceremony, the royal festivities and the assembled crowned heads, was a hairy American backwoodsman from Iowa.

On 14 April 1887 the steamship *State of Nebraska* anchored at Gravesend, carrying the latest American sensation, Buffalo Bill's Wild West Show. The star of the show was Buffalo Bill himself, Colonel William Frederick Cody, soldier, cowboy, showman, promoter and celebrity. He was already a household name in America, the superhero of dime-store novels, an actor playing himself in theatricals about fighting savage 'Indians'.

In the flesh Cody was a giant of man, ruggedly handsome, his features 'as perfect as if they had been chiselled out of marble'.[79] His life was the stuff of American folklore. He was fourteen when he joined the Pony Express, fitting the bill for the advertised position: 'skinny, expert riders willing to risk death daily'. He became a scout for the US Cavalry and fought in nineteen battles and skirmishes with native Americans, won the Congressional Medal of Honour for gallantry, then made a living hunting and killing buffalo to feed railroad crews, acquiring the nickname that defined him as an Old West legend. In 1883 he founded his own show, Buffalo Bill's Wild West, a circus-like extravaganza that toured widely for three decades in the United States, starring the likes of sharpshooter Annie Oakley, 'Wild Bill' Hickok and Chief Sitting Bull. Now he was in London for the first time, in the role which had made him famous.

Buffalo Bill's Wild West show had all the now-familiar tropes of the Wild West. There were native Americans attacking a wagon train, gun battles with cowboys, shooting exhibitions, native American dances, horseback races and bucking broncos. Most of the actors in the show had never set foot in the West and never fired anything but blanks, but the illusion was convincing and the public were completely won over. The show took London by storm and the critics raved. 'Buffalo Bill's entertainment is assuredly the most remarkable ever seen in this country!' gasped the *Illustrated London News*.[80]

Two days after opening, on 11 May, Queen Victoria herself went to see what the fuss was all about, at a private showing at Earl's Court. It was remarkable because since the death of her husband she had stopped going anywhere; shows came to her, usually at Windsor or Balmoral, but as Cody would boast later, 'my show was altogether too big a thing to take to Windsor Castle, and as in the case of Mahomet and the mountain, as the Wild West could not go to the Queen it became absolutely necessary for the Queen to go to the Wild West, if she desired to see it, and it was evident that she did'.[81]

The Queen was smitten. By October over a million of her subjects had also taken William F. Cody to their hearts, and they would do so for generations to come.

Of course George Sanger didn't thrill to the prospect of Buffalo Bill riding into town, but in his memoir he was dismissive of the latest foreign competition, avowing he had 'nothing to learn from America, at least as regards the show business'.[82] For all that, George was suspiciously well

informed about the latest developments across the Atlantic. In fact, having acquired a couple of real buffalos and several Liverpudlian 'Red Indians', he had already been presenting his own 'Buffalo Bill' and 'Wild West' shows for at least a year before Cody showed up.

In addition to his skills as a performer, Cody was a supreme self-promoter. His commanding reputation was inflated by a publicity blitz the likes of which had never been seen on this side of the Atlantic. Wherever his show toured, ahead of the performance he despatched members of the company in full native dress to mingle with the locals and hand out flyers. There were posters featuring illustrations of native Americans shooting rapids in canoes and other stirring episodes from the Wild West plastered across fences and walls from London to Birmingham.

Cody's agents also employed the standard American practice of over-sticking the bills of every rival show in town. When they found George Sanger's showbills offering 'Scenes from Buffalo Bill's Wild West', Cody took legal action. In August he secured an injunction forcing his English rival to remove the words 'Buffalo Bill' and 'Wild West' from his posters. Sanger altered the billing for his London shows, but continued to hand out programmes for his show promising 'scenes from Buffalo Bill and the Far West'. A week later Cody received a copy of Sanger's programme by post, accompanied by what he described as a 'vulgar and insulting' letter in Sanger's name, declaring his intention to continue his parody Wild West show 'for some time to come'.

George Sanger was summonsed to appear before a judge charged with contempt.[83] In September, William

Cody and George Sanger met face to face for the first time at the Law Courts on The Strand. The two showmen presented strikingly opposite figures. What George lacked in height he always made up with his ubiquitous silk topper, but he wasn't allowed to wear it in court. There was Cody, looking every bit the legend: tall, ramrod-straight, buckskin-clad, with his trademark auburn moustache, goatee beard and great flowing mane of golden hair. Beside him was the small, pale, balding middle-aged Sanger. Next to Cody, he was dwarf-like.

Sanger denied any intent to plagiarise Cody's posters or his show, or to mislead the public. He argued that the programmes he issued were simply notices that his entertainment was not connected with that of Buffalo Bill. Cody's legal team pointed out that the pictures in Sanger's programmes and bills were still exact copies of the plaintiff's, right down to the same expression of horror on the stagecoach driver's face and a picture of the real Buffalo Bill, in a blue shirt, riding up to the rescue of the coach. Mr Justice Kekewich agreed that this obviously constituted 'a pictorial lie'. He ordered Sanger to pick up the court costs and warned him never to publish the pictures again.[84] It was an embarrassing defeat for the English showman, but George's court battle with Cody may have produced one unexpected benefit and a rather odd footnote in the history of popular entertainment – the creation of the 'circus peerage'.

Throughout his court proceedings with the American, George had been irked by repeated references to 'the Honourable William Cody'. Cody acquired his honorific justly. He was a former member of the Nebraska state

legislature and he always used it on his show bills. The Englishman meanwhile was referred to throughout the court hearing as plain Mr Sanger, and it rankled. Cody had made George look small, figuratively and literally, and he didn't take the humiliation lightly.

According to his grandson, after the court appearance George Sanger said nothing on the subject until he was back in his wagon, then he broke a long, brooding silence by banging his fist on the table with a force that made the contents of the caravan rattle: 'If that Yankee **** can be Honourable then I shall be a Lord.'[85] George's sign painters were kept busy through the following days announcing their proprietor's new status, and telegrams were dispatched to printers ordering them to insert the prefix 'Lord' on all the posters. The pretence was so successful that from then on, the self-ennobled circus proprietor was almost never referred to by the press or anyone else without his fake title.[86]

Several years later, George would claim that when he was presented to Queen Victoria after a command performance, she said to him, 'Lord George, you are looking younger than ever.' If she said it at all she must have been teasing him, but George took it as an official validation of his title. He later claimed that he had since been offered a knighthood by the Queen on three occasions but had declined, because as a 'Sir' he couldn't be a 'Lord' as well, a notion that would no doubt have amused the Queen's Private Secretary Sir Arthur Bigge, Lord Stamfordham.

That at least was how his grandson remembered it, but 'Lord' George could be careless with the facts in the cause of telling a good yarn, and he often told the story differently.

He confided to the scene painter Joseph Harker that it was the outcome of a deal when he offered to buy some horses from 'Buffalo Bill' Cody. The American sent a message to Sanger to the effect that 'The Honourable William F. Cody' refused to take a penny less than the amount he was asking. Sanger, on the spur of the moment, sent a message back: 'If you are the Hon. W.F. Cody, then damn it, I'm Lord George Sanger, and I won't give a ha'penny more.' George also told reporters, including one from the *Daily Mail*, that as a boy he was 'rather more of the well-mannered young gentleman than the rest of the family ... the "Lord" was tacked on by my father purely in fun'.[87] Randall Williams, also known as 'King of the Showmen', was a close friend and claimed that it was he who first named him 'Lord George', at one of the circus proprietor's suppers. The author Garrard Tyrwhitt-Drake was quite certain that it came about when the circus proprietor Robert Fossett billed himself 'Sir'; Sanger was irritated because his show was bigger than Fossett's, so he started calling himself 'Lord'. Or he could have been first styled Lord Sanger 'when the Burgomaster [sic] of Ostend presented me with a gold medal in commemoration of the assistance I was able to give to the poor of Belgium in a terrible flood year'.[88] Take your pick.

William F. Cody was far from the first 'Yankee' circus proprietor Sanger locked horns with. Since the 1840s, Britain, ancestral home of the circus, had experienced 'an American invasion'.[89] The Americans brought with them a new kind of circus, bigger, bolder and brasher than anything ever seen on this side of the Atlantic. One by one Britain's homespun circuses were crushed under the juggernaut of

the newcomers. Although their operation was relatively small by American standards, George and John Sanger alone had taken on the Americans on equal terms in a fierce, cut-throat battle of clashing dates and rival billing. Eventually the Sangers tested themselves against the greatest of them all, Phineas Taylor Barnum.

In 1874 at the Agricultural Hall in Islington, the Sanger brothers had broken box office records with their spectacular pageant, *The Congress of Monarchs*. There had been nothing like it staged in London before, a grand parade of costumed performers representing famous kings and emperors from around the world, past and present, with chariot races, horseback riding and high-wire acrobatics. This glittering extravaganza was their most ambitious, most expensive show to date, and it drew audiences upwards of 37,000 people a day. Barnum made occasional trips to England to find new talent or simply to raid British circuses for fresh ideas. In 1874 he went to London hoping to buy some of George Sanger's impressive stud of horses, but he came away with considerably more. At the show in Islington, Barnum liked what he saw, and paid George £33,000 to copy his *Congress of the Monarchs* show, complete with duplicates of the original equipment, wardrobe and other props associated with the pageant, including over 1,100 suits of armour. This was not all that Barnum copied, allegedly. George Sanger claimed that he built the first ever three-ring circus at Plymouth as early as 1860, and revived the idea at the Agricultural Hall, but found that his audiences struggled to follow the bewildering multiplicity of acts. Barnum took the three-ring circus idea back to America and later claimed it as his own.

Barnum's purchase of Sanger's *Congress of Monarchs* was the foundation of his circus celebrity. He also went on to acquire the rights to use Sanger's name in America, but neglected to keep up the annual £2,000 payment for use of the Sanger name, to George's undying fury.

In November 1989 P.T. Barnum was back in the UK with his most spectacular production yet, in partnership with James Anthony Bailey, and he was greeted in London as a returning hero. George Sanger may have been the Lord of the ring, but Barnum was king, as he was demonstrating with a 100-performance run at Olympia. Twice daily, 12,000 people came to see his Greatest Show on Earth, among them Oscar Wilde and Britain's former and future prime minister, William Gladstone. *The Era* tried to cover the show in detail but found it impossible: there was 'more than one pair of eyes could take in'.[90] The grand finale for each show was a historical production, *Nero*, featuring epic gladiatorial combat scenes. London's *Evening News and Post* noted: 'the stage is strewn with enough corpses to keep all the coroners in England busy for a month'.[91] The press heaped praise on Barnum, according to the American circus historian Ernest Albrecht, 'as if they had never heard of Sanger'.[92] When Barnum & Bailey's closed at Olympia in 1890, over 2.5 million people had seen the show.

In public George Sanger poured scorn on his 'Yankee' rivals, averring 'there is nothing that American showmen have ever done that Englishmen have not done first and done better', but privately he hated them with a passion. Barnum was a crook and a fraud who'd stolen his name and his ideas. 'Barnum's Greatest Show on Earth,' he spat, 'is a

combination of the greatest American liars on earth.' He and Cody had beaten him on his own turf; they were parasites, fastening on to his territory and sucking the lifeblood out of his business. Adding insult to injury, the Queen had made the effort to see them all perform, an honour George had yet to receive. In truth, the competition from America did George Sanger a huge favour. By setting the bar higher, they had forced him to think even bigger.

⏤

For all his fantastic success in London, it was in the provinces that George Sanger established his reputation as the nation's favourite mass entertainer. Every year at the end of February, he took his mighty show on the road, and for nine months it roamed the country, covering over 2,000 miles and visiting around 200 towns, giving two shows a day every day except Sunday. George boasted that there was not a town or village with over a hundred people in the United Kingdom he hadn't visited.

The man in a pony-drawn cart, chased by dogs and followed by curious children, was the first sign that life for locals was about to change, at least for a day or two. This was Sanger's Circus advance agent. His cart was full of posters, vivid, brilliantly coloured lithographs of the extraordinary, with fierce and snarling lions and tigers, elephants and trick-riders, hair-raising feats on the high wire and trapeze, and girls in pink tights being shot from the mouths of cannons. If he did his job properly, there soon wouldn't be a wall within five miles that didn't have a poster on it blazoning: SOMETHING NEW UNDER THE SUN, TWICE DAILY.

Name	Rating	Ship	Other clasps
Robinson, Thomas	L.M	Belleisle	
Robinson, Thomas	Ord	Captain	
Robyns, John (Army Medal) Capt R.M		Neptune	
Rogers, John	Pte, R.M	Neptune	
Rogers, John	Boy	Pompée	
Rolls, William	A.B	Ringdove	GUADELOUPE
Rose, Edward	A.B	Ringdove	FORSE LE BRUNE 1810 / GUADELOUPE 1809
Ross, James	Master	Demerara	
Retely, Lewis	Lieut R.M	Cleopatra	TRAFALGAR
Russell, Peter	A.B	Neptune	OFF THE PEARL ROCK
Ryland, John	Pte, R.M	Belleisle	GUADELOUPE
Sabben, James	Mid	Neptune	GUADELOUPE / ANSE-LE-BARQUE 1810 / TRAFALGAR
Salter, William	L.M	Cherub	CHERUB 28 MARCH 1814 / GUADELOUPE
Salter, William	Vol.	Fawn	
Sambler, Stephen	A.B	Neptune	GUADELOUPE
Sanger, James	Ord	Pompée	
Saul, John	L.M	Belleisle	
Saville, John	L.M	Gloire	GUADELOUPE
Scott, James	Master's Mate	Pompée	AFT NAVY, ROYT SERVICE / POMPEE 10 JAN 1814

MARTINIQUE

Name	Rating	Ship	Other clasps
Seale, George	Ord	Haughty	
Seale, Charles Henry	Mid	Neptune	GUANTANO... CLAN 1810 / GUADELOUPE / BASQUE 11 AUG 1807
Sear, George	Ord	Pompée	GUADELOUPE / POMPEE 17 JUNE 1809
Shaddock, Elias	Q. Gunner	Belleisle	TRAFALGAR
Shakeshaft, Edward	Ord	Eolas	4 NOVEMBER 1805
Shanks, Thomas	Corpl, R.M	Belleisle	
Shasory, Edward	L.M	Intrepid	
Shaw, James	L.M	Neptune	
Shepherd, Benjamin	Mid	Neptune	CRAFTON 21 MARCH 1813 / GUADELOUPE / TRAFALGAR
Shisler, James	Master's Mate	Penelope	
Shirley, George	Gunner	Cleopatra	EGYPT / NILE / 14 MARCH 1795
Shutland, Pierce	Pte, R.M	Eolas	
Shreeve, William	A.B	Pompée	GUADELOUPE / POMPEE 17 JUNE 1809
Shuttleworth, George	L.M	Acasta	JAVA
Suddeworth, George	Pte, R.M	Penelope	
Silvers, Robert	Boatswain's Mate	Cleopatra	
Summers, Edward	Mid	Ethalion	OFF TAMATAVE 20 MAY / TRAFALGAR (1811)
Simpson, James	Ord	Ulysses	
Simpson, John	Mid	Cuttle	ACHERON 3 FEB 1805
Simpson, John	Commander	Wolverine	JUNE 1804

The only action James Sanger saw was the battle of Martinique on HMS *Pompee*, for which he was awarded a Naval General Service Medal clasp. His son George claimed that his father was given a pension for his heroism on HMS *Victory* at Trafalgar. *Photo author's collection*

Photographic print of George Sanger (centre) with his wife Ellen (above), daughter Harriet Sanger (right), daughter Laurina Sanger (left) and grandchild (below, probably Georgina Coleman, first child of Laurina Sanger and Alexander Coleman).

Sourced from The National Fairground and Circus Archive, The University of Sheffield

Ellen Sanger, lion-taming wife of George Sanger. She performed under the name of Madame Pauline de Vere the Lion Queen at Wombwell's Menagerie before joining Sanger's Circus.

George Sanger's wife Ellen 'the Lion Queen' in 1893, aged 61. She died six years later.

Sourced from The National Fairground and Circus Archive, The University of Sheffield

George Sanger and his wife Ellen, with elephants and camels in the foreground. George is marked on the photograph in pen as 'Dada' and Ellen as 'Mama'. The man standing on the right is William Sanger, George's brother. The photograph was taken at the Hall by the Sea in Margate.

Sourced from The National Fairground and Circus Archive, The University of Sheffield

Harry Austin, on the shoulders of his brother George. The Austin Brothers stayed with Lord George Sanger's circus for over 30 years as a double jockey act. Harry married Sanger's granddaughter Ellen Coleman.

Sourced from The National Fairground and Circus Archive, The University of Sheffield

George Sanger's granddaughter Ellen and her husband Harry Austin with their circus living wagon.

Sourced from The National Fairground and Circus Archive, The University of Sheffield

Cabinet card studio photograph of Ellen Austin, equestrian performer and granddaughter of George Sanger.

Sourced from The National Fairground and Circus Archive, The University of Sheffield

ABOVE AND LEFT:
P.T. Barnum collaborated with George Sanger, but to George's undying fury Barnum failed to pay for permission to use his name in the US.

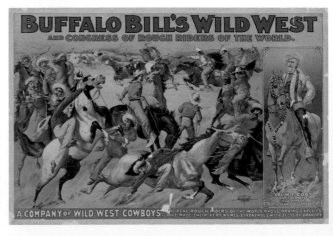

George Sanger plagiarised William F. 'Buffalo Bill' Cody by stealing his Wild West act and copying his posters, despite being scornful in public of his 'Yankee' rival.

George Sanger's
circus comes to
Beverley, Yorkshire,
in 1901. The parade
was up to half-a-
mile long and took
half an hour to pass
any given point.

MURDER of LORD GEO. SANGER.

HUNT FOR THE WANTED MAN COOPER.

SEEN CYCLING TO LONDON.

A SURPRISE ENCOUNTER ON HIGHGATE HILL.

POLICE DESCRIPTION of the WANTED MAN.

Wanted, for murder, 28th, Herbert Cooper; 6ft.; 26; complexion, hair and medium moustache dark; smart military appearance; may be taken for actor or City clerk. Recently worked as a labourer. Dress: Dark blue suit, light cap; clothing probably bloodstained; has money, and may endeavour to leave the country.

The police invite the co-operation of the public in their search. Information will be welcomed at every police-station.

Herbert Cooper, the man wanted for the murder, with a hatchet, of Lord George Sanger—as the Circus King of former days must inevitably be known—was still unapprehended at the time of going to press.

Hundreds of police and civilians, continuing a search that had lasted all night, were still investigating every likely hiding-place for miles around Park Farm, East Finchley.

It appears practically certain, however, that, by means of a bicycle, Cooper reached London last night, for a friend, who has been interviewed by *The Evening News* is positive that

HERBERT COOPER,
Whose description has been furnished by the police in connection with the murder of Lord George Sanger.

playing the royal arms. is approached from the road through a yard.

In front of the visitor as he opens the yard gate rises a high barn with glass doors—Sanger's elephant house.

The farmhouse is on the left, and on the right the yard slopes down to a fair-sized

Grange Wood, which extends for over a mile, and would provide good cover for a man anxious to hide.

Many of the men went through Marylebone Cemetery, stepping over the graves and turning the light of their lanterns into trenches and corners to make sure that Cooper had not taken refuge among the

---

First reports on the murder of George Sanger and the fugitive Herbert Cooper.

Findmypast.com newspaper archive

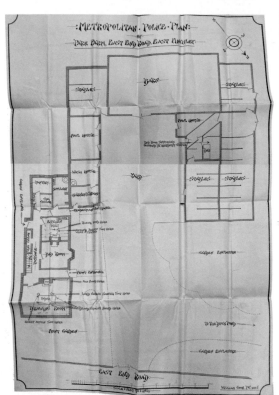

Police drawing of the murder scene at Park Farm.

Photo author's collection

Detail of the murder scene at Park Farm showing the locations of the three assaults and the place where the alleged murder weapon was eventually discovered.

Photo author's collection

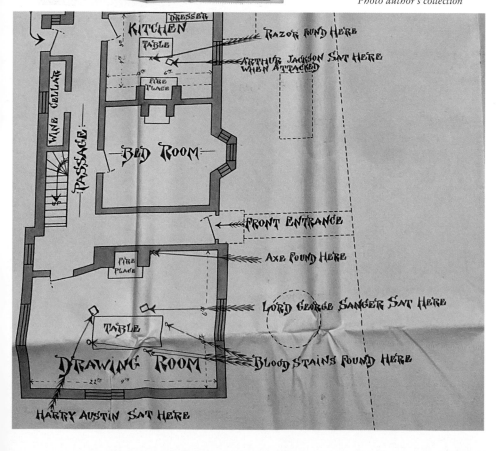

George Sanger's funeral cortège leaving Park Farm in East Finchley. The whole route from Finchley to Margate was lined with people sheltering under umbrell from torrential rain.

© *Alamy Stock Photo*

Home Office pathologist Bernard Spilsbury. His word in the witness box was unimpeachable.

© *Alamy Stock Photo*

An Inquisition

taken for our Sovereign Lord the King, at *The District*

Middlesex	Council Offices, Friern Barnet in the *parish*
to wit.	of *Friern Barnet* in the *county*
	of *Middlesex* on the *second*
	day of *December* A.D. 19 11 [and by adjournment on the
	day of , and the day of],
	before *George Cohen* one of

the Coroners of our said Lord the King for the said *county*

of *Middlesex* upon the Oath of

_____ being good and lawful Men of the said *county*

of *Middlesex* duly sworn to inquire for our said Lord the

King, on view of the Body of *George Sanger*

of *Park Farm Finchley*

as to h *is* Death, and those of the said Jurors whose names are hereunto subscribed,

upon their Oaths duly administered to them, do say That the said *George Sanger*

died of Coma due to haemorrhage caused by fracture

of skull caused by being struck with an axe

on 28th Nov 1911

and so the Jurors aforesaid do further say That the said *Herbert Charles*

Cooper of *Park Farm his Finchley*

on the *28th* day of *Nov.* A.D. 1911

did feloniously ~~wilfully and of malice aforethought~~

~~did murder~~ against the Peace of our said Lord the

King, his Crown and Dignity, the said *George Sanger*

and the Jurors aforesaid, upon their Oaths do further

say that the said *George Sanger*

at the time of h *is* Death was a — male person of the age of *88 years*

years, and a *retired Circus proprietor*

In Witness whereof, as well the said Coroner as the said Jurors have hereunto
subscribed their Hands and Seals the Day and Year and Place first above written.

G. Cohen — Coroner.		Geo. Kidd
Harry A. Foy	Chas A Penny	M B Baddeley.
Fred J. W. Soole	Edward Palmer	A. S. Mills
Edward H. Cleese	J. W. Morris	
H. J. Pooley	R. D. Brown	
J. S. Walford	Geo. Stewart	Frank Paige

The verdict on George Sanger's death in the hand of Coroner George Cohen
and the signatures of the sixteen men who agreed that Sanger
was wilfully murdered by Herbert Charles Cooper.

Photo author's collection

THE DAILY MIRROR

"LORD" GEORGE SANGER MURDERED.

Famous Showman Struck Down in His Own House by a Man Armed with Axe and Razor.

FORTY CONSTABLES SEARCH FOR ASSAILANT

Lord George Sanger, the famous circus owner, who was in his eighty-fifth year, was murdered last night at his house, Park Farm, East Finchley.

Struck on the head with an axe in his own dining-room shortly after 6 p.m. by a man who entered the house by the back door, he lingered till eleven, when he died, in spite of the efforts of three doctors.

The assailant, who made good his escape and up to a late hour had not been captured, was reported to be a young man employed on the farm.

Two other persons, one a youth named Austin, who was employed to read to the aged circus proprietor—and another employee, were both wounded with a razor by the man, who succeeded in escaping.

TWO EMPLOYEES WOUNDED.

Lord George Sanger, it appears, shortly after 6 p.m. was being read to in his room, when the door burst open and the assailant, with an axe in one hand and a razor in the other, rushed in, and, without warning, aimed a smashing blow at his head. A moment later he turned on Austin and cut his throat with the razor.

The alarm had already been given, and as the man was leaving the house by the scullery another employee, named Jackson, tried to overpower him, but the man cut at him with the razor, and, leaving him also badly wounded, made good his escape into the grounds which surround the house.

No motive so far can be assigned for the crime, and it is supposed that the assailant suddenly went mad.

Search was made for him in the extensive grounds of the farm and estate, but up to a late hour he had

few days by a system of his own in which he was fond of saying the chief thing was kindness. "Look the lion full in the face and talk to him as you would to a man," was his dictum.

As showing his influence over the animals it may be recalled that on the day of thanksgiving for the restoration to health of King Edward when Prince of Wales a full-grown African lion trained by him was allowed to ride on the summit of one of the large gilded cars with Mrs. George Sanger by his side in the character of Britannia.

He had also a fine lion that took part in a pantomime, coming up on a great lift from the cellar of the theatre to seventy feet above the level of the stage.

THE LION THAT WAS "SCARED."

On another occasion when told at midnight that one of his fiercest lions had escaped, and was hiding in a narrow court at the entrance to which, in their fright, soldiers were waiting with fixed bayonets and the fire brigade were turning their hose on the beast in the darkness, he rushed to the scene in his pyjamas.

"Get out of the way," he said to the police.

"What are you here for?" he then asked the volunteers. Then, walking into the darkness alone, he pulled the lion out by the ear.

"Come home, you silly ass!" he said, and the lion went home quite calmly.

Sanger was the only man who knew how frightened the lion really was and how glad it would be to get home to its nice warm bed!

Lord George Sanger probably appeared before more "crowned heads" than any other performer of recent years, theatrical or otherwise.

Lord George Sanger photographed on the steps of one of his travelling vans.

not been taken. The razor was found, but the axe was missing, and it is believed that the assailant has it still with him.

He several times gave performances before Queen Victoria and visiting monarchs.

The *Daily Mirror* reported that Sanger's assailant had rushed at the elderly George Sanger with a razor in one hand and an axe in the other.

Findmypast.com newspaper archive

THE MURDER OF "LORD" GEORGE SANGER: PORTRAITS OF THE "WANTED" MAN.

Herbert Cooper, who is wanted.

Another portrait of Cooper.

Police photograph of Cooper.

Mr. Austin, wounded by assailant.

Lord George Sanger.

FARM WHERE "LORD" GEORGE SANGER WAS MURDERED: SEARCH FOR CLUES YESTERDAY.

"Lord" George Sanger. The Groom. Cooper's father. Cooper.

The wanted man with an axe. The window of the room in which the murder was committed. Searching for clues yesterday.

In a double-page splash, the *Daily Mirror* published a photo of Herbert Cooper holding a large felling axe – probably the felling axe used in the attack.

Findmypast.com archive

Herbert Cooper's suicide note.
Photo author's collection

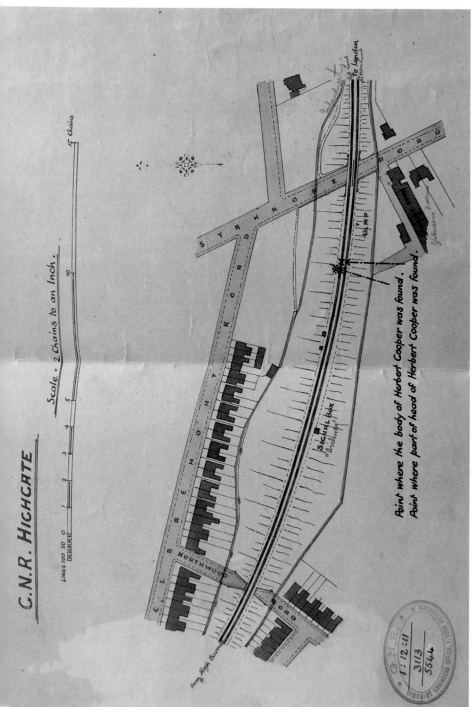

Police drawing of the scene of Herbert Cooper's suicide.

Photo author's collection

MAN=HUNT ENDED.

LORD GEORGE SANGER'S MURDERER DEAD ON RAILWAY.

The body of Herbert Cooper, the man who was wanted for the murder of his master, "Lord" George Sanger, at Finchley, was found on Friday morning on the railway between Crouch End and Highgate. He had evidently placed his head on the line, for it had been severed from his body by a train.

The discovery thus put an end to a search which had been in progress for two nights and a day. It was between eight and nine o'clock on Friday morning that some railway employees found the body on an embankment just outside a tunnel between Highgate and Crouch End stations.

The spot was some little distance away from the scene of the murder, but in the same district of North London. The body was lying on the up line, the feet being towards the embankment pointing towards the premises known as Spencer's Farm.

The police were summoned, and a sergeant who arrived agreed with the suspicions of the railwaymen that the body was that of Cooper. Later the body was identified by Thomas Cooper, a brother, and two detectives.

A number of documents were found, including a pocket-book containing the man's name and address, and a paper containing a rambling, badly-written statement, addressed to his father, in which Cooper ascribed what had happened to the "lies" which had been told about him.

An old East Finchley resident, who was a close friend of the late Mr. Sanger and knew Cooper also, says it is more than likely that, when the will of the veteran showman comes to be proved, it will be seen that Cooper would have benefited largely under it.

News of the discovery of Herbert Cooper's body.

Findmypast.com newspaper archive

Even if Sanger's circus wasn't putting on a show in your village you might still experience the thrill of watching the great mysterious closed vans swooping by and perhaps catch a glimpse of the exotic animals in their mobile cages. Sanger's show on the move was an astonishing sight. The whole comprised 62 horse-drawn wagons from front to rear, extending up to two miles long, every wagon blazing with gold leaf and painted scenery. There were twenty-odd cages of wild animals, a stud of more than 200 horses and a company of performers, grooms, stable-hands, tent-men, musicians, womenfolk and children rarely less than 200 strong.

Tours around mid-Victorian Britain were physically testing for man and beast. They might move only twelve miles a day, and journeys between the principal cities could take up to a week. In summer, the roads were bone-breaking hard, and the daily sandstorm of dust and grit kicked up stuck in the eyes and throats of those behind. In hot weather they moved by night to spare the horses. Drivers dozed off on their boxes from fatigue, the horses blindly following the lead of those in front. When it rained the roads became sticky, impassable swamps. Horses dropped dead in their tracks from exhaustion and overwork, wagons were smashed to pieces. During the great snowstorm of 1886 in Yorkshire, they battled through several weeks of blizzards in March and April, travelling up to their knees in snow along turnpike roads with drifts six- or eight-feet high. No matter how atrocious the weather, or how bad the roads, the show kept moving.

George and his family travelled in handsome living carriages, magnificently comfortable 'palaces on wheels' drawn

by teams of powerful horses. These were luxuries afforded to the very few. For most of Sanger's ensemble, wagons were forbidden. George required obedience and punctuality from his performers but above all he prized appearance. He believed that the merits of his travelling circus were judged by the quality of his horses and as he owned one of the finest studs in the country, he wasn't going to allow his employees to ruin the effect with shabby carriages drawn by nags. Some of his better-off performers could afford to find overnight accommodation in the nearest town, in low-class lodging houses where the rental was payable in advance and the cutlery was chained to the table. Tent men and other minor employees were content to doss down in the straw, or wherever they could, on the ground or under the beast cages and tableau wagons.

Normal life was suspended when Sanger's came to town. Schoolchildren went missing from classrooms and factories closed for the day. At one o'clock promptly, an hour-and-a-half before the first performance, the grand parade began, a taste of the wonders to come. The parade was perhaps half-a-mile long and took the best part of half an hour to pass any given point, 'a panorama of constant interest from end to end'.[93]

Then the show began, lasting about two hours. Anyone who could afford the modest entrance fee was rewarded with a sensory overload of spectacle and skill. The thirteen-metre ring was packed with a galaxy of talent from all over the world, an ever-changing cast of human performers offering breath-taking stunts that required great strength, nerve and, quite probably, clinical insanity. The Danish strongman

John Holtum caught 50-pound cannonballs fired at him at point blank range.[94] Women and men were stuffed into the mouths of large pieces of artillery and fired through the air. George's granddaughter Georgina, tiny, lithe and fearless, was one of the show's star trapeze artists. As a finale to her act, she carried an audience member across the high wire on her shoulders, then abandoned them on the other side, leaving the volunteer stranded with no means of descent other than walking back across the wire to the ladder and inevitably falling into the net beneath. Nineteenth-century health and safety being what it was, you wouldn't bet on the volunteer being an audience plant.

The highlight was usually a pantomime or a hippodrama. This entertainment, driven by George Sanger's ardent patriotism, was full-blooded. His audience loved to be reminded that Britain's glorious empire was sustained with cold steel. The Egyptian Campaign, the Fall of Khartoum, the Zulu War, the Sudan Campaign, the Boer War; for the price of sixpence you could see them all fought twice daily.

After the first show, everyone ate and rested until the evening, then the second performance began at seven, finishing at about ten o'clock. The house takings were scooped into tins and counted. Heaps of dirty copper and silver coin were transferred into canvas bags, dumped in a pony trap and driven to the nearest bank once a week. It was a strictly cash economy, with no accounts kept. Nellie Sanger took care of the money side. She couldn't read or write but she could reckon money faster than anyone. In London and on the road, she took the cash at the entrance, counted the receipts, made up the twice-weekly pay packets and settled

all of the bills. Like Mrs Grudden in *Nicholas Nickleby* she also did all the odd jobs that needed doing but were nobody else's business in particular: mending costumes, managing the wardrobes, getting the tickets ready for opening, shopping for the weekly provisions for the entire crew, doling out piping-hot tea topped up with Scotch whisky to the tent men. Somehow, she found the time to cook and clean for her own family and made sure all the children with her husband's circus attended at least two hours of education every morning. Nellie's ability to combine so many roles was a mystery and a wonder to her family.

George demanded the operation always function like clockwork, that the arrival in any given town on the date announced became fact. Most of the time it was a miracle of punctuality, but there was hardly ever a journey completed without some minor disaster or other along the way. Hundreds of farmers and smallholders had cause to regret the progress of Sanger's entourage through their district. They came like an invading army trampling all before them. The combined weight of men, horses, elephants and heavy wagons destroyed turnpikes and bridges, meanwhile the crew helped themselves to any stray livestock that crossed their path. George was constantly harassed by farmers and landowners demanding compensation for damages or theft. At Cardiff he was pursued by the railway company when his elephants escaped and caused thousands of pounds worth of damage to an embankment, and there were hundreds of similar nuisances to attend. His star elephant Ajax went on regular nocturnal walkabouts, and one morning was found stuck fast in the doorway of a grocer's store. Half the shop

front had to be demolished before Ajax could be dislodged, but he had already helped himself to everything in reach of his trunk, eating or destroying hundreds of pounds' worth of stock. There were days when George paid out more compensation than he could hope to make in profits, but he always reimbursed whatever was asked with little fuss.

Tent men were essential to the proper running of the circus, but the work was hard and attracted only the most desperate. They were notoriously unreliable and walked off the job at a moment's notice, to be quickly replaced by random strangers begging for short-term work. George's tour manager advertised for men who were 'sober and steady', and threatened to dismiss them on the spot if they proved otherwise. But tent men made themselves useful in other ways. During a show they provided security, prowling the perimeter of the tent keeping an eye out for people trying to sneak in under the canvas. They were also Sanger's foot soldiers, and were expected to be handy with their fists if called upon. Circus workers were often regarded as fair game for abuse and conflicts with the locals often turned physical. Although he was small, George learned to use his fists at an early age, and he relished a scrap as much as anyone. His grandson recalled a flashpoint at Motherwell when the circus owner, in his mid-sixties, appeared at the door of his caravan and offered to take on an entire crowd of belligerent locals. It descended into a raucous brawl involving dozens of men wielding tent hammers and chains. In Ireland, he goaded a local audience of republicans by flying the Union Jack above the main tent, and a pitched battle ensued. The circus crew were overcome by greater numbers and the tent was

destroyed. George refused to perform anywhere without his beloved Union flag flying, so he cancelled all the shows and went home to London.

Canvas tents were vulnerable. They blew away in high winds and a mass of snow could easily rip them apart. At Goole in March 1886, a heavy snowfall caused the main tent poles to snap like twigs. George, standing in the middle of the ring organising the dismantling operation, had a split-second to react, dropping to the floor between two sturdy elephant tubs. The small pocket of safety saved his life. Local newspaper reports described in graphic detail the mishaps that occurred when Sanger's Circus took their menagerie on the road. Employees lost scalps and hands. At Plumstead, hired hand Alfred Jukes had his right arm ripped off at the shoulder while feeding two polar bears. Dozens of people were injured in attacks by circus animals, some proving fatal, others leaving victims permanently disabled, but the onus was always squarely on the keeper or the public to keep out of harm's way. People loved to visit the site of a recent blood-bath. When one of Sanger's lions caught a groom unawares and ripped his throat out, 4,000 flocked to the next perform-ance to see the killer beast. Exotic escapees made great news copy, and there was flippancy in the reporting of them.[95] Newspaper reports of wild animals roaming the countryside attacking hapless horses, animals that periodically attacked their trainers, high-wire dancers losing their debate with gravity, tents occasionally collapsing onto crowds – it all helped inject a frisson of danger and excitement.

In an era when few people ventured beyond the near-est market town, Sanger's touring circus was a glimpse into

another world, an exotic, thrilling place full of strangeness and wild animals, of colour and glitter, music and movement – all for a day or two, and then it was gone, leaving only yellow grass. At the end of the season, when the leaves turned red, the exhausted performers and the gold carriages full of snarling wild beasts made their mud-splattered way back to London. Then, without pause, after nine months on the road, they began preparations for another, no-less-demanding schedule, playing to packed houses at Westminster Bridge Road. Thus, the pattern of Sanger's circus year was fixed around the exhausting twin orbits of long summer tours and winter at Astley's. The effort required to survive such a balancing act was exhausting, gruelling and dangerous, but hugely rewarding. The proof was in George's bank account.

11

Autopsy

On 30 November 1911, a handsome young doctor stepped onto a train in north London, his Gladstone bag in hand. Thirty-four-year-old Dr Bernard Henry Spilsbury lived in Harrow-on-the-Hill with his wife Edith and the first of their four children. He travelled to Paddington every morning by the recently electrified Metropolitan line, to his workplace at St Mary's Hospital. To his fellow rail passengers on this brisk November morning, Spilsbury looked more like a matinée idol than a doctor. Over six-foot tall, dark haired and firm of jaw, he was immaculately turned out in his bowler hat, spats and red carnation in the buttonhole of his expensively tailored morning coat. Spilsbury's precise grooming and aristocratic bearing belied rather more humble origins. He was born above his father's chemist shop in Leamington Spa, the town where his grandfather also ran a pub. His father paid for Bernard to attend the best schools so he could become a doctor, but there was frankly little in the young man's academic performance to show that the money was well spent. He was an unexceptional scholar and his grades were at best average, but his persistence and his

father's funding paid off. Bernard graduated from Oxford with a second-class degree, enough to secure him a place studying medicine at the University of London and to get him a post as an intern at St Mary's, Britain's pre-eminent centre for forensic medicine. Little did anyone suspect that the young man would one day be revered as some kind of crime-fighting superhero.

Bernard Spilsbury became a forensic scientist at a time when the profession was very unfashionable. Pathology was known as 'the beastly science', its practitioners faceless men who spent their days probing the recently and the not-so recently departed. The work was arduous, low status and often deeply unpleasant. They used knives, saws and chisels to open up corpses and often spent their days up to the elbows in blood and gore. Britain had once led the world in forensic science, with the most momentous discovery in criminology – that no two people have identical fingerprints – but now it lagged behind. After a series of embarrassing high-profile courtroom blunders, the British legal system had lost faith in the ability of men in white lab coats to solve crimes. When confronted by complex medical issues, juries were confused by the jargon and contradictory interpretations of what were supposed to be objective facts. If the so-called experts couldn't speak plainly or make their minds up, what chance did a layman have? Forensic science was crying out for someone the public could believe in.

It was an unusual, well-publicised death that first brought Bernard Spilsbury to the fore. In 1909, Helena Elphinstone-Dalrymple, aged 29 and the daughter of a baronet, had an exceptionally bad hair day. She had booked an appointment

for a dry shampoo at Harrods. The process entailed applying a lotion containing tetrachloride of carbon. It was a technique the Harrods salon had been using for years, although it was noticed that the well-heeled clients often felt faint during the application, so an electric fan was used to disperse the fumes. On this occasion, however, the customer collapsed and died. Very unwisely, Harrods continued to use the treatment, even as customers were turning blue during their weekly shampoo and set. The young Spilsbury was able to prove that Helena had inhaled lethal fumes contained in the shampoo. Harrods was censured for employing an unskilled operator and told to stick with soap and water but was otherwise exonerated. The Director of Public Prosecutions paid Spilsbury just one guinea for his sterling work. More importantly, he had forged the beginnings of a working relationship with the Metropolitan Police, who noticed his gift for explaining complicated forensics in clear, simple language that anyone could understand. His opinion was increasingly sought by the police in the investigation of difficult-to-solve crimes. Within a year he would be giving evidence in the most sensational murder trial of the century.

In 1910, Cora Crippen, an aspirant music-hall singer living in north London, luxuriating in the stage name of Belle Elmore, was reported missing. Anxious friends said no one had seen her since a party at her home some five months earlier. The police called on her husband, Harvey. The man they encountered was a quietly spoken, unprepossessing American, small, balding and myopic. If Crippen was at all troubled by a visit from two detectives, he gave no inkling of it. He explained that his wife had gone back to America. The

police walked away, reassured that there were no grounds for further enquiry. But Harvey Crippen was spooked. He fled the country the next day and boarded an ocean liner to Canada, accompanied by his young mistress and secretary, Ethel Le Neve, disguised as his son. The police took another look at his house. Number 39 Hilldrop Crescent was situated in a nearly perfect semi-circle off the north side of Camden Road, the main thoroughfare in the district. A thorough search revealed the gruesome remains of a body, laced with poison, buried beneath the coal cellar. Crippen's flight from justice was an international sensation. It had a fittingly dramatic end when Chief Inspector Walter Dew of Scotland Yard, pursued by the world's press, tracked the couple across the Atlantic and apprehended them, Crippen having been identified by the ship's captain after the vessel received a description of the pair via a telegraph dispatch. It was the first ever use of wireless to make an arrest. The world was suddenly less safe for criminals on the run.

The decomposed corpse in the cellar on Hilldrop Crescent was assumed to be that of Cora Crippen, but the body was without a head, arms or legs, and what was left of the torso was so badly mutilated that there was no way of telling what sex it was, let alone identifying it. Harvey Crippen said the corpse must have been there before he moved in. The case against him would stand or fall on whether the prosecution could truly establish that it belonged to his wife. At the Old Bailey, Bernard Spilsbury took the spotlight. He had extraordinarily good eyesight and could spot detail that others couldn't see without a microscopic lens. A fragment of skin no bigger than the end of a matchbox had been

recovered from the cellar, fringed with what appeared to be pubic hair. He found a mark on the skin tissue which corresponded to an abdominal scar Cora Crippen was known to have as the result of a hysterectomy. It was flimsy evidence. The defence team, wrong-footed by Spilsbury's youthful and dandyish appearance, brought forward two pathologists who lamely dismissed it: the mark, they said, was not a scar. Spilsbury stood his ground. His assuredness under pressure on the witness stand carried the jury. Harvey Crippen was hanged on 23 November at Pentonville Prison.

From there, Spilsbury's fame and reputation in the mortuary and in the courtroom spiralled. So incredible were his deductive powers that the public came to think of him as a living, breathing Sherlock Holmes. He was adored by the media and his hold over courts was little short of hypnotic. Unshakeable in the witness box with his good looks and easy courtroom manner, he cut through the jargon of the laboratory like the blade of his scalpel, clearly, directly and precisely delivering his expert opinion in terms any layman could understand. Juries were dazzled by his charisma and convicted on his say-so. Even judges in their summaries were more inclined to favour Spilsbury's word over those of pathologists called by the defence. Of almost 200 criminal trials at which he would speak for the prosecution, very few ended in an acquittal. A minority thought that Spilsbury was held in dangerously high esteem and some of his fellow pathologists grumbled that he was no more than an average technician, that his success was a triumph of style over substance. But for now, and for the next 40 years, the word of Bernard Henry Spilsbury was virtually unassailable.

⌒

Looking back, the first decade of the new century had seemed, at least for the privileged, a kind of long, golden, Indian summer, but in 1911 Britain was on the cusp of a new era, straddling the twilight of Edwardian gentility and the upheavals of 20th-century modernity, bringing with it a mixture of excitement and anxiety. It was the first year of the reign of King George V, son of Edward VII and his wife Queen Alexandra. Britain was the seat of an empire that still controlled a quarter of the world's land and population, but the rapid growth of Germany's military and naval power had rattled the nation's sense of security. Britain's technological advances however were increasingly impressive. In Belfast, an immense ship said to be as tall as a New York skyscraper and 'practically unsinkable' was built. From Hendon, a monoplane completed the first non-stop flight to Paris in just under four hours, and the world's first airmail post service flew to Windsor. In London, sophisticated engineering enabled the sinking of a new underground line from Charing Cross to Heath Street at a depth of 150 feet below the earth. In Hampstead, the Heath Protection Society feared that the new subterranean trains would shake the trees to death. The roads were becoming more dangerous. The stink of horse manure competed with the stench of diesel fumes from cars. In October notice was given that horse-drawn fire engines would soon be withdrawn. Four-legged animals were no match for the speed of their automated equivalents.

A thrilling innovation was meeting the popular appetite for entertainment. In cinemas people could now see but not hear the screen stars Sarah Bernhardt in *Camille*

and Lionel Barrymore in *The Battle*. Pathé too introduced a novel medium to British audiences, the cinema newsreel. In June, the oldest man in the world recalled for the camera his memories of the Battle of Waterloo, while the Kaiser, in London for the coronation, was filmed taking in the popular tourist sites.

The old structural pillars of class and entitlement were still firmly in place. The census of 1911 confirmed the widening gulf between rich and poor. One in seven working men and women was a domestic servant. Their masters, the 1 per cent of the people who owned 70 per cent of the nation's wealth, enjoyed lives of seemingly unending aristocratic privilege. The new King George V went hunting in Nepal and shot 21 tigers, eight rhinos and a bear. 'A record', he boasted, 'and one I think will be hard to beat.'

The 36-year-old Home Secretary Winston Churchill was relieved to note that the suffragettes had agreed a summer truce in their increasingly disruptive crusade, but there was much agitation elsewhere. Temperatures soared and the sun blazed day after day. As the country sweltered, a wave of industrial action paralysed the country's ports and railways. Ben Tillett, who ran away from home before his seventh birthday and became an acrobat in a travelling circus, led a dockworker strike and food was left to rot at ports, increasing the threat of shortages. The heatwave stretched into September, turning pastures to tinder, and farmers raised the price of milk. In Hyde Park soldiers were camped in the sweltering heat, mobilised in case the strikes turned to violence. Rioters were shot dead in Liverpool and South Wales. It seemed half the country was burning while the other half was on strike.

Everyone in the country was united in their preoccupation with the weather. Men repairing the roof of Lincoln Minster dropped their tools and fled when the lead started to melt at 130 degrees. City dwellers were worst affected. The East End of London with its narrow, cramped alleys was unbearably hot. Disease spread rapidly and child deaths were an agonisingly familiar part of daily life – 2,000 in August alone from diarrhoea associated with rotted food and bad milk. *The Times* began a regular column under the heading 'Deaths from Heat'.

On 11 September the temperature suddenly dropped. *The Times* had good news: 'The condition over the kingdom as a whole is no longer of the fine settled type of last week and the prospects of rain before long appear to be more hopeful for all districts.'[96] *The Lady* magazine was already devoting several pages to new autumn fashions including sumptuous fur coats. The long, hot summer was over. By November, the weather was bitterly cold and wet. The cold snap was a timely reminder that the brave explorer Robert Falcon Scott had begun his dash to the South Pole for the glory of Britain and her empire.

For the mortuary at the end of Avondale Avenue, Finsbury, 1911 had been an exceptionally busy year for post-mortem examinations of suspected murder victims. Here in April, Bernard Spilsbury examined the body of Alice Linford, her throat cut by her ex-fiancée George Pateman. Spilsbury was back in Finsbury in early November for an autopsy on the exhumed remains of 49-year-old spinster Eliza Barrow. They were recovered from Islington Borough Cemetery where, eleven months earlier, the remains of Cora

Crippen were interred. According to Eliza Barrow's doctor, she was a victim of an outbreak of diarrhoea, but her land-lord, an insurance clerk called Frederick Seddon, had taken an unhealthy interest in her financial affairs and this made her relatives suspicious. Spilsbury found that Eliza had died from acute arsenic poisoning. In fact, when her corpse was fully exhumed two months after burial, it still contained more than enough arsenic to kill her. As in the Crippen and Bateman trials, Spilsbury would dazzle in the witness box, elegant in dress and manner, easily dealing with cross-examination by the defence barrister and securing the prosecution and subsequent hanging of her murderer Seddon.

Spilsbury had a growing collection of little black med-ical notebooks in which he kept details of his work, but he was also in the habit of jotting down the highlights of every case on little filing cards. They were thought to be the basis of a book he was writing, but it was uncompleted at the time of his death. Eventually there were thousands of these case cards, covered in untidy, spidery handwritten notes. The card collection covered everything from sudden deaths from a variety of natural causes, to accidents, suicides and criminal abortion, suspicious deaths of infants, as well as cases of murder and manslaughter. Spilsbury had seen many abnormal and strange deaths over the course of his career: 'Poisoning from Rhubarb'; a woman who died after taking the 'Nelson Lloyd safe reducing treatment'; 'electro-cution during electrical treatment in a bath'; a suicide who'd complained to his mother that there was something wrong with his private parts; a pair of legs neatly severed from the knee abandoned under a train seat at Waterloo Station. Each

filing card included the name of the deceased (if known), approximate age, the date and the place. Finally, the card gave answer to a simple question. What was the cause of death of the person laid before him?

There was still a pinch of winter in the air when Spilsbury arrived at the Avondale Avenue mortuary at 10.30am. On this day his attention was on the corpse of a man in his mid-eighties. Carefully placing his black Gladstone bag on the slab on the large slate-topped table next to the recumbent figure, he swiftly set about his job. Pathologists at the time had to work quickly because mortuaries had no refrigeration or effective means of preserving bodies. Finchley mortuary was a bare, stone-floored, limewashed room, bitterly cold in late November. Spilsbury worked more quickly than most of his colleagues because he craved nicotine. He chain-smoked cigarettes at the rate of 50 a day, but never in the mortuary because it disguised the odours he needed to smell. He bent over the corpse and sniffed it, as was his custom, as if it was a rose garden.

The post-mortem commenced with an external examin-ation of the surface of the corpse. The body before him was that of a slight, well-nourished, male octogenarian, about five-foot-four-inches tall. The body had good muscle tone for a man of his advanced years. The crown of his head was completely bald, but a ring of dyed black hair framed his ears and the back of his head. The man's face had a roughness befitting someone who had worked a great deal outdoors, the skin stretched thin across high cheekbones.

The pathologist noted several external injuries. Focusing on the head, Spilsbury saw a swelling on the right side above

the ear measuring about three by two-and-a-half inches. On the top of the head was a lacerated wound, shaped like the letter 'Y', surrounded by an area of bruising. On the left side of the head, behind the left ear, was another lacerated wound, also surrounded by bruising. On the back of the man's right hand there was a large bruise with a small wound in the centre. He could also see a small bruise on the right ring finger and another bruise on the back of the left hand. There were marks on the legs, including a small bruise on the right shin and a tiny abrasion on the left. There was a lot of blood in the right ear, but no sign of a wound.

Next, Spilsbury subjected the cranium to his blade and the probing of his forceps. He found that the swelling above the man's right ear was caused by haemorrhage in the scalp and the bone beneath the swelling was fractured. A fragment of bone was detached from the skull and there were also fractures running from this point to the top of the head and down the base of the skull. This accounted for the blood Spilsbury found in the man's ear. Tracing the line of the fracture with his forceps, he found that a large artery had been ruptured. There was also a considerable amount of blood between the skull and brain, producing compression on the brain as well as blood around the spinal cord. There was a slight injury to the surface of the brain in the vicinity of the fracture, but no serious brain injury.

After making a longitudinal incision down the chest and drawing back the abdominal walls, Spilsbury now considered each of the old man's internal organs. Heart, lungs, oesophagus, stomach, liver, kidneys and pancreas – the pathologist turned them over in his hands looking for visible

signs of potentially fatal disease. He saw that the heart was enlarged, the cavities dilated and the muscles showed a good deal of senile degeneration. The arteries were also diseased. All perfectly normal for a man in his eighties.

The investigation was complete. After removing his long white apron and his rubber gloves, Spilsbury made his customary jottings on a card. All that remained was to write up his findings in full for the coroner's inquest. He knew how the old man had died. In two days' time the world would find out why.

12

Elephant

IN THE EARLY 1880s, if you took an early-morning stroll along the beach at Margate, you might have encountered a smartly dressed gentleman in a dark frock coat, britches and black riding boots, wearing a black, custom-made silk top hat, accompanied by what would appear to be a couple of large dogs on a leash. He's in his sixties, but at a distance could pass for someone twenty years younger. You would have noticed his erect bearing, his shoulders pinned back to make the most of his short stature, although the topper also helps give the impression of someone much taller. Getting closer, you may have recognised his face as one you have seen many times from posters and handbills. You would have seen the hooded eyes, the imperious yet benevolent level gaze, the high cheekbones, the slightly receding chin disguised with a little beard carefully tonsured into the shape of a ring. It is unmistakeably Lord George Sanger, every inch the showman from the top of his hat right down to the lifts in his patent-leather riding boots. As you got nearer still, the top hat and the smartly tailored clothes would not be what immediately caught your eye. The thing

that held your attention would be that he's walking a pair of tigers.

Margate was the home of the latest enterprise in George's expanding entertainment empire. It was once a playground for London's wealthy, but railways were changing the habits of the nation and for the first time people of all classes could enjoy pleasure excursions to the seaside. Thanks to a new rail terminus, the once-genteel seaside town was now a thriving coastal resort and was making the most of a new Act of Parliament promising four new annual national public holidays. Directly across the road from Margate's seafront there was a substantial new single-storey property known as the Hall by the Sea. It was built as a ticket hall to serve as a rival to the existing railway line by the London, Chatham & Dover Railway Company, but the frenzy of railway building had exceeded need and the building stood empty. The catering contractors Spiers & Pond bought the premises and converted it into a restaurant and dance hall, but the business struggled. In 1870 the owners sold the lease to local businessman Thomas Dalby Reeve for 3,750 pounds. Reeve was a wealthy local entrepreneur, property developer and one-time town mayor. Large, stout and bewhiskered, he was the very model of a successful Victorian businessman. Having made his fortune from various family business interests, including the manufacture of carbonated drinks, he bought a brickworks, which he used to stamp his name on the local landscape by building Dalby Square, a classy residential area away from the more boisterous activities of central Margate. Reeve would soon find himself in an unlikely partnership with Lord George Sanger, building Britain's very first permanent seaside amusement park.

It was George's youngest daughter, nineteen-year-old Harriet, who put them together. George's son died in infancy, but his two daughters Harriet and Laurina grew up strong and healthy and they were put to work in their father's circus as child equestrians as soon as they were able to sit upright on a horse. When Harriet was six, she and her eight-year-old sister were performing side by side as 'the youngest riders in the world'. Laurina continued to perform in her father's circus and emerged as a formidably talented haute école rider.

Laurina's sister had ambitions elsewhere. When Harriet was eighteen, she fell in love with Arthur, the eldest son of Margate's luminary Thomas Dalby Reeve. She and Arthur were married on her father's 48th birthday, 23 December 1873, at Holy Trinity Church in Lambeth, a stone's throw from Astley's Amphitheatre. Having grown up living in her parent's caravan, Harriet had now risen to become a member of one of Margate's wealthiest and most respectable Victorian families. She celebrated her arrival in polite society by announcing her immediate retirement from the circus ring. Harriet was now, she grandly informed her parents and her sister, 'above the sticks and canvas'.

When George Sanger saw a business opportunity he pursued it with the single-minded determination of a shark. When Harriet told her father that her wealthy in-laws had acquired the Hall by the Sea he immediately offered himself as business partner and within days he was executing a plan. With the property came a large plot of low-lying land at the rear. George would jointly manage the new venue with Harriet's husband Arthur, with Arthur running the

dance hall while George developed the adjoining four acres of rough land. When 61-year-old Thomas Dalby Reeve died suddenly two years later, George assumed full ownership of the site, and turned the Hall by the Sea into a palace of dining and dancing with a spectacular ballroom, while the land behind the venue was landscaped and transformed into a pleasure garden complete with ornamental ponds, classic statuary and a bandstand.

The entertainments on offer were aimed at snaring the widest possible market. There were rides, fairground booths and stalls, shooting galleries, swings, roller skating and a steam-powered roundabout. The venture also saw the return to the family business of George's older brother William. His travelling waxworks show had failed and he was facing debtor's prison, when George rescued him with the offer of a permanent home at Margate managing the fairground rides.

One of the most popular features of the Hall by the Sea was a zoo. It also served as a retirement home for those animals for whom age or illness had terminated their performing careers in Sanger's circus, and as a breeding ground for their replacements. George Sanger went to great expense to procure the rare, strange and hard to get. Most of his wild animals had a recognisable taxonomy, others not so much, for example his 'Brazilian zebras' and 'vedo, or Peruvian god-horse'.

Elephants were the perpetual Victorian circus favourites and nothing approached them in size and impact. All of the leading circus proprietors competed over elephant displays, each seeking to show the most, the biggest, the whitest. At any one time George owned around thirteen elephants, and

every November from 1876 they were pressed into service for London's biggest annual jamboree, parading and defecating all over the Lord Mayor's Show. White elephants had unicorn status.[97] The Prince of Wales was once anxious to have a close-up of Sanger's latest acquisition at Astley's, 'the only White Elephant ever seen in the Western World', but the Prince was disappointed to learn that it was a bog-standard elephant coated daily in whitewash.

With patience and/or bullhooks, the leviathans of the animal kingdom could be trained to accomplish extraordinary feats. They formed pyramids, uncorked bottles and drank their contents, even (if the posters were to be believed) walked tightropes. In the late 1890s George's brother John trained elephants to play football and staged 'elephant vs human' contests. Famously, four members of the local football club at Leicester competed in a penalty shoot-out against Sanger's star elephant, which was unbeaten in penalty-kick competitions until William Keech stepped up and dummied the beast, sending it the wrong way. Some elephants refused to join in the fun. The *Burnley Express* reported that during a game one of the players suffered broken ribs and a pierced lung when an elephant 'seized him with its trunk and several times raised him in the air and banged him to the ground'. A yellow card offence at least.

Sanger claimed that in 70 years in the business he'd never known an elephant kill a keeper or trainer unless the animal had been abused. This was disingenuous. He had been around them long enough to know that male elephants had a propensity to kill their trainers and often did. The longest serving and most popular among his herd was a bull

named Charlie. He was born in the wild, most likely in Sri Lanka. Charlie was forcibly separated from his family as a baby, then shipped in a deep, dark hold on a four-month sea voyage to an animal dealer in Germany, then on to the docks in London. Charlie was a docile giant and most of the time he posed no danger to humans, but if he so chose he could snuff out a keeper's life with little effort. In adulthood he grew to over eleven-feet tall and weighed over three tons, and was reckoned to be bigger even than the famously hyped Jumbo.[98] By 1900 Charlie had been with Sanger's for about 38 years and had reached the time in a male elephant's life when musth transformed him into an unpredictable, lust-crazed monster.* One Sunday morning at Crystal Palace, Charlie's regular handler was called away and he was left in the care of a handyman, Emmanuel 'Chips' Baker. The stand-in, who it was alleged had been drinking heavily, picked up a military lance used as a show prop and advanced on the elephant in a menacing way. Charlie, who had already broken his chains that day and was in no mood to have a spear pointed at him, broke free, grabbed Baker with his trunk and dashed him to the ground, then knelt on the life-less body and squashed it to a pulp. The elephant escaped from his stable into the south nave of the Crystal Palace, scattering a crowd at a music concert. The confused beast was eventually cornered with his trunk wrapped around a large statue of a man with a raised arm. It was thought Charlie mistook it for a man about to strike.

* Musth is a periodic condition when bull elephants become aggressive and sexually active.

Rogue circus elephants are notoriously difficult to take down. The favoured methods were to have them shot, strangled or poisoned. Charlie was offered an industrial quantity of prussic acid hidden in a loaf of bread, which he sensibly refused. George sent word to Churchill, the Strand gunsmith, who despatched three marksmen to Crystal Palace armed with large-calibre rifles. The executioners delivered the coup de grace with a single volley from each, firing two into Charlie's head and one behind his shoulder. When the ghastly business was done and the huge elephant lay silent, George had the presence of mind to call in the press and pose for photos while seated on the stricken Charlie's head.[99] Amid the chaos, a second, much younger elephant, called Archie, took the opportunity to take an extended tour of Sydenham. After sixteen hours of freedom he was cornered in a gravel pit near Bromley, but not before he'd killed 22 dogs and destroyed swathes of property including several garden walls. One resident was in his conservatory, listening to his wife playing 'Just A Song at Twilight' at the piano, when Archie walked through one side of the building and out the other.

There were two unsettling postscripts to Charlie's execution. It emerged at the inquest into the death of Emmanuel Baker that the handler had once been fired by Sanger for mistreating animals, but was allowed to return as a labourer fifteen months later. It also came to light that three years earlier, Charlie had killed in chillingly similar circumstances. Sanger kept part of his menagerie in stables in Dalston in north London. One of the employees was 27-year-old Alan Baker (no relation). This Baker had also been employed by

Sanger as an elephant trainer, fired several months earlier over some unspecified mistreatment of the animals in his care while at Bedford, but then re-engaged as a stable hand. On Sunday 23 January 1897, shortly before 6pm, Baker called on a work colleague who was feeding Charlie to ask if he was joining him for tea. Elephants have relatively poor eyesight but are guided by incredibly well-developed senses of hearing and smell. Although it was dark, Charlie recognised his former keeper's voice. Breaking free from his chains, he impaled Baker on his tusks like a marshmallow on a toasting fork, then tossed him to the floor. At the coroner's inquest Charlie was described as a quiet, tractable animal of previous good behaviour. He was assumed to be settling an old score for rough treatment by his former handler. The jury was reminded that elephants had long memories: a beast called Blind Bill had killed his keeper at Alexandra Palace for improper treatment despite having not seen him for seven years. The jury returned a verdict of death by misadventure.

Charlie was one of thirteen elephants that died in George Sanger's care over a period of roughly 35 years. His last elephanticide probably occurred in 1902, when a 25-year-old male called Mammy became dangerously unstable and again Sanger had to rely on the services of the London gunsmith E.J. Churchill.

〜

Sanger's sick or elderly elephants were housed at his Margate zoo, a brick-built structure comprising 23 cages. The living conditions for the enclosed beasts were grim, their

cages cramped, bare and rat-infested. Mixed species lived in unhealthy proximity. A local natural historian reported seeing a single large cage housing monkeys, big cats, a jackal, a porcupine, a boa, pigs, geese and ducks, a small dog and her two pups, rabbits and guinea pigs.[100] In the early days the animal cages offered poor protection for public and employees alike, resulting in several reported injuries. A visiting vicar was luckily none the worse for being allowed to feed a polar bear 'which would take a piece of biscuit out of my hand as gently as if he were a dog', but a keeper was severely mauled by a leopard, and a little girl who put her hand between the bars of the cage to pass a piece of cake to a leopard lost an arm.[101]

The Hall by the Sea employed 160 people, and for the first nine years it ran with losses of up to 5,000 pounds a year, but by the mid 1880s George Sanger could justifiably boast that it was 'one of the best-known and best paying concerns in the United Kingdom'.

George and Nellie made Margate their home and George served as a member of the local council. George's seafront exercises with big cats and his general insouciance when handling wild animals were the stuff of legend. Once at Weymouth, five caged lions were fighting furiously with each other and covered in blood and even the fearless lion-tamer Crockett refused to intervene, but George, whip in hand, stepped into the cage alone, beat the lions to one side and coolly built a barrier between them with boards. He told a disbelieving newspaper reporter that his secret was simply to 'look the lion in the face and talk to him as you would to a man'.

George had started out as a business partner with his son-in-law Arthur Reeve, but their relationship was never less than toxic. Harriet's marriage was happy and by all accounts Arthur was a likeable man, but he was heartily detested by his father-in-law. Under the terms of their original business agreement, Arthur managed the Hall by the Sea, but as soon as George took sole control he got rid of him. To humour his daughter, he gave Arthur a job as his touring manager. George couldn't write and avoided any kind of clerical chores, so Arthur was left to sort out all of the paperwork and serve as general dogsbody. George never disguised his contempt for his son-in-law, and this led to many rows. One morning, after a typical fallout between the Sangers and the Reeves, Harriet and her husband awoke to find that the circus had moved on and they had been left abandoned in a field without any horses to pull their caravan. The Reeves left to run a hotel in Margate and never worked for the circus again. George continued to use his wealth to expand his operations in new directions. There was a much less controversial addition to his empire in 1883, when he bought a large chunk of land in Margate's sister resort Ramsgate and built a new amphitheatre with an adjoining hotel and several shops. As usual everything was gloriously overstated. The theatre was a huge, ornate affair crowned by a larger-than-life-size figure of a rearing horse and rider, the front guarded by eight scantily clad female bronze figures in the neoclassical mode, each holding aloft elaborately ornamented gas lamps. Their number was reduced to two after an attack of local prudery and six were removed to Sanger's Margate business.

George's eldest daughter Laurina took the traditional circus family route. In the ring she found fame as a trick rider known by the family's pet name for her, 'Topsy' Sanger. When Laurina was 21 she fell in love with a rising star of the Victorian circus called Alexander Coleman, known professionally as Little Sandy. Alexander 'Little Sandy' Coleman was a clown in a million. He was one of a stellar cast at Charles Hengler's Circus in Argyll Street and already on his way to becoming one of the most talented jesters of the era. He was known in his trade for his extraordinary versatility. He could reduce an audience to tears of uncontrollable laughter, but he was also a first-rate tumbler, equestrian and pantomimist. As a trainer of animals he had few equals and he even filled in as ringmaster. George Sanger was enraged when he found out that his daughter was seeing one of the top performers with a celebrated rival. His stubborn opposition to the courtship drove them to elope. In March 1874 Laurina and Alexander were secretly married at St James's, Piccadilly. George reacted with blind fury. In time he forgave his errant daughter, smoothing the path to reconciliation by gifting her his Ramsgate amphitheatre as a belated wedding present, but he never let go of his hatred for his son-in-law.

For a while, Little Sandy and Topsy were the golden couple of the thirteen-metre ring, Sandy the celebrated multi-talented comic hero, while his wife was given top billing in her father's shows as star equestrienne. The marriage was also blessed with four children inside five years: Georgina in 1875, followed by Alexander, Ellen and finally George in 1880.

Her career as a performer was burning as brightly as ever, but it was a difficult time juggling the demands of her husband with her job and the needs of the children. As a busy working mother, Laurina Coleman was keen to limit the size of her growing family. In a world where contraception was not widely available or reliable, illegal termination was often the only option. On 14 October 1982, in a room over the ticket office of Astley's Amphitheatre, just a stone's throw from St Thomas's Hospital, the mother of four died of blood poisoning after a botched abortion, another silent victim of the terrifying inadequacies of 19th-century family planning. She was 29 years old.

13

A very god of a man

'SANGER'S WOLVES ARE LOOSE! Bolt your doors! Bar your windows!'[102]

Lambeth, south London, shortly before midnight on 12 February 1888. The neighbourhood is awakened by the news that there's a wild wolf pack on the streets. They have escaped from their cage at Astley's Amphitheatre on Westminster Bridge Road. It is rumoured that a couple of disgruntled employees left the cage door open deliberately. The police are already at the scene in numbers, warning locals to stay indoors. Sanger's employees are frantically running around raising the hue and cry. Gradually, the panic subsides as word gets around that the predators have been isolated in a stable at Astley's. It is safe for the public to come and see for themselves, which they do, in their thousands.

An hour later, Lord George Sanger is holding court with the press, punctiliously suited and booted as always, not looking in the least like a man who has just been disturbed in the middle of the night by a life-and-death crisis. In Astley's stable courtyard, he invites newspaper reporters to inspect the mangled remains of a white horse, which

163

the circus proprietor describes as a 'superb Hanoverian cream' named Shrewsbury. Struggling to keep his emotions in check, George reveals that the dead horse was one of his finest performing mares. Poor Shrewsbury was in the stable yard when the Siberian wolves broke free. They fell on the hapless mare in a frenzy, ripping out her throat, then her stomach. Fortunately, the beasts were quickly rounded up and safely caged by their heroic handler Frank Taylor, a menacing slab of manhood with deep, sunken eyes and a heavy jaw, known to the public as Alpine Charlie. Sanger confirms for the assembled reporters that the wolves were let loose in his stables deliberately by two grooms who had been disciplined for misconduct. He has reason to believe that the miscreants have already fled London and are half-way to France. There's nothing more to fear, but just in case, the keys to the cage are in the safekeeping of his trusted assistant manager Mr Oliver.

The next day, the story of the escaped wolves was splashed in newspapers across the country and in the following days was repeated across Europe and as far afield as Australia and New Zealand. The popular *Illustrated London News* gave a page to the story, accompanied by a drawing of men in bowler hats armed with sticks, bravely beating off the wolves as they circled the mangled carcass of the stricken horse. In recognition of Frank Taylor's valour in averting a public disaster, George Sanger advertised the time and place of a public presentation to his courageous employee, the gift of a hundred gold guineas. The newspapers commended Taylor for his bravery, having saved the good people of Lambeth from being eaten by wild beasts,

and saluted Lord George for his extraordinary generosity. That night and for every night over the following week the show at Astley's sold out, all 4,000 seats filled by punters anxious to judge the ferocity of Alpine Charlie's Siberian wolves for themselves.[103]

Throughout the crisis, George Sanger had turned in a first-rate performance, one so completely convincing that only a handful of people knew that they were watching an act.

George was ever mindful of opportunities to draw the attention of the press and he didn't particularly care how it was achieved. Recently, business at Astley's had been slower than usual. A couple of days earlier he instructed Frank Taylor to starve his wolves. Old Shrewsbury, past her prime and of no further use as a performing animal, was summarily executed in her stable and dragged into the yard. Late that evening the wolves were let loose. Frank Taylor's Siberians were said to be 'tame as lambs', but when a wolf smells blood the primal need to hunt and kill takes over and Shrewsbury was an easy meal. Apart from Taylor, only two of George's immediate family were in on it. For maximum authenticity, Sanger's company were kept in the dark so they could play their parts to perfection, reacting with genuine horror when they encountered the hungry wolf pack tearing at the carcass of the old horse. The presentation of the hundred guinea purse was also part of the performance. The employee was supposed to hand it back after the reporters had gone home. But the purse stayed in Frank Taylor's pocket, to George's impotent fury. One word from his employee could bring the whole miserable, embarrassing stunt down around his ears. George waited to the end of the season before he fired Frank Taylor.

Lord George Sanger's largesse was legion. It was a reputation he worked hard to maintain. Whenever he was on the road, in every town he visited, he would find the most prominent bar and announce drinks for all on the house. He only allowed himself one glass, but while George was present no one else was allowed to put a hand in their pocket. The fake lord loved to play the part of a feudal lord, distributing alms to the poor. If he was in a town or city that was famous for a particular product – knives in Sheffield, or pots in Stoke – on the day before the show he bought a barrowload of the local ware and walked the streets handing out gifts to everyone he passed. Nowhere was he received with more enthusiasm than in his birthplace, Newbury. Every return was fêted as though royalty had arrived and the band struck up 'Home, Sweet Home' as George and his wife made their entrance into town riding cream-coloured horses. Every occupant of the local workhouse received free tickets to his show and for those who couldn't attend he sent gifts; free tobacco for the old men of the town, and for the ladies a pound of tea, sweets and other small luxuries.

Everyone loved Lord George. He had a gift for charming one and all, making them feel he was a personal friend to each. Unfailingly suave in manner, he was 'capable of toadying to the highest in the land and coping with the aristocracy and gentlemen on equal terms, to the mutual delight of both parties'.[104] You would see nothing in his demeanour or appearance to suggest the hardships he endured as a youth and he bore himself at all times like a gentleman of the highest rank. Fine clothes helped him project the necessary image and at his neck, his silk tie passed through a gold ring and

was held in place with a jewelled pin and gold watch-chain spanning his waistcoat.

In his late sixties he had lost most of his hair and his face was more lined and weather-beaten, but in every other respect he was the same as when he was 30 years old, weighing not a pound more nor less. Throughout his adult life he was as slim and agile as a jockey and blessed with (and in the end cursed by) great physical courage and stamina. He never touched tobacco and lectured on the evils of smoking, nor did he drink alcohol before 6pm and only then in moderation. His wife Nellie, who loved a drop of gin more than George ever knew, could make a bottle vanish at the hint of his approach with the skill of a stage magician.

It was only when you got up very close that you might notice a couple of small details hinting that George's world was very much unlike yours. His elegant clothes were usually covered with horsehair and a patina of bird droppings. You might also scent the commixed odour of lamp-oil and animal fodder on his coat and the whiff of miscellaneous animal ordure and straw lingering on his expensive leather boots.

As the years passed, while the hair of his great rival William 'Buffalo Bill' Cody turned snowy white, George's hair, or what little was left of it showing beneath the rim of his hat, remained determinedly jet black. He tinted it himself by regular application of a secret darkening agent of the type used to blacken horses. His eyebrows were similarly coloured, as was his beard, meticulously trimmed into the fashionable doorknocker style favoured by Charles Dickens. On each gaunt cheek he wore a dab of rouge. Often the black dye and the rouge were misapplied and it gave him

the appearance of an end-of-pier ventriloquist's dummy, to the great amusement of his grandchildren.

His roaming lifestyle had denied him any formal education. He never learned to write, but in his later years George taught himself to read and he could sign his own name. He was an avid consumer of the daily newspapers until his eyesight let him down and he had his personal assistant read them for him. His memory was prodigious and in his seventies he would test this faculty by reading a half-column of newsprint, then repeating it word for word two hours later. He loved his Shakespeare and could declaim lengthy passages, recitals the younger members of his family learned to dread. Curiously, he hated seeing his employees reading and would grumble that it was a waste of useful time. His command of foreign languages was good enough for him to operate his business all over Europe, but he regretted never having learned any Russian.

He rarely concerned himself with the financial side of the business. No one knew quite what he was worth, and he probably didn't know either because he never kept any books. Expenses were paid in cash out of the takings and the remainder banked or left in heaps of coins and notes lying around his living quarters. If George was going out somewhere, he just grabbed handfuls of gold coins, no questions asked. No one was sure where the money went – presumably into the hands of useful people or those who needed it.

He liked to spend money and loved to be seen spending it. Show business made him prodigiously rich and the more he made, the more he flaunted it. In his business dealings it suited him to behave as though he had an inexhaustible

supply of cash. Joseph Harker, the pre-eminent theatrical scene painter of his age, was hired by George to do some work for one of the great Christmas pantomimes at Astley's. When Harker broached the subject of his fee, the proprietor waved him away: 'I like the look of your mug. Charge what you think fit.' Harker went on to paint scenery and design sets for George Sanger for years but never once saw a contract or received a word in writing about these projects, nor did he ever have cause to complain about their business arrangement because George always paid him promptly.

He was generous to those in his industry who were down on their luck. He gave money to associates and strangers alike, even helping out rivals. Among his employees George inspired great loyalty and to most of those who served at his pleasure he was 'a very god of a man'.[105] Like the court of some mediaeval king, every New Year's Eve at the stroke of midnight his entire company would assemble in a room above Astley's Amphitheatre with George at the head, seated on a sort of throne, while a black member of the crew toasted the health and prosperity of 'the Master', then each member of the company would file past and do the same.[106]

But George was a capricious Old Testament god. He concerned himself with every detail of the show and his word was law. He expected high standards and long hours from his performers and he was ruthless if anyone didn't come up to the mark. Those who stepped out of line could expect a tongue-lashing, or worse. He carried a little malacca cane and during rehearsals would stride among his performers, his cane twitching in his hand, delivering stinging cuts to

the backside of anyone he thought was slacking, like some demented Victorian schoolmaster.

He was sadistic if an artist failed during a performance. His grandson once saw a young wire walker fall from her perch several times. When she finished her act George was waiting for her in the wings with an arctic blast of froideur. He pulled out an open penknife from his pocket and offered it to her with the instruction: 'Here, don't cut your throat, cut your bloody head off.' Scores of performers came and went and only the bravest or most loyal stayed the course. Those who fell short had their contracts terminated with a curt: 'Call yourself an actor? Get off my stage!' He demanded fealty from family members. When one of his granddaughters left Sanger's circus to perform in the music halls he remarked bitterly, 'Marie's gone over to the enemy.' When his daughter Laurina married her clown from a rival circus he considered it a betrayal of Shakespearian proportions.

Where other circuses failed, George Sanger's greater business acumen and deeper pockets always prevailed, but as the century entered its final decade his extraordinary run of good fortune stretching back to Stepney fair in 1853 was coming to an end. After eleven years of touring Europe, his continental audiences were dwindling and he was forced to abandon his European conquests and concentrate on turning around a slump in audience attendances in London.

Under George's management, Astley's Amphitheatre at Westminster Bridge had enjoyed a long Indian summer. Over the 22 years that he was in charge he had restored the old building to its rightful place as the greatest circus in the world. But by the start of the 1990's George was making

some poor business decisions. The shows were becoming bloated, too elaborate and ruinously expensive to stage. The properties in Ramsgate and Margate were mortgaged to keep Sanger's empire afloat.

Astley's was losing its lustre too and was desperately in need of modernisation. Having burned down and risen Phoenix-like three times, the life of the old venue was finally snuffed out by health and safety officials. The new London County Council was given the job of licensing entertainment venues and showed its teeth. In what seemed to George like a campaign of persecution, the LCC demanded expensive rebuilding works at Astley's. Swimming in debt, under mounting pressure from his ground landlords who wanted to sell the plot to the nearby St Thomas's Hospital, on 4 March 1893 George bowed to the inevitable and surrendered the keys. The old amphitheatre was demolished soon afterwards.

Astley's was gone, but there was still the magnificence of Lord George Sanger's travelling circus to look forward to. When George and his brother John dissolved their partnership they vowed to keep their rivalry on a friendly footing. But now George was back on the road full-time in direct competition with his brother. It quickly descended into a bitterly fought contest for primacy.

Sanger was a brand long before anyone knew there were such things, but George always understood the value of his name and he didn't like sharing it with anyone. As owner of the biggest and most successful circus company in Europe he complained, with justification, that John's much smaller operation with much lower overheads was reaping the harvest of his reputation and stealing his customers. The tactics

each camp used to gain an advantage over the other were often brutal. They could have arranged their schedules to avoid competition. Instead, the rival Sanger brothers would show up in the same town, each in a deliberate attempt to kill off the other's business.

Eighteen-eighty-nine was an *annus horribilis* for the Sanger family. In May that year 63-year-old George suffered severe injuries when he was attacked by a bull and tossed in the air several times. The press reported that he lay 'in a dangerous state'. Three months later, on 16 August 1889, 70-year-old John Sanger fell ill with a 'violent cold' on his way to perform in Ipswich and he died of pneumonia six days later. He was interred in the family plot in Margate Cemetery, within a mausoleum topped by a life-size marble horse with a bowed head. John Sanger's funeral was an opportunity to heal the family rift, but the moment was lost. Following the briefest interregnum in hostilities, as one war of the Sangers ended, another began. The John Sanger & Sons Circus was continued by John's children John, George, James and Lavinia, under the management of the eldest, 35-year-old John junior. George's nephew styled himself 'Lord' John Sanger, deliberately muddying the waters and cranking up the tension between the competing branches of the family. George retaliated by billing himself 'Lord George, the Original Sanger, the World's Greatest Showman'.

The bitter rivalry continued as both Sanger outfits doubled down on their efforts to destroy the other's livelihood, but George had been in the business long enough to know that internecine battles with nephews were only the beginning of his troubles.

14

Inquest

SATURDAY 2 DECEMBER 1911. The joint inquest into the deaths of George Sanger and Herbert Charles Cooper opened promptly at 1.30pm at Friern Barnet Council offices with the coroner for Central Middlesex, Dr George Alexander Cohen, presiding. Cohen was a former barrister from Scotland and the first and only Jewish coroner among 280 in England and Wales. He had been in his new role for a little over twelve months. One of his very first appointments was to investigate the death of Alice Linford, whose murderer George Pateman was arrested by two of the men in court on this day, Detectives George Wallace and Henry Brooks.

The council offices at Friern Barnet were temporarily housed in an architectural oddity, an eccentric 18th-century mock-Gothic turreted mansion in Friern Barnet Lane, formerly a private house known as The Priory. The coroner's court within was similar to a regular court of law, but much smaller, and instead of a dock there was a chair for witnesses. Dr Cohen sat on a platform slightly raised above the floor of the court with the witness chair to his left and

the jury to his right. At the plain oak table below him was the solicitor representing the Cooper family, Mr Forbes. Facing Dr Cohen and filling the rest of the room were pew-like benches for witnesses and the press. The hearing was open to the public, but anyone who came in hope of gaining access to the day's proceedings was disappointed. The room was too small to accommodate anyone else besides the families of the deceased, who occupied two rows at the back of the court. A uniformed officer stood at the doorway, admitting only those with signed passes from the coroner. Outside the building, a handful of curious spectators peered through tall, narrow windows, perhaps straining to catch a glimpse of the star expert medical witness and man-of-the-moment, Bernard Spilsbury.

Dr Cohen's role was an ancient one. He investigated sudden, suspicious or unexplained deaths and if possible reached conclusions about the causes. The coroner and his jury could also consider whether enough evidence existed to prove that a crime had been committed. If the facts pointed to a suspect, they could also formally accuse and recommend a warrant for arrest. Silencing the shuffling of the courtroom onlookers, Dr Cohen signalled for the inquest to commence. Sixteen local men, all living a few-hundred yards from the scene of the crime and selected from two parallel-running streets in East Finchley, Church Crescent and Clifton Avenue, were sworn to the jury with John George Kiddy of 17 Church Crescent appointed foreman. Briefly, the coroner outlined the purpose of the proceedings, reprising the circumstances that brought them there. No one needed reminding that the elderly George Sanger was a famous man of that parish

and that his death was one of the most notorious in their experience. The bare facts of the case were known to everyone who had read a newspaper: the razor-and-axe wielding employee, his violent struggle with three members of the Sanger household, the brutal slaughter of the elderly showman, the flight of the suspect and the subsequent discovery of his decapitated body on a railway line.

Over the next two-and-a-half hours, the packed court would hear the testimonies of key witnesses as reporters scribbled notes they hoped would provide eye-catching content for Sunday's papers. None were expecting anything new to emerge that might cast doubt on the premise that Cooper murdered Sanger then took his own life, but they were looking forward to the first-hand accounts of the brutal attacks from Jackson and Austin, and to perhaps learn more about the discovery of Cooper's body on the railway track. Most of all, as the *Observer* reported the following day: 'the great interest aroused by the tragedy was maintained in expectation of a sensational story of the motive for the crime said to be contained in a letter written by Cooper'.[107]

For the benefit of the jury, S Division's draughtsman P.C. Cook produced an A2-size hand-drawn plan of the crime scene at Park Farm. It was beautifully detailed and rendered in black and crimson ink, crimson signifying the key positions in the unfolding drama – where the attacks took place, the location of blood stains, where the razor and the axe were found, the makeshift bedroom occupied by Herbert Cooper and so on.

The first witness to be called was a short, stout, elegantly dressed woman who announced herself as Harriet Reeve.

She was George Sanger's daughter and lived in Tottenham, on the pig farm she owned with her husband Arthur. She had last seen her father alive and well on the Saturday before the assault. She received an urgent message on the Tuesday evening to go over to the farm. When she arrived she found her father lying injured in bed. The following day she identified his body at Finchley mortuary. She told the court that her father was 85 years old: 'he would have been 86 this month'. All previous reports assumed he was 83 going on 84. Dr Cohen recorded Sanger's age in his deposition thus: '86?' It wasn't the most auspicious start.[108]

Next up was Arthur Jackson, his head covered with large patches of sticking plaster. According to the reporter from the *Observer* the witness was 'evidently suffering pain'. Jackson said he'd been working for Sanger as a servant for just two months, but hadn't known his employer before he saw the job advertised in a local newspaper. When asked to describe his duties, Jackson replied: 'It depended on the old gentleman's mind.' Most evenings he acted as nurse attendant to Sanger, a job previously occupied by Herbert Cooper, with whom he had always been on friendly terms. Then Jackson offered a fresh revelation not known to the press. About five weeks ago, he heard his employer mention that someone had stolen 50 pounds from the household.

Cohen: 'Did you hear who was supposed to have taken it?'

Jackson: 'No.'

Describing the night of the assaults, Jackson said he had been sitting in the kitchen reading for about twenty minutes when Cooper walked in. Cooper said he'd come for

his gramophone. Jackson indicated he thought it was in the pantry. Cooper went into the pantry, then withdrew, saying it was dark and he would need a light. Cooper walked around to the back of the chair where Jackson was sitting – to reach a cupboard, so Jackson thought. The next thing he knew, Cooper had seized him from behind and had his hand over his mouth and he felt a burning sensation on his throat. He didn't realise he'd been cut by a razor until later. There was a struggle and both men fell to the floor. Jackson said he was dazed and didn't remember what happened next. When he recovered his senses, probably after a couple of minutes, Cooper had gone. Jackson ran outside to summon help. When he returned, he found Sanger lying on the floor near the hearthrug, barely conscious and unable to speak. At this point, the razor used in the attack on Jackson was passed among the jury for examination. Dr Cohen drew attention to the fact that the blade was tied open with a piece of string. The implication was clear – the weapon had been made ready and this showed that Cooper had intent to inflict harm.

Now it was Harry Austin's turn to take the witness chair, his head swathed in bandages. The *Observer* reported that Austin's face was 'very pale, but he appeared to have recovered much more readily from the shock than his fellow-sufferer [Jackson]'. Austin gave his evidence clearly and unhesitatingly. He knew about the theft of 50 pounds. Mr Sanger told him he believed that Cooper had stolen it, then had tried to make it look as though there had been a break-in. The police weren't brought in because Mr Sanger didn't wish it. Austin had overheard Mr Sanger voice his suspicions to Cooper directly but said that if he put the money

back 'no one shall ever know anything about it'. Dr Cohen pressed Austin. Had the money been put back?

'No.' Cooper had told his employer 'I'll draw it out of the bank and give it you back that way', but Sanger had replied; 'I would not take 50 pounds of your money. Go back to your business and think about it.'

Now Austin described the night of the attack. At around 6pm he was sitting in the drawing room with his employer, reminiscing about the old show days, when they heard shouts and screams as a fight broke out in the kitchen. Austin went to the door to see what was going on and saw Cooper advancing on him with an axe held high above his head. He tried to close the door, but Cooper forced it open, knocking Austin backwards. Cooper lunged at him three times with the axe. He'd managed to fend off the first couple of blows and had cried out 'have mercy!' but on the final blow the axe bounced off his arm and the blade hit him directly on his head, leaving a gash three-and-a-half inches long.

Austin added: 'If I had not broken the blow with my arm I should have been killed.'

After being struck, he fell back into the fireplace fender, stunned. When he regained consciousness – he estimated that it was no more than fifteen seconds later – he saw Sanger prostrate on the floor. 'I said to myself, My God, poor Mr George is dead.' At this, Austin jumped out of the drawing room window to seek help, but collapsed unconscious in nearby Church Lane, where someone found him and sent for a doctor.

Cohen asked Austin if he saw what happened to Sanger.

'No. He was at the back of me.' At this, Sanger's damaged felt hat was produced. It had a huge cut at the front. Austin said that Sanger always wore this hat in the house.

Cohen asked Austin about his former employee's relations with Herbert Cooper. Austin replied that Cooper was 'not in favour at the time … he [Cooper] used to live there and had been made a fuss of, but that was some time ago. I told Cooper not to come to the house'.

'When did you tell him?'

'On November 4th.'

'After the question of the 50 pounds?'

'Yes.'

'Why did you tell him?'

'Because Mr Sanger did not want him about the place.'

The coroner then took evidence from Herbert Cooper's brother, Thomas John Cooper. He described Herbert as 'usually very jolly' but said that for the last few weeks he had seemed subdued and had taken to hiding in a shed on the farm for long periods. This behaviour began after the allegation about the stolen money. Herbert had spoken to him about it and said he had pointed out to his employer that he had often picked up money that was lying around the house and put it away. If he had wished to rob him he could have very easily done so before.

Tom Cooper reprised the deposition he had given the police on the evening of the assaults. He was at home that night when at 5.45pm he was alerted that there was something going on at the farm. He found his employer lying on his back, comatose but still breathing. He lifted him up and spoke his name but there was no response. He'd called out

to see if there was anyone else in the house but there was no answer so he left to fetch a doctor. Tom Cooper last saw his brother alive at 5.30pm. They had been working together that evening and his brother was very quiet, as though something was preying on his mind.

Cohen: 'Was your brother a quick-tempered man?'

'Yes.'

'Have you ever heard your brother say anything spiteful against Mr Sanger or Jackson or Austin?'

'No.'

The Irishman Dr William Orr told the court that he had been called from his home in High Road, East Finchley to Park Farm at about 6pm. He found Mr Sanger sitting in a chair in the drawing room. Someone must have washed his head because there was no blood to be seen, just a large wound on the top-right-hand side of his crown with the bone laid bare. Someone told Sanger that the doctor had arrived and the old man raised his head as if in acknowledgment, but he didn't speak. Dr Orr and others helped him to bed where he at once lapsed into unconsciousness. He never recovered and died five hours later. Dr Orr confirmed that he had been by Sanger's side for almost all of that time.

PC Frederick Nicholls from Albany Street station was the first officer on the scene at exactly 6pm – he remembered hearing the hour being struck on the church clock as he entered the farm gates. He found Jackson in the kitchen, bleeding from cuts to his neck, then in the drawing room he found Sanger sitting in an armchair, bleeding from wounds to the head and unable to speak. Nicholls searched the ground floor rooms and found a broken razor lying on the

kitchen floor. Austin told him that Cooper had attacked him with an axe, then attacked Sanger with the same weapon, then left the way he came in.

Next there was evidence from one of the senior officers on the case, Detective Inspector John Cundell. He said that, because of the remoteness of the farm and the lack of nearby telephones, the police were unable to take witness statements until about 8.15pm. He asked Thomas Cooper senior if he knew where his son was. The father had replied: 'If you find him, you will find him dead.'

There was a hush in the tiny, packed court room while Dr Cohen read aloud the suicide notes found on Herbert Cooper's body.

Harry Austin's wife Ellen lived at Park Farm with her grandfather George Sanger. At the time of the incident she was visiting friends, but she returned to the farm around 7.40pm. She too was aware that some money had gone missing. She had not heard her grandfather directly accuse Herbert Cooper of theft but had guessed from remarks made that he suspected it was so. Her husband had told her that Cooper was banned from the house 'on account of the loss of the money'. Since then, as far as she was aware, Herbert Cooper had not been inside the farmhouse except to enquire if there was any mail for him.

William Venables, a butcher's assistant, told the court that he had known Herbert Cooper for about four years. He had last seen him on Sunday evening when they were drinking together at The Five Bells public house. The rest of his evidence was basically a repetition of the story he'd told the police. He was riding his bicycle past Park Farm Lodge

on the night of the murder when he saw Arthur Jackson run into the road shouting for help.

The assembled representatives of the press were hoping for something more interesting from the next witness, Jane Beesley. This was the Jenny mentioned in Cooper's suicide note. She had been employed as a live-in domestic servant at Park Farm for about sixteen months and resided at the adjacent Park Farm Lodge. She was on her half-day off when the assault happened. She returned to the farmhouse at 6.30pm when she heard that someone had been 'knocking the governor about'. Arriving by the tradesman's entrance, in the kitchen she found a doctor bandaging her employer's head. The last time she saw Herbert Cooper was on the previous Monday. She also knew about the missing money and of Mr Sanger's suspicions. Then another new fact slipped out, almost in passing. Whenever Harry Austin was away, Cooper occupied a bedroom adjacent to that of Austin's wife Ellen, although he'd been ordered to stay away from the house. She told George Austin (Harry Austin's brother) about it. That night she overheard Harry Austin accuse his wife Ellen of having an affair and he said he could prove it. The next morning, she also heard Mrs Austin tell Cooper he shouldn't come to the house again. Since then, as far as she knew, Cooper only went into the farmhouse to fetch his post.

Could Jane Beesley account for the reference to her in the note found on Herbert Cooper's body addressed to Harry Austin?

She said that she had spoken previously about Cooper's conduct at the farm – she assumed it was something to do with that.

Next, attention was focused on George Sanger's brother-in-law, James Holloway, husband of Ellen Sanger's sister Amelia, 'comedian clown' and formerly show manager working for the deceased. He arrived at the farm around 6.20pm and found his brother-in-law sitting in a chair having his head bandaged by Dr Orr. He helped Thomas Cooper and his son lift the chair into the adjoining ground-floor bedroom and put Sanger to bed. It was Holloway who found the blood-stained axe in a recess by the sitting room fireplace and handed it over to the police.

At this, the large axe was produced and shown to the jurors.

Holloway returned to his seat. Now it was time for the witness everyone was looking forward to, Dr Bernard Spilsbury. He had been the last to arrive at the coroner's court, averting his gaze as he entered the building by tipping his hat to cover his face. Dapper as always, his customary red carnation fixed in the buttonhole of his suit, now Spilsbury took his place in the witness chair. The courtroom was still as he read from his longhand notes, reprising the examination of Sanger, describing the prominent 'Y'-shaped wound on the top of the victim's head, the bruising and the internal bleeding. Finally, he gave details of the general degeneration of the old man's organs.

Dr Cohen pressed him: 'From the age of the deceased it was what one might expect?'

'Yes.'

'And for a man at that age of his life, the body was particularly healthy?'

'Yes.'

'What do you think he died from?'

'He died from a coma, due to compression of the brain by haemorrhage following a fracture of the skull.'

The coroner's deputy brought forward the heavy felling axe discovered in the Sanger drawing room by James Holloway and held it aloft.

'Assuming that the injuries you state you found on Mr Sanger caused his death, can you say if these injuries could have been caused by that axe?'

For once, the pathologist's testimony was equivocal. Spilsbury paused.

'Yes … they may have been, but not by the cutting edge of the axe. I think more probably they were caused by the side or the blunt edge of the axe.'

When the last witness stepped down, Dr Cohen summarised the post-mortem results. He asked the jury to consider, on the basis of the evidence, whether a crime had been committed. If they concluded it likely that Herbert Cooper had played a part in the murder of Mr Sanger then they must return a verdict of wilful murder against him. It took the jury less than a minute's consultation to return their verdict: George Sanger had been wilfully murdered by Herbert Charles Cooper.

After a brief adjournment, the participants in the inquest reassembled and turned their attention to the death of Cooper.

Thomas Potter, a ticket collector at Highgate Station, told the court that at around 7.40am a passenger arriving from King's Cross had reported seeing a body by the side of the rails further up the line. They didn't have time to get

the passenger's name because his train was on the move. Potter went in the direction of Crouch End to search the line with the platelayer James Roberts, and they found a body 50 yards from Stanhope Road bridge, about half a mile from Crouch End Station. William Woodcock, acting stationmaster at Crouch End, informed the police and called for Dr Thomas Parry to attend to Cooper's body at about 9.20 on the Thursday morning.

There were audible gasps from the jury and witness benches as Dr Parry detailed the scene he encountered. The body was lying parallel to the line, feet towards Highgate and the head towards Crouch End, having been flung about six feet from the line by the force of impact. From the neck down, the body was untouched. About three-quarters of Cooper's head had been sheared off and lay crushed and mutilated about nine feet away from his torso. Dr Parry said he thought Cooper had not thrown himself under the train: he'd laid his head on the line and waited for the next train to pass. The body had been struck from the right side. He had no doubt that death was instantaneous. He estimated that Cooper had been dead for two hours. An examination of his stomach showed that he hadn't eaten for a considerable time.

Another meticulously executed ink drawing of the scene of Coopers death was produced, an 'x' marking the location of the torso next to the railway line, another 'x' nearby marking the position of the severed head.

George Sanger's former coachman, Harry Grierson, took the witness chair. He had been employed as a driver by the deceased for fifteen years and knew Herbert Cooper well. His contribution was otherwise limited but there was

one useful insight. A couple of weeks before the incident, he said he had had a conversation with Cooper, who was clearly upset, because Sanger suspected him of taking some money. Cooper told him he might leave for Australia, but before he left he would give Jenny (Beesley) 'a good hiding'.

Then the final witness, Herbert Cooper's 55-year-old father Thomas. Looking drained and much older than anyone remembered him, his words barely carried to the members of the jury and the people sitting at the back of the court room. He had last seen his son alive at about 5.30 in the evening of 28 November. For the past weeks, Herbert had been 'very quiet in his manner and if spoken to twice on any matter he would get very irritable'. Then, is if by way of an apology or explanation, he volunteered that Herbert's great-uncle, the brother of his maternal grandmother, had died in a lunatic asylum, aged 35.[109] At this point the interrogation of Thomas Cooper was interrupted. A doctor representing the Cooper family told the coroner that the witness had suffered great anguish and was evidently unwell. Mercifully, Dr Cohen ruled that Thomas Cooper would not be required to give further evidence. The courtroom was still as the witness collected himself and made his way back to his seat.

The jury considered in private for just a few moments, then returned a verdict of 'suicide, whilst of unsound mind'.

The light was fading over Friern Barnet as Dr Cohen closed the proceedings at 4pm. The coroner and his jury were satisfied beyond all reasonable doubt that Herbert Cooper murdered his employer and had escaped justice by taking his own life. Everyone was eager to get home. The room emptied and as they dispersed, the sixteen men from

East Finchley discharged their final duty by adding their signatures to the coroner's reports. Cohen filled in the last space in each. On the first he wrote: 'George Sanger died of coma due to haemorrhage caused by fracture of skull caused by being struck with an axe on 28 November 1911.' On the second he wrote: 'Herbert Charles Cooper was found dead on the G. N. Railway between Highgate station and Crouch End station lying against the outer up rail. [illegible] he died of crushing of the brain.' Coroners' inquests, especially those in which foul play was suspected, could take days, weeks, even months. The combined inquests into the deaths of George Sanger and Herbert Cooper took less than three-and-a-half hours. Afterwards, Dr Cohen was effusive in his praise for PC Cook and his maps of the murder and suicide scenes, which were 'excellently done'.

The murder of George Sanger and the suicide of the chief suspect had put the story on the front pages of the newspapers for most of the previous week, but as far as the press were concerned, the inquests had little new to offer. The coroner's rulings on the deaths left no room for speculation. The Sunday papers, which were obliged to compress a whole week's news in one issue, gave the story very little space, the *Observer* alone dedicating two columns of coverage. Monday morning's papers gave just a couple of inches to the contents of the notes found on Cooper's body and little else. His suicide had been the subject of taproom conjecture in The Five Bells public house and at breakfast tables all over the country, but apart from those details now being revealed there had been few surprises. The facts, or most of them, had already been established in the days following

Sanger's murder. Cooper had lost his job and reacted badly – that much was already known – now they knew why. He was a thief.

Apart from that there were just a few more blanks to be filled in. Harry Austin was the last person to see Herbert Cooper alive. No one saw the murderer flee or the direction he took and no one could be sure where Cooper was hiding or what he was doing in the 48 hours before he met his end. The area where his body was found, including the local woods and nearby pavilions in Manor Farm fields, had all been thoroughly searched by police over the previous day but there was no trace of him. The police surmised that he made his way along the road to Highgate Woods, then could have spent his last couple of nights holed up in one of several empty farmhouse outbuildings near the railway line. He probably got onto the line by climbing over a stone wall in Stanhope Road. Again there was widespread mis-reporting. In North America a story was circulated that he had thrown himself from a moving train two miles from the scene of the murder.

George Sanger had one last audience. On the following Tuesday morning, driving rain fell on the black umbrel-las sheltering the growing crowd outside the entrance of Park Farm, East Finchley. The curtains of the house had been drawn since the owner's death a week earlier, and the Sanger family had exchanged their usual clothes for deep-est black mourning. As the rain coursed into the gutters of East End Road the black-plumed horses outside waited motionless under the leaden sky as the coffin was carried out to the hearse. The funeral cortège left the main gate at

just after 8am, taking a left turn towards the High Road, where it broke into a trot. Despite the early hour and the dreadful weather, large crowds gathered at every road junction, and the route was several lines deep with bareheaded men, hats respectfully tucked under arms as the cortège passed by. Following the hearse came four carriages filled with flowers, drawn by two of the late showman's famous white horses. Behind, a single mourning coach was occupied by the Sanger family. The solemn procession passed down Highgate Archway, along Holloway Road to The Angel, Islington, through Smithfield meat market and on to Holborn Viaduct Station, where the body in its oak coffin was placed on a special train bound for Margate, accompanied by family mourners for the almost two-hour journey east. The route all the way from London was impressively lined with people, some walking miles just to see the train go by. Many people came out of respect, but many more did so out of curiosity. The gory details of the Sanger killing had been avidly read by the public and now they knew they were seeing a piece of history. A heavy gale was blowing when the train arrived at Margate West station shortly before noon. No one was prepared for the display of public concern which awaited them. For many years George Sanger had owned local theatres, shops, a zoo and a huge amusement park in Margate, and was an important presence on dozens of local committees of local governors and tradesfolk. Meeting the coffin at the railway station were dozens of civic dignitaries and representatives from all the great circus families. Among the rain-sodden mourners, Frank Wilson, 'Lorenzo the Lion King', caught a fatal chill and expired a

few days later. Around 50 carriages followed the hearse on the two-mile route from the station yard, as the cortège and its followers made the slow progress to the Parish Church of St John the Baptist, and then on to the cemetery. Again the route was thronged with people, many of them skipping work to see Lord George's final homecoming. Shops were shuttered, all business suspended and cabmen in the streets tied mourning bows to their whips.

George Sanger's body was laid to rest in the family grave with his wife Nellie, his brothers John and William, and his daughter Laurina. Dominating the plot was the marble sculpture of a life-size mourning horse with a bowed head. It stood on a tall pedimented plinth, decorated in relief with equestrian emblems entwined with roses and poppies. On the base of the plinth in bold relief was the name 'SANGER'.

In Newbury, the flag on the municipal building was lowered to half-mast as a wreath was placed in the Market Place in memory of the town's most celebrated son. The press coverage the following day was worthy of a state funeral. Newspapers around the world offered sympathy for the tragedy that had overtaken the Sanger family and there were more extraordinary demonstrations of the high regard in which the old man was held by his peers.

There was no hearse and pony parade for Herbert Charles Cooper, laid to rest that same day. His body was reunited with his head and transferred from Hornsey mortuary into a plain wooden coffin and conveyed to St Marylebone Cemetery on East End Road, only a fifteen-minute walk from Park Farm and the spot where George Sanger was slain. There, without ceremony, his body was lowered

into an unmarked grave among those of his extended family. It's likely that only his immediate family were present, the stigma of suicide alone enough to keep old friends and work colleagues away.

Long before the coroner had reached his conclusion, the wider public had already settled upon the question of innocence and guilt. Herbert Cooper had killed his employer and had wounded two others in a series of unprovoked, frenzied attacks. The body of evidence only pointed in one direction and no reasonable hypothesis existed to suggest otherwise. Cooper's flight and subsequent suicide confirmed it beyond doubt. What the public didn't know is that there was one extraordinary detail that had not been revealed in any of the press reports, a detail that would cast the case in a very different light.

15

Winter

'MY FATHER WORE A PIGTAIL and fought on the *Victory* with Nelson at Trafalgar.'

Christmas Eve 1895. The nation's favourite showman is delivering his annual speech at the Gala Dinner of Margate's Conservative Association, of which he is president and founding member, waxing loquacious about his long and colourful career. Having started on the very lowest rung of the ladder as a cocky fairground spieler, Lord George Sanger is now a titan of the British entertainment business and can use his influence and his considerable fortune to promote not only his many businesses, but also the political causes he holds dear. The boy who grew up sharing a chilly wooden caravan with his family of twelve is now a staunch Unionist and among the first to join up for the Primrose League, a vast, loyal band of working-class Conservatives, named in honour of their poster-boy and George's hero, Britain's late prime minister Benjamin Disraeli.[110] George was an ardent admirer of Disraeli and liked to think he saw something of himself in the statesman. They were both outsiders who'd climbed the greasy pole and reached the top. His devotion to

Disraeli extended to copying his flashy style of dress. George once had a chance encounter with his idol on a railway station in Belgium and it made him quite giddy. 'I stammered out a few words of thanks and a humble congratulation on the splendid manner in which he had served our country. This was met with a kindly smile and a good-humoured shake of the head.'[111] To commemorate this momentous event, George named one of his lions Lord Beaconsfield.

For all George's celebrity, he faced mounting pressures. He fought long and hard against the expansion of magisterial powers designed to erase nomadic Gypsy, Roma and Traveller communities from public life.[112] Parliamentary regulation was threatening to tame some of the brutishness of working conditions in the circus and there were new sensitivities about child welfare, not to mention a growing animal rights movement. As senior spokesman for his industry, George also worked hard to resist government efforts to regulate the circus, but he knew he was swimming against the tide. The British circus had enjoyed a golden age, but the seeds of its decline were already sown.

In 1897 George Sanger made what he came to regard as the worst judgment error of his show business career. The 72-year-old showman was laid low for several weeks by illness. While he was recuperating, his daughter Harriet and her husband Arthur Reeve came to him with a business proposition. If he made his circus and zoo a limited liability company and opened it up to potential investors, he could shed some of the financial burden and still have a flourishing business. The Reeves would even arrange it all for him. The very mention of Arthur Reeve gave George dyspepsia,

but he agreed to hear them out. He was at a low ebb and battling to keep his circus empire profitable. Falling attendances and competition from Barnum, Cody and his own nephews had taken their toll. George's wife Nellie, always the more practical when it came to finances, saw trouble and warned her husband against deals with jossers,[113] but the old showman saw the prospect of an easier life and found it appealing. Arthur Reeve introduced him to a broker named Openshaw who persuaded George that he would receive a large lump sum while retaining control of the circus. On 1 July 1897, Lord George Sanger's circus and menagerie business, 'together with the whole paraphernalia connected with this gigantic concern', including 'one of the finest groups of ostriches ever got together in this country', was floated. His profits for 1897 were estimated at 14,000 pounds, although it was pointed out that the owner never kept any books; his 'system' was to simply bank surplus cash at irregular intervals. Openshaw introduced George to a potential business partner, Clement Howarth, a millionaire cotton baron from Lancashire. As a sweetener, Howarth was offered a ride in George's yellow carriage in the pre-show parade. The cotton baron enjoyed the experience so much that before the ride was over, he was begging George to sell his syndicate all of the shares.

From this congenial beginning, however, relations between the new business partners quickly turned sour. As a high court judge would point out later, all the expenses came out of Sanger's end, while Howarth's syndicate enjoyed the profits. At a showdown with Howarth at the office of Sanger's London solicitors Lewis & Lewis, the cotton baron

simply refused to speak to the showman. In a fit of pique, George threw his silk top hat on the floor and trampled on it. He and Howarth were locked in litigation for years, while the old showman was, in his own words, 'nearly worried into my grave'. When Howarth's syndicate missed a payment by a few days, George seized on it as an excuse to take back control. He sued Howarth for recovery of the 35,000 pounds he was owed. A settlement was agreed. Sanger bought back all the shares and withdrew unreservedly what was described in the press as certain 'heated words' and 'imputations' against Howarth's character. At the High Court hearing the puzzled judge, Mr Justice Ridley, queried the plaintiff's counsel Mr Rufus Isaacs. 'Is he *Lord* George Sanger?'

'Yes, m'lud, but I don't think I am justified in conferring a peerage upon him, I think the name was part of the advertisement.'

Once again George had control of his business, but he bitterly regretted putting himself in the hands of the Reeves and he never let them forget it.

﹌

On 30 April 1899, George's wife Nellie followed her brother-in-law John Sanger into the family mausoleum at Margate. She died aged 67 at her daughter Harriet's farm in Tottenham, where she had been nursed through an undiagnosed illness for the last eighteen months of her life. In her distressing final days Nellie experienced terrifying hallucinations and believed she was being burned alive. Her family were convinced her illness was the result of the head wound she received during her early lion-taming career.

Throughout her terminal illness, Nellie's lifelong stubborn faith in snake oil remedies didn't help. History has left little trace of Ellen 'Nellie' Sanger, just a few photographs and posters, a Staffordshire figurine and handful of write-ups in provincial newspapers, but she was undoubtedly a remarkable woman who did more than her share of the heavy lifting in the 48 years she and her husband were together. Just as George had to combine the knowledge of a dozen trades in his working day, Nellie was expected to meet all the contingencies of the travelling season and much more, as housekeeper, mother, secretary, accountant, worker and business partner. At her funeral George fell on Nellie's coffin and wept.

With the cruellest of timing, just a couple of weeks after his wife's death, George Sanger received the invitation he had long dreamed of when he was summoned to a royal command performance at Windsor. The circus always had a special place in Queen Victoria's affections. As a young girl she thrilled to Van Amburgh's circus lions, and later she took her children to Astley's.[114] Throughout her reign she would visit, or more usually be visited by, circuses; there were private performances at Balmoral, Sandringham and elsewhere. It had taken a frustratingly long time for George's fantasy to become reality. He was annoyed when she favoured his American rivals 'Buffalo Bill' Cody and Barnum, and furious when his nephew Lord John beat him to it with a private showing at Windsor Castle. George had once been invited to perform at Balmoral in 1898 when Nellie was still alive, but he was detained on business in London and had to leave the show in the hands of his road manager, so was

robbed of a chance to meet his Queen in person. After this event, Victoria, as confused by the existence of more than one Sanger circus as everyone else, wrote in her journal: 'It was a remarkably good circus, in fact the same as I saw several years ago at Windsor, but that Sanger has since died.' On 17 July 1899, Lord George achieved what he considered to be the apex of his career when he put on a show for his ageing monarch and was afterwards received for a private audience.[115]

⌐

George began the new century with a bang, or quite a few bangs. In 1901 Sanger's circus presented another Imperial shoot-'em-up at Hendon, this time representing British soldiers giving the Boers a kicking in South Africa, featuring 'one hundred trained horses enacting the dying and slain beasts upon the field of battle'. In June that year George also became the last surviving member of the original Sanger magic roadshow when his brother William died aged 73, after an attack of bronchitis 'brought on by the east winds'.

To mark Queen Victoria's passing, in 1903 George gifted his birthplace of Newbury a statue, erected at his direction on the spot his father's stall had once occupied, and where George and his siblings once sold fish and fruit. His present, a rust-brown terracotta likeness of the late Queen, stood on a tall plinth guarded by four recumbent lions and a mysterious second female figure called Fame, grasping a wreath of laurel and gazing up at the monarch. The latter, an afterthought by the donor, delayed the unveiling by twelve months. On 24 June 1903, thousands turned out in

Newbury's marketplace to see George's daughter Harriet unveil one of the ugliest monuments to Queen Victoria of that year or any other.[116]

For all his munificence, the early years of the new century found George struggling financially. All was not well with his touring company. Every year there was an expectation that it would be bigger, more impressive, more extravagant than the last, but the masses who once went to the circus now streamed into football matches and other new forms of entertainment. Music halls could also offer circus performers more comfortable gigs with better pay. George had always carried his years lightly, but now he was feeling his age, hopelessly confused by the accounts his wife had always kept for him. In 1904, his 79th year, the nation's favourite entertainer decided to retire.

George had acquired an 18th-century brick farmhouse in East Finchley to serve as his winter quarters. There was enough land and stabling for all of his horses and he converted the outbuildings to storage rooms for his circus props. He also laid out a ring in which new acts could be rehearsed and animals trained. The locals were occasionally startled by the sight of elephants grazing alongside cows and oxen in the lush meadows that would become, in a few years, Hampstead Garden Suburb. Park Farm would be his retirement home, but first there was one last victory lap.

George Sanger's career ended on a high, his most lucrative British tour in six years. From March to October his circus travelled a record 3,300 miles, playing twice a day, every day except Sundays. It was, he noted with satisfaction, 'an excellent finish for a man who had been on the road

for three-score years and ten'. He retreated to his winter quarters at East Finchley with the applause and acclaim of the public still ringing in his ears. A couple of days after his last hurrah, George gave a newspaper interview from Park Farm. He reminisced about his life as a showman, his father's peep-show business, his audience with Queen Victoria and the other 'millions of adventures' he'd experienced. He spoke of his plans for the future: 'There's life in the old dog yet ... I want to go to St Petersburg, for one thing and try my tongue.' Explaining his decision to retire from show business, he blamed the rising cost of pitch rentals and advertising costs, changing public tastes and, weirdly, the working class: 'The working element have got out of hand ... They're a rough lot, dreadfully fond of pubs. And I've done with 'em.'[117]

Finally, he announced that he was putting all his circus properties up for auction. He was selling up and that was the end of it. 'It's got to be,' Sanger told the reporter. 'There's no one to take up the reins when poor old George drops 'em.' During the interview they were joined briefly by a stocky, bearded, straw-hatted man, introduced by Sanger as his farm bailiff, Thomas Cooper. The bailiff addressed his employer respectfully throughout as 'my Lord' and was described in the article as 'humble but beautifully agricultural'.

The sale was held over two days from 31 October, at Park Farm, conducted by the auctioneer Mr J. Ord.[118] The auction proceeded at breakneck pace. Almost everything went under the hammer – circus props, costumes, horses and wagons. Most of the prices fetched were a bitter disappointment for the old showman, but he was in a combative mood and joked

his way through the sale. The press noted later: 'It says much for the philosophic effect of circus-running that at the end of fifty-four years spent on the road the king of English show-men was able to watch without a tear the dispersal of his famous caravan at prices which would have wrung the heart of a second-hand clothes dealer.'[119] When Mr Ord succeeded in squeezing another half-crown from a bidder for one of the famous gilded wild beast wagons that had toured Europe for many years, George turned on the new owner and remarked sarcastically: 'He ought to be locked up for taking too much of your money.' The prospective buyers had little respect for antiquity. Sanger forced a hollow laugh when an item optimistically listed as 'a coach built for Queen Anne in 1702 and used in the coronation of Queen Victoria' fetched a single sovereign. A box of new musical instruments valued at fifteen pounds was sold for twelve shillings. The famous 'Indian car' once drawn by 40 ponies, fetched top price at 31 guin-eas, the King's tableau went for just ten pounds. Finally, Lord George's famous yellow-and-gold barouche was sold for just six guineas. All that remained were a few pieces of scenery and costumes he couldn't get rid of and some ponies he couldn't bear to part with. A few months later, his old friend the auctioneer and former freak-show mogul, Tom Norman, had the consolation prize of arranging the sale of Sanger's menagerie at the Hall by the Sea, Margate. When the last item was sold, George Sanger led everyone in singing *Auld Lang Syne*, then it was over. The next morning Park Farm's housekeeper found the receipts of the sale, including cheques, gold and silver, heaped carelessly on the living room table exactly as George had left them the night before.

George's decision to sell, effectively ending any chance of founding his own circus dynasty, came as a surprise to many people, perhaps even within his own family. He had a business that could still make a profit if it was run properly, the strongest brand name in British circus and a large family including a dozen grandchildren almost entirely groomed in the business from birth. The abdicating king had simply decided that there was no successor worthy of picking up his crown. In January 1908 George retired as Chairman of the Showman's Guild, capping his farewell with a long valedictory speech ending with a downbeat warning: 'We all have winters and summers, but I fear the winter of the travelling show business is now with us.'

Shortly afterwards he sat down with a ghostwriter to document his life story in words. In the memoir, originally serialised in *Lloyd's Weekly* titled *Seventy Years a Showman, my life and adventures in camp and caravan the world over*, George Sanger reprised many of the stories he never wearied of telling. It was published in book format later that year. His unidentified collaborator is assumed to have been George Robert Sims, a prolific and talented Victorian journalist and playwright.[120] Most travelling showmen either didn't or couldn't write, so Sanger's ghosted autobiography was received as a very rare, unfiltered account of life on the road and considered a classic in circus literature.

In his memoir George describes himself as 'the last man on earth to desire to spoil a good story' and he was as good as his word. He was pushing 80 and had never been able to keep a diary of his life on the road, so there were bound to be errors, remembrances dulled with time and no doubt

coloured by ego, but George was also an unabashed connoisseur of tall tales. If he was to be taken at his word, his father had an amazing knack for turning up in the right place at the right time and had seen history unfold before his eyes. In his twilight years, during his endless rounds of speech-making, George invariably began with the tale about how James Sanger fought at Trafalgar and was at the actual scene of Nelson's death on HMS *Victory*, but like many of his stories, it doesn't bear scrutiny. There's an in-joke among naval genealogists; if every family who claimed to have had an ancestor on Nelson's flagship had actually been there, the *Victory* would have sunk under their weight. It's highly unlikely that James Sanger was ever seized by gangers or forced into naval service. In all likelihood, he ran away from home and volunteered to join the navy to escape the drudgery of his apprenticeship and farm chores. The archived muster rolls show that James Sanger did not serve on HMS *Victory* or any other ship at Trafalgar. Nor was there any Royal Prescription conferring special privileges on navy veterans or anything like it. His magical 'Freedom of England' letter was probably an ordinary discharge certificate. According to George, his father also invented the smallpox vaccine, witnessed an infamous murder and had a front-row seat at the last large-scale armed rebellion on mainland Britain.[121] Surprisingly little of his memoir has ever been fact-checked.[122] Historians have also raised a sceptical eyebrow at his claim that Barnum stole from him the three-ring circus. Perhaps the old showman retold these tales over the years so often that he convinced himself they were real. In his memoir George passed off his fake title as a bit of

harmless fun, but his grandson attested that it was done in real anger. Most of all, George loved being around famous people and he was flattered to think of them all as his friends. According to his grandson, he never wearied of telling the story about how he'd taught Charles Dickens to ride a horse. It was another lie, of course.[123] There was also an odd omission. George sorrows over the baby son he lost but does not once acknowledge the existence of either of his daughters, although both were star performers in his circus. Despite the many shortcomings, George's memoir carried enough raw truth to make it a unique and fascinating insight into the trials of the itinerant showman. It was all a bit too raw for some of his fellow entertainers, who were very unhappy about his exposé of certain frauds involved in their industry.

The publication of *Seventy Years a Showman* in 1910 was to have put the seal on the final chapter in the epic, show-stopping life of perhaps the country's most famous and best-loved entertainer, and it seemed that the old showman would finally enjoy the serene and honoured old age he deserved. His memoir concluded with a humble admission: 'I feel that the latter days of my career … have not the interest for my reader that attaches to the earlier period.' But there was a footnote yet to be written, one so incredible that even George Sanger would have blushed to make it up.

16

Hubris

IN 1956 THE WRITER JOHN LUKENS was recovering from the flu when he received a mysterious parcel. It contained a small bundle of manuscript, neatly clipped together and typed on half-quarto sheets. Attached was a note from a friend, expressing the hope that he might find it of interest. The manuscript contained the reminiscences of another famous member of the Sanger circus family, 75-year-old George Sanger Coleman, one of Lord George Sanger's four grandchildren by his daughter Laurina. The content fell far short of a reasonable size book and it was full of technical detail about the circus, but there was something in it, not least the magic of the Sanger name, that made John Lukens want to know more. He arranged to meet the manuscript's author and encountered a little old man, much wasted by illness, with a powerful story to tell. The result of that meeting and many subsequent interviews was their collaboration on *The Sanger Story*, Lukens' ghost-written autobiography of George Sanger Coleman.[124]

Coleman had long since reached the end of a very long and successful career as a circus performer. He was

born in 1875 in a room above the stage door at the famous Astley's and from the age of six he performed as an equestrian, clown and tumbler. He worked all over the world and rubbed shoulders with just about every great showman of that golden era, from P.T. Barnum to 'Buffalo' Bill Cody, but the book is dominated from the first page to the last by his grandfather, the greatest Victorian showman of them all.

George Coleman learned about death at a very early age. He was two years old when his mother Laurina died after an illegal termination, he was six when his older brother Sandy died after swinging on a tent guide rope and falling on his head. Little Georgie and his two sisters Ellen and Georgina were raised by their grandparents and so he was able to offer a unique insight on the life of the man they were brought up to call 'Dadda Sanger'. His grandfather had never learned to write, so the melodramas and pantomimes that entertained Victorian England were dictated and it was young 'Georgie' who was given the job of transcribing them. *The Sanger Story* showed that Georgie dearly loved and was quite in awe of his famous grandfather Lord George, but he doesn't sugar-coat what was often a very difficult relationship.

In his memoir *Seventy Years a Showman*, George Sanger presented himself as an enlightened employer who presided over his entertainment empire with a serene benevolence, a civic-minded patriarch committed to good causes, winning people over with his charm and good humour and his patriotic zeal for monarch and country. In *The Sanger Story* his grandson describes another side of the famous impresario, hitherto unseen by all but his family and those who worked for him. Behind the public smile and the displays

of largesse, you get an authentic account of his grandfather's quick-tempered ruthlessness, of a despotic and unforgiving man so competitive that he would try to drive his own brother out of business; someone completely intolerant of any sign of weakness in his employees, especially when they were members of his own family. Georgie was only too well acquainted with the little malacca cane his grandfather always carried with him. The book is an invaluable reference source for anyone with an interest in Lord George Sanger's life, but it is what Georgie had to say about his grandfather's death that is truly extraordinary.

George Sanger struggled with retirement at Park Farm in East Finchley. After eight decades of travelling in a caravan and moving with the seasons, he wasn't accustomed to laying his head down every day in the same place he woke up. According to one source he slept in a coffin-sized box so he could enjoy the familiar feel of wood knocking against his elbows.[125] But in his new life as a farm owner, some things remained the same. George's writ was absolute. He expected his farm hands to put in the long hours and high energy once displayed by his lion tamers and trapeze artists. Life at Park Farm was a daily ordeal for the staff. They were bewildered and occasionally terrorised by their elderly employer's whims and autocratic behaviour. Everyone was expected to address him as 'my Lord'. It confirmed the suspicion that after years spent successfully presenting himself as a member of the peerage, George too was convinced he was the genuine article. If one of the workhands had reason to call at the farmhouse, perhaps to deliver a message, his Lordship would offer them a meal. If the employee declined his offer, he

would command: 'Sit down, damn you, and eat!' Employees crept by the main house, fearful that the old man would catch their eye and embroil them in some crazy scheme or other. He was easily bored and would often find some outlet for his energies in bizarre and unpredictable ways. One day he unexpectedly announced his return to show business. *Mazeppa*, a spectacular horse-based drama usually featuring a cast of several hundred animals and performers, had been one of his greatest showbiz triumphs and George felt the urge for another shot at glory. He was planning to stage a new production of the show in a music hall in East Ham, a fantastic and lavish spectacle with the set alone costing 2,000 pounds to build – in today's values about a quarter-of-a-million pounds. It was so big that a special train was needed to transport the materials to East Ham. But in his confusion, the old showman had every piece of scenery and equipment built at a scale to accommodate the vast stage at the old Astley's. Less than a quarter of it would fit the tiny stage at East Ham.[126] When he realised his mistake, George announced that the hippodrama would be staged in his own farmyard instead. All of the farm hands were obliged to perform as actors, George himself wearing a long false beard and playing the important role of Abder Khan. There were tense moments when, as the old man was in full flow declaiming one of Khan's great speeches, an employee forgot himself and burst out laughing.

Another manifestation of George's steadily loosening grip on reality was his huge collection of handsome silver trophies. They were once part of his show parade, displayed in an enormous glass case on wheels drawn by cream horses.

George told everyone the trophies were gifts from the crowned heads of Europe and they were labelled accordingly. But he had in fact bought all the silverware himself. His grandson recalled writing out the cheque for him to sign when part of the collection arrived. Before the ink was dry, George was telling everyone that they were gifts from his many admirers.

His famous acts of generosity became more erratic. When one of Harriet's daughters got married, it was a huge, lavish affair. Everyone was expecting George to provide his granddaughter with a more than generous wedding present, as was his custom. There was embarrassment all round when he presented the bride and groom with a couple of cheap, terracotta busts, one of himself and one of Nellie, which he had dug out of his attic and hand-painted gold.

One Sunday morning a farmhand went to the Park Farm stables and discovered that several horses were missing, presumably stolen. George was alarmed by the incident, which at the very minimum demonstrated that none of his employees had noticed a gang of intruders on the farm. Everyone assumed the matter would be reported to the local police, but George did nothing. He may have been a card-carrying Conservative, but he didn't trust or cooperate with the police. Never did and never would.

His eccentricities, as his family saw them, became more marked. George's lifelong obsession with birds was well known: he had always travelled with a small aviary in his living caravan, sharing a space with up to fourteen larks, two canaries and a jackdaw. The latter's favourite perch was George's silk top hat. In January 1907 his friends and family

were puzzled when each received a postcard with a photograph of the retired showman standing against a sundial with a parrot perched on his hand, taken in front of a backcloth of a woodland scene. On the back of the postcard was printed:

Please to accept this with my very kindest regards, taken on my 80th birthday, 23 December 1907. I sincerely wish you a Long, Prosperous and Happy Life. LORD GEORGE SANGER*

One day his grandson came to visit and found that the old man had redecorated the living room at Park Farm in bizarre fashion with wallpaper printed with massive peacocks. The room was ablaze with blue-green birds, many of them upside down. He hadn't removed any of the many pictures on the walls and had simply papered around them.

Even as the years advanced, he cut a striking figure. He maintained his lithe, compact frame and was rarely less than immaculately dressed in his silk top hat and frock coat. Retirement had barely lowered his standards and he groomed himself each morning as though preparing to receive his public. It was only in the last two years of his life that he stopped wearing his top hat indoors. The ubiquitous topper gave way to a bowler hat, bought for tuppence at the Caledonian Market in Islington. He occasionally travelled there in style in his carriage, drawn by two miniature piebald horses and surmounted by his liveried coachman Harry Grierson, known to all as 'Fairy'. A couple of times a year

---

* He was 82 years old.

George went to Margate to visit his daughter Harriet and his wife's grave. His progress on these occasions was like a mini show parade, the old man reclining in his golden landau, waving his silk topper as though he was royalty, acknowledging his admiring subjects. On the trips to Islington market and to Margate he was generally accompanied by his valet, young Herbert.

෴

Herbert Cooper was born in Beckenham, Kent, in 1887, the year of Queen Victoria's Golden Jubilee. His parents were from Buckinghamshire, his father Thomas born in Ludgershall, his mother Jane in nearby Grendon. They both went to, and probably met at, the new National school in Butt Street. They married in their early twenties and moved to Bromley in Kent where Thomas made a living as a dairy farm worker. In 1880 the Coopers had a daughter, Mabel. She was the first of six children, followed by Carrie two years later, then Thomas junior, Herbert, Florrie, who went by the nickname 'Dick', then finally George, known to the family by his middle name Leonard. In 1882 the family moved to Beckenham, where Thomas senior became a reasonably successful dairy farmer. When the 1891 census was taken, he was running his own dairy farm just a couple of miles away in Wickham Road, Bromley. At that time the family was sufficiently well-off to afford their own sixteen-year-old live-in servant, but Thomas Cooper saw good times and bad at the farm. A recent outbreak of pleuropneumonia struck the national dairy herd and many cows and calves had to be slaughtered. Presumably the Coopers' business did not

thrive, because for reasons unknown they moved to a house in Manor Park Road, East Finchley, where Thomas took a job as a bailiff at Park Farm working for a dairyman called Edmund Gunning. Jane Cooper also took on a housekeeping role for the farm owner. To the family's huge relief, when George Sanger bought Park Farm he kept Thomas Cooper on as his farm bailiff for a wage of 29 shillings a week, but his wife Jane died in February 1906, aged 46 years old. By this time their two eldest daughters had left home and Thomas was alone with three sons and the youngest daughter. The youngest of the three Cooper boys, Leonard, took a job as a butcher's apprentice working for Pulham & Sons. Leonard's employer Samuel Pulham had seventeen businesses in and around Finchley and showed off his considerable wealth by buying Elmhurst, the grandest of all the big houses on East End Road.

The two eldest sons, Thomas junior and Herbert, were employed to look after the farm owner's horses. When the 1911 census came around the family occupied the cottage across the road from Park Farm and the Cooper household comprised Thomas senior, Thomas junior age 26, Herbert 24, Florrie nineteen and Leonard age sixteen.

Thomas's second-eldest son Herbert was taller and slimmer than his father but had his dad's broad shoulders and thick, muscular arms. He also enjoyed a drink at The Five Bells where he met his friends and talked about horse racing. Herbert liked a flutter, but as his acquaintance Charlie Norton would tell the press later, he didn't bet heavily, he was fonder of whist drives. Herbert was an enigma. The press would later describe him as unpredictable, unstable

and violent, but most of the people who knew him well found him quiet, courteous and personable.

George Sanger was fond of both of the Cooper boys, but he was particularly indulgent towards Herbert. The old man was impressed by his smartness and good manners. He probably taught Herbert a few circus moves. Neighbours recalled seeing the youth performing tricks on a bicycle around the farm. He was a fast and willing pupil and picked them up easily. Herbert was soon promoted to the post of personal attendant to 'the Guv'nor'.

The old showman's vivacious, talkative, granddaughter Ellen was intrigued with Herbert too. This was George Coleman's elder sister. Ellen was four when their mother Laurina died. Previously one of the most famous clowns in the Victorian circus, after the death of George and Ellen's mother, Alexander Coleman drank to excess and the touch of comic genius left him. He was crippled by one of the leaps that so delighted his audience, having landed awkwardly after entering the ring at Astley's one day with one of his trademark high somersaults. His light never shone again.[127] Ellen and her brother and sister didn't understand why their father was an increasingly distant figure in their lives, but the reason for his absence was clear to anyone familiar with Alexander Coleman's acrimonious relationship with his father-in-law. George Sanger despised him from the day he eloped with his favourite daughter and he blamed him for her death. George Coleman's last memory of his father was when he turned up at Astley's out of the blue one day with a woman. There was an almighty row between his father and his grandfather – the young boy didn't understand why.

His father left and never returned. Alexander 'Little Sandy' Coleman drank himself to an early grave and died aged 53.

George Sanger had eight grandchildren by his two daughters, but Ellen was always the apple of his eye. Confusingly, both Laurina Sanger and her daughter Ellen were known professionally and within the family as 'Topsy'. George showed his affection for his favoured granddaughter by spoiling her. On her birthday every 1 May, George threw a huge party at which Ellen was seated on a tall throne with a glittering tiara on her head and was crowned the May Queen. Ellen spent money easily and ran up bills, but she could always rely on her grandfather to bail her out. She soon became an asset to the family business as a good all-round circus acrobat, on horseback, on the high wire and on the tightrope, where she excelled. While all sweetness and grace in the ring, she was a firecracker outside it. Ellen had her grandfather's hot temper and she and her sister Georgina fought with horse whips and anything else that came to hand.

Ellen enjoyed her reputation as the best looking of the sisters and she grew up to be a ringer for her late mother, petite, dark-haired and voluptuous. She was eighteen when 24-year-old John Henry 'Harry' Austin came to work for Sanger's Circus. Harry and his younger brother George were the sons of a circus acrobat from Liverpool. They were trick riders and together they performed a double jockey act. One stood on the horse's back while it galloped round the ring with the other on his shoulders. The Brothers Austin were famous in Europe and all over North America and would work with Sanger's Circus for over 30 years, to the bitter end.

Harry Austin was small, slight and likeable. A photographer captured Harry and George in one of the publicity photos, where he has a boyishly handsome, earnest face and a large walrus moustache. Everyone in the Sanger family was delighted when he and Ellen were married. The union quickly produced three daughters, Florence in 1896, followed by Victoria, who died in infancy, then in July 1898 Georgina, known to all as Cissy. In 1909 they had another daughter, Winifred Olive.

Although Harry Austin was now a member of George Sanger's family he remained in complete awe – and like most people was also slightly terrified of – 'the Guv'nor'. To some degree Harry had a similar relationship with his wife Ellen, because there is no doubt she wore the trousers in the Austin household.

George Coleman was 8,000 miles away in South Africa when his grandfather died. He was in a Johannesburg teashop when he saw the newspaper headline:

LORD GEORGE SANGER
MURDERED
ASSASSIN AT LARGE

He could scarcely believe his eyes. Over the next week, more details appeared in the press and each day the story seemed to the grandson more unbelievable than the last. He had no reason to doubt the basic facts of the case as he and everyone else had received them from the newspaper reports, that

someone had murdered his grandfather in a callous, cold-blooded attack and had attempted to kill two more members of the household. But something didn't sit right with George Coleman. The Herbert Cooper that emerged in the press was at odds with the young man Coleman knew very well. The Cooper family were good people, loyal employees and liked by all of the Sanger family. Herbert Cooper had been treated by his grandfather more like a son than a servant. The idea that Herbert was capable of harming the old man, yet alone killing him, was as bewildering as it was disturbing. The grandson was haunted by a nagging feeling that the full story hadn't been told, but he was several thousand miles away and it was weeks before he was able to talk to his family to try to make some sense of it all. When he got home to East Finchley he found out that his suspicions were justified.

17

The valet

BY JANUARY 1912, the violent deaths of George Sanger and his presumed assassin Herbert Charles Cooper were already fading from public memory. The popular press had wrung the story dry and moved on. The nation was absorbed with the dispiriting news that the British polar explorer Robert Falcon Scott and his team of four had reached the South Pole only to find that the Norwegian Roald Amundsen had easily beaten them to it. Elsewhere, New Mexico became the 47th state of the Union and Alfred Wegener had presented a new and startling theory of continental drift. A new Republic of China was created, while in Russia, Vladimir Lenin and his followers formed a new breakaway Bolshevik party. The old world was passing.

In early January, just over a month after the funeral of his grandfather, George Coleman returned from South Africa to the shaken household at Park Farm. He'd had a couple of months over which to ponder the savagery of the crime against his grandfather and all the grisly evidence he had read about in the newspapers. Now he had many questions. When he sat down with his family, they revealed to him in

confidence information which had been withheld from the public. A whole new story began to unfold, and although not as horrific in every detail as the account told in the press, it troubled him much more than anything he had read.

From first-hand accounts, George Coleman was able to piece together what happened in the final few weeks leading to the tragedy on the evening of 28th November.

After the death of Nellie Sanger, a notable eccentricity of George's life at Park Farm was his increasing dependence on a valet or 'nurse attendant'. It was not because of infirmity or any particular need for someone to take care of him – he was still very independent and age-defyingly sprightly. George simply craved company. He was grieving for his wife and in his final years he was heartbreakingly lonely. His grandson recalled visiting Park Farm one day to find the old man, having taken up his usual position on a chair to the right of the drawing room hearth, staring deep into the large fire. George explained that he'd been reading all about the new craze for spiritualism. At the time, the whole country seemed engaged in the hunt for proof of an afterlife. The late Queen herself was rumoured to have consulted often with a medium who claimed to be in touch with her dear dead husband. George said he searched daily for some sign from Nellie, but it wasn't working.

George tried to fill the gap in his life with some young male employee or other who he would more or less adopt as a son. This relationship followed a predictable course. He would quickly form a very close attachment with his new favourite, shower him with presents and take him wherever he went. In Herbert Cooper's case at least, this intimacy

included sharing a bedroom. Then just as quickly, George would drop him and replace him with another. This was the fate of Herbert Cooper, usurped in Sanger's affections by Arthur Jackson, just as surely as Herbert himself had been a substitute for someone else. One day he was the old man's special friend, the next he was effectively ostracised, excommunicated from the Park Farm inner sanctum.

In Arthur Jackson's case, 'young' was a relative concept. According to his military record he was 38 years old, born in Hampstead in Middlesex. He gave his occupation as a former infantryman in the 2nd Royal Fusiliers, also known as the City of London Regiment. The 1891 census finds Jackson as a nineteen-year-old private stationed at the Shaft Barracks at Hougham near Dover. When he was 29 years old his regiment sailed from Gibraltar to the South African Cape to fight in the second Anglo-Boer War. The brigade was present at Colenso, where the British were heavily defeated and were lucky to take few casualties. Later Jackson's regiment was part of the drive to relieve Ladysmith and Mafeking and the capture of Pieter's Hill. By 1902 the British had crushed the Boer resistance, and in June that year Jackson's unit sailed home, but it had been an unpopular war and there was little mood for celebration.

Beyond that, Jackson's life is a closed book. Further proof of his army record, for example, doesn't appear to exist. Perhaps he lied about his age when he signed up, maybe he was using someone else's name. One way or another it makes it impossible to separate him from a hundred or more Arthur Jacksons. There's little else to discover about the man himself, but we can draw some conclusions

from the few available facts. The late-Victorian Army was the poor relation of the Navy and had more than its fair share of desperate unemployed. It's likely the young Jackson was picked up by one of the many recruiting sergeants that haunted public houses. With little education or professional skills, his return to civvy street would have been difficult and he was most likely cast in the role of drifter, without a settled life, someone who changed jobs frequently. No doubt he could read well enough, and you imagine he knew how to dress smartly, how to be charming and that he possessed a knack for conversation, all traits that would have endeared him to his new master. George was needy and susceptible to flattery. Jackson was used to obeying orders and George liked that as well.

As revealed at the coroner's inquest, the precipitous decline in Herbert Cooper's status was triggered by an alleged theft. George Sanger voiced his suspicions explicitly to Harry Austin, but also made it perfectly clear to everyone in the household that he believed Herbert Cooper was the culprit. Whenever Cooper was within earshot, Sanger would say: 'You know, I could put my hands on the very chap that took that money.' At this, he would turn and look Cooper up and down.

George's grandson did not believe that any money had been stolen. He was convinced that the allegation of theft against Cooper was another unfortunate sign of his grandfather's increasing eccentricity – today we might call it dementia. He didn't for one moment think that his grandfather was being deliberately malicious, he was simply not in his right mind. Whether it was meant or not, the effect

on Herbert Cooper was the same, and the employee's distress was apparent to everyone. The casually cruel remarks, with Cooper constantly made an object of public contempt by George Sanger and by other members of the household, continued in this grim fashion for several weeks. Finally, in desperation, Cooper confronted his employer. If George Sanger really thought he had stolen the money, then they should go to the police together and put the matter in their hands. Sanger flatly refused to cooperate. He told Cooper that if the police were involved, he would simply deny that any money had been stolen.

A local police sergeant told Harry Austin later that Herbert Cooper did go to Finchley Station and he reported that Sanger had lost 50 pounds and that he had accused him of theft. Cooper begged them to investigate. The police agreed to do so, but only if George Sanger would agree to prosecute if proof was found that there had been an actual theft. This was a condition that Cooper, the police and everyone else knew the old man would never meet. There had been thefts at Park Farm before, including that of the horses, but the owner wouldn't report the crimes. The local constabulary had no interest in getting involved in another time-wasting exercise and so the opportunity to prove Herbert Cooper's innocence was denied him. However uncomfortable the situation was, it was soon to become a lot worse.

When the census was taken in April 1911, Ellen and Harry Austin had been married for twelve years. At the time Harry was working in North America and Ellen was living at Park Farm. Their children meanwhile were staying with their aunt Agnes, the wife of Harry's brother George,

in Kitchener Road, East Finchley. We don't know what caused this arrangement, but perhaps whenever Harry was away, Ellen would keep her grandfather company while her sister-in-law took care of the children. She stayed at the farm again later in the year while Harry was in hospital following a routine procedure. When Harry came home, he heard that Herbert Cooper was having an affair with his wife.

George Coleman speculated that the dalliance probably started after the family turned against Cooper. Herbert was desperately in need of a friend and Ellen Austin offered more than tea and sympathy. Coleman knew his sister well and his sympathies were entirely with Cooper. Herbert was 24 years old, still living with his parents, fond of whist drives. Ellen was a sexually predatory 33-year-old woman and a mother of three.

After the theft allegation, Cooper was allowed to continue his old job as a farmhand, but he was banned from the house. Park Farm's live-in servant Jane Beesley put the cat among the pigeons when she found Herbert using a spare bedroom adjacent to Ellen's room while her husband was away. She told Harry Austin's brother George. There was a showdown between Ellen and Harry. Ellen denied all but agreed to tell Herbert Cooper that he should never again visit the farmhouse.

When Herbert lost his job as George's personal valet, instead of returning to his family home just across the road, he'd fixed up a living space for himself in one of the farm outbuildings and furnished it with some old theatrical props. Whether it was wounded pride that prevented him from going home, or he did this because it made it easier for him to

keep his clandestine affair alive, is moot. Most people in the household knew about Cooper's den and turned a blind eye.

Meanwhile, Harry Austin and Arthur Jackson continued to goad Cooper about the stolen money at every opportunity. It must have seemed to the 24 year old that the world had turned against him. It was in this state of mind that he and Arthur Jackson crossed paths in the kitchen of Park Farm at 5.45pm on 28 November 1911. According to George Coleman, this is what happened next, as described to him confidentially by Harry Austin.

Herbert Cooper told Arthur Jackson that he'd come to pick up his gramophone. Jackson called him 'a thieving bastard' (probably the author's cleaned up version) adding, 'what else have you come to steal?' Jackson's taunt was one too many and Cooper snapped. In a kitchen cupboard there were several cut-throat razors. Cooper grabbed one of the razors and slashed at Jackson's throat. As the two men grappled, Jackson screamed. From the sitting room, Austin heard the noise, went to the door and shouted down the passage, 'What's going on there?' On hearing Austin's voice, driven perhaps by sheer rage and jealousy, Cooper charged towards it, seizing as he went a full-size felling axe that was leaning against the passage wall. In the drawing room, a fight broke out between Cooper and Austin. Even at his great age, George still had an appetite for confrontation – perhaps even a relish for it. He sprang from his chair and joined in the fray. The old man grabbed a bronze candelabra from the mantlepiece and lashed at Cooper. Cooper saw the blow coming and deflected it with his arm. The heavy ornament accidentally caught Sanger on the side of his head. The old

man reeled backwards, hitting his head on the edge of the table as he fell. The next thing anyone knew, George Sanger lay motionless on the floor.

There were more revelations. Harry Austin confided to Coleman that the injuries inflicted by Cooper as reported in the press had been very much exaggerated. Jackson's wounds were the most superficial. When Cooper went at him with the razor, his neck had been mostly protected by his high, stiff shirt collar and he shed some blood, but only the amount you would expect from a razor nick. Harry Austin also confessed that his own injuries amounted to no more than a few bruises.

Was George Coleman's retelling of the story completely reliable? On one point it diverged a great deal from the version heard at the coroner's inquiry. He was told that his grandfather's injuries were also less extensive than was reported. Contradicting the depositions provided by Dr Orr and others at the scene, Coleman heard that his grandfather was stunned by the blow on the head from the candelabra, but he seemed to have recovered and was 'quite normal' for a while. He refused help and went to his room, undressed himself and went to bed unassisted. This was completely at odds with other witness statements which confirmed that the elderly victim was barely conscious and had to be carried from the drawing room to his bedroom. There was a lengthy delay before the attack was reported to the police, enough time perhaps for the old man to have rallied temporarily. In classic brain haemorrhages resulting from blunt trauma injury it is not unusual for there to be a period between accident and death when the victim appears to be recovering.

According to Harry Austin, Herbert Cooper didn't immediately flee from Park Farm after the attack, as the police and everyone else had been led to believe. He returned to his den in the outbuilding and stayed there for some time, at least long enough to scribble two suicide notes, before disappearing into the darkness. Everyone at the farm knew where he was hiding and felt sorry for him, but no one dared go near.

For the Sanger family, Herbert Cooper's suicide was convenient. There would be no trial, no awkward questions asked about the way he was bullied, or about Ellen Austin's alleged extramarital affair and the disgrace that might bring. Any remorse they may have felt about Cooper's death was outweighed by relief that the matter was closed. Harry Austin admitted that he lied to the police and perjured himself in the coroner's court because the family was 'frightened by what a trial might reveal'.[128] The grandson assumed Austin was referring to his wife's affair and that everyone was trying to protect her.

Harry Austin also knew that the stolen 50 pounds was most likely a figment of George Sanger's confused imagination and that Cooper had never intended to harm the old man. Austin regretted that the family hadn't come clean about what happened and they had hoped the story would go away.

Herbert Cooper's suicide would weigh heavily on his conscience for many years afterwards, but he and subsequent generations of the Sanger family remained tight-lipped about their knowledge of the alleged murder at Park Farm and a code of silence prevailed. The events of 28 November 1911

were a private family matter, something best forgotten; old ghosts should not be disturbed. George Coleman wrestled with his conscience for many years before he told the family's secret to the author John Lukens, hoping at least that the book would ensure that for future generations the story would be told differently. But when *The Sanger Story* was published in 1956, Harry Austin's confession that Cooper had been wrongfully accused of murder for the sake of the family's reputation went largely unnoticed. The revelation was just a footnote in the reminiscences of an elderly retired circus entertainer, a book that received little attention. The original version of events, as determined by the coroner's inquest and reported in the world's press, that Lord George Sanger had been slain by a crazed employee named Herbert Cooper, proved impossible to erase.

The Sanger Story didn't right a wrong, but at least it was a step in the right direction, an acknowledgment that George Sanger's death was an unfortunate accident. Most people would probably agree that death by hitting yourself over the head with a candelabra while grappling with someone hefting an axe is, by any stretch of the imagination, a very peculiar and unfortunate way to go, more farce than tragedy. The author John Lukens and his source George Coleman had no reason to doubt Austin's account – he was the only person in the room at the time who lived to tell the tale – and as far as they were concerned, that was the end of that. The last chapter in this story was written.

Except it wasn't, because someone was obviously lying.

18

In plain sight

AFTER THE CORONER'S INQUEST into the deaths of George Sanger and Herbert Cooper, the original police files on the Sanger murder enquiry were closed. All of the details of the investigation, including the written statements, the forensic evidence, Scotland Yard's internal documents and the coroner's inquest report were hidden from public view for 75 years. Now more than 110 years old, these records held in the National Archives at Kew and at the London Metropolitan Archives at Farringdon are open for public scrutiny. The documents contain information that John Lukens did not have access to when he wrote *The Sanger Story*. When put together, they provide a compelling new insight into the murder, suggesting that something altogether more sinister took place at Park Farm on the evening of 28 November 1911.

The public never knew about Herbert Cooper's alleged affair with Ellen Austin. The press had failed to appreciate the significance of it. At the coroner's inquest, Jane Beesley's testimony that Harry Austin had accused his wife of having an affair with the murderer was not picked up or reported by any newspaper. *The Times* alone made an oblique reference

to a 'familiarity' between Cooper and a woman who was not named. The affair was also known to the police – Jane Beesley had mentioned it in the statement she gave them – but they didn't seem to think it was important.

There was one part of the coroner Dr. Cohen's examination of Arthur Jackson to which the press, while noting, also attached little value. This brief, seemingly perfunctory exchange was, in fact, a significant moment in the proceedings. In his original statement to the police, Arthur Jackson went into great detail about what he saw. After Cooper attacked him, he said he watched as his assailant charged down the hallway, wielding an axe, towards the drawing room where Austin and Sanger were sitting. Jackson said he shouted after him and followed down the hallway, but had stopped short of going into the drawing room because he had blood on his clothing.

In the formal surroundings of the coroner's court, Jackson offered an alternative version. He said that he had been knocked temporarily unconscious and had did not know where Cooper went after he left the kitchen. In fact he had no recollection of anything after he regained consciousness, he hadn't seen the assault on his employer or been near the drawing room. He could only remember leaving the farmhouse to summon help.

This leaves Harry Austin as the only living person who was in the drawing room when the assaults took place. It was his word against that of Herbert Cooper, the man he suspected was sleeping with his wife.

Harry Austin was also less sure of his facts at the inquest. In his deposition to the police, he said that he had been

stunned by a blow to the head from Cooper's axe, but just before he passed out, he definitely saw Cooper standing over Sanger with his arm raised, holding an axe, then saw him bring it down. Under interrogation from the coroner his story changed. Austin said he didn't see what happened to Sanger because the old man was behind him. He was only aware of seeing him lying on the floor afterwards. It was a considerable step back from his original statement.

One very important aspect of Harry Austin's story as revealed in John Lukens' book is corroborated by the case records. The blood-stained brass ornament found lying on the drawing room floor was mentioned twice in the police reports and was obviously significant, but it was not spoken of at all at the coroner's inquest. An autopsy had revealed that George Sanger died as result of blunt-force trauma to his head, but there was no evidence to definitively state that he had died from a blow from an axe. Nor was the injury to George Sanger's head as described by the Home Office pathologist Bernard Spilsbury – the Y-shaped indention to the skull and several hairline fractures – consistent with the injuries you might expect from a blow to the head from an axe blade. Spilsbury's unconvincing explanation was that perhaps the blunt end of the axe was used, but even then it would surely have crushed the old man's skull and killed him instantly. Spilsbury's account went unchallenged. Wasn't it much more likely that the wound was caused by the blood-ied brass ornament found on the floor near the body? The coroner didn't ask, therefore Spilsbury didn't speculate. Spilsbury also mentioned the defensive injuries he found on George Sanger's hands and legs. They suggested that the

old man had been in a fight, but the coroner did not pursue this line of enquiry either.

The supposed weapon, the axe, was literally the most striking feature of the whole case. There is something uniquely dreadful about the slow, blunt power of an axe that makes it a potent symbol of unspeakable evil. So powerful is this imagery that in the public imagination an axe murderer is a uniquely deranged and merciless killer. The graphic newspaper reports of the old showman hacked down and lying amid puddles of blood in his drawing room sent shivers down the spine and lived long in the memories of everyone who read them.

Axe murders are the stuff of horror films, but they are extraordinarily rare events in real life. The people who lived in that time and read the press reports would have recognised how unusual it was for someone to be murdered with an axe in their own home. They may have heard the name Lizzie Borden, the young American woman who was accused of butchering her parents in the case that abides as one of the most famous in American criminal history. The horrible identity of the alleged murderer is immortalised by the children's rhyme passed down across generations.

> Lizzie Borden took an axe,
> And gave her mother forty whacks.
> When she saw what she had done
> She gave her father forty-one.

Axe murderers like Lizzie Borden may be prominent in the imaginations of people who write murder fiction, but she was exceptional.

In fact, the Lizzie Borden rhyme is incorrect in one very important detail. A small hatchet, rather than an axe, served as her actual weapon. The distinction is not known to many, but it is a key one.

The axe allegedly used by Herbert Cooper to injure Harry Austin was a large felling axe, the kind you would use to a chop down a tree. They work by being very heavy, the weight giving the axe momentum at the point it hits the target. The head of a typical felling axe weighs around four– five pounds. This makes it a very slow and cumbersome murder weapon. Depending on the strength of the person using it, it can take at least five and up to ten seconds to lift and swing a large felling axe.

We've already established that British axe murders were very rare. Coincidentally, however, around this time there were a series of notorious axe attacks in America known as the Villisca murders. It's not our story, but it's worth mentioning because it is relevant.

Shortly after midnight on 10 June 1912, a stranger hefting an axe entered the back door of a two-story timber house in the little Iowa town of Villisca and bludgeoned to death six children and two adults. At the time the crime was thought to have been an isolated incident. Subsequently, however, it was linked to a spate of axe murders across America, involving perhaps as many as a hundred victims including the slaughter of entire households, mostly in the Midwest, during the first two decades of the 20th century. The signature element of the crime was that the murderer always struck with a heavy felling axe, usually the blunt side. The case was never solved. There was no FBI, no federal crime

databases and most investigations were left to small-town police or private detectives. Forensic science as we know it didn't exist and fingerprint records were still in their infancy. Crime scenes were regularly overrun by nosy neighbours who inadvertently tampered with evidence. For one reason or another, somehow the killer always slipped under the radar. However, the investigation yielded a great deal of information about the mechanics and consequences of axe attacks. Thanks to the anonymous Villisca axe murderer, we know quite a lot about what actually happens when someone is hit over the head with a large felling axe.

Felling axes have very long handles because a great deal of leverage is needed for chopping down big trees and other heavy work. You need a lot of room to swing one, at least an 'axe-length' – that's the length of the handle and blade plus the length of the arm. Harry Austin said that Herbert Cooper struck him on the top of the head, so it would have required a vertical swing, a downward chopping motion. He would have needed a lot of clearance space above his head. It is believed that the Villisca axe murderer was very short. This is generally held to be true because when he swung the axe over his head – the killer was assumed to be male because of the brute strength required to swing a heavy axe – it only grazed the ceiling, whereas if he had been of average height or taller, the axe would have taken a chunk out of it. Herbert Cooper was over six-foot tall.

When an axe of this size hits a skull, the weight of the axe transfers to the entire skull and the skull invariably shatters. The immediate cause of death is extensive brain contusion following fragmentation of the neurocranium. However,

the momentum of a such a powerful weapon is such that it would not only pass through the entire skull, but most likely the tissue beneath it as well. Some of the Villisca murder victims left fragments of their brains on the murder weapon and on the ceiling. To put it bluntly, if someone hits you over the head with a felling axe you are immediately dead. You are not going to live to tell the police about it. Despite his reputation as a forensics superhero, it's clear that Dr Bernard Spilsbury had never seen a body hit hard in the head with a heavy felling axe and had no idea how completely a human head could be destroyed by one blow.

Picture the scene playing itself out in the drawing room. According to Harry Austin at the inquest, Cooper swung the axe at his head at least three times. Since the axe was heavy and took several seconds to swing, assuming that Austin didn't just stand there waiting to be hit, he had plenty of time to react and try to evade the blows raining down on him. It follows that there must have been some kind of murderous, desperate chase around the parlour. The police reports mention signs of a scuffle – a broken clock, a few shards of glass on the floor, a damaged hat, some fire irons knocked into the grate – but none of the chaos you would expect to find after a man has chased another around the room with an axe. In the kitchen too, where Cooper was alleged to have fought Arthur Jackson, apart from the discovery of the razor on the floor, the police reports made no mention of any sign of a fight, let alone the drama described by Jackson.

Another thing that the Villisca axe murders taught us is that when a person hits another person on the head with an axe there is going to be flying blood. Not just a few specks,

a lot. By 1911 experts had learned to analyse blood patterns. Blood droplets falling from a height of several feet make a larger splash pattern than those falling from only a few inches. Those falling straight down produce a round splatter, while those falling from a body in motion produce an oblong splash, with the narrower part of the drop indicating the direction. Contrary to the lurid press reports, there was very little blood spilled at Park Farm that evening, just a small amount on the floor where George Sanger fell, on the edge of the table and on the base of the brass candle holder. Curiously, there was no blood found on any other surfaces at the crime scene.

These may seem like two very obvious questions, but they didn't occur to the police or the coroner or any of his jury.

1. If Harry Austin was hit three times with a heavy felling axe, why were there no tell-tale spatterings of blood?
2. Why were his injuries so trivial?

There is one telling detail hidden among the police files that may explain why.

The police report states that the murder weapon was not discovered until 2am the following morning, more than eight hours after the assault. It was found in the drawing room, resting in a shallow recess in the wall to the right of the fireplace. In other words, it was right under their noses all along, a matter of a few feet from where George Sanger fell. The police files also reveal another even more curious fact. The discovery of the axe was made, not by a policeman, but

by George Sanger's brother-in-law James Holloway, who handed it in to an officer.

How was it possible that a room full of police officers investigating a crime scene spent six hours without noticing the very large axe they were specifically searching for, and only then when it was delivered to them by a member of the Sanger family? Did it strike the police as odd that the murderer, before fleeing into the night, had made some attempt to conceal the weapon in a recess next to the fireplace? Why did he try to hide it where it could be very easily found? Why not take it with him? Why hide it at all when there were potentially three witnesses to the attack? The senior police investigating team didn't consider any of these questions. Perhaps they thought Herbert Cooper was simply a very tidy killer.

According to the police report, there was blood on the axe, but it could have been anybody's – Sanger's, Cooper's, Austin's or Jackson's. In 1911 even Bernard Spilsbury didn't have the technology to differentiate blood types. Had the blood on this axe been tested to prove that it was human blood and not from a farm animal? If it had, there is no mention of it in the police files or in the coroner's report.

There was also something very odd about Harry Austin's comment to George Coleman that he knew Herbert Cooper never wanted to deliberately harm the old man. After all, according to Austin, Cooper took a heavy felling axe to a fight in a parlour. It was a terrifying, imprecise weapon capable of murderous mayhem. Surely the man wielding it bore responsibility for the outcome.

None of it made any sense, unless the axe was planted after the fact.

19

False witness

HERBERT COOPER'S NEMESIS was a housemaid who knew more than she could be persuaded to tell, or told more than she actually knew.

Jane Beesley was a 42-year-old spinster, born in Crosby, Lancashire, the youngest daughter of Joseph Beesley, a Liverpudlian watchmaker and his wife Anne. Jane had a close connection to the Sanger family through her sister Agnes, who was married to Harry Austin's brother George. The couple lived in nearby Kitchener Road and often looked after Harry and Ellen Austin's children when their parents were working.

In 1911 Jane Beesley was one of a shrinking army of 1.27 million indoor domestic servants. Her position was unenviable. Employing a servant was a sign of respectability, but for households where money was tighter, it was often the case that they could only afford one – the 'maid of all work'. Dwindling servant numbers reflected the fact that there were new opportunities in factories and shops, where workers received something unheard of in domestic service – evenings and weekends off. Jane Beesley was on call at Park Farm six-and-a-half days a week, with only half a day

to herself. For most in her situation it was a life of relentless drudgery. She was in an odd situation, related to the Sanger family by marriage, yet also expected to wait on them hand and foot, cleaning, washing, tidying and cooking. This seems to have bred a certain amount of resentment, at least enough to make her interfere in a matter that was none of her business and snoop on her mistress.

Jane Beesley had been working in the Sanger household for sixteen months and was well-placed to know at least some intimate details of the Austin marriage. We know that Harry Austin's job took him away from home for long periods. When he was away, the children stayed with their aunt Agnes while Ellen Austin slept at Park Farm alone. Recently, Harry had also spent some time in hospital. It is less clear what Jane Beesley actually saw. She hadn't found Ellen Austin and Herbert Cooper naked together in the bedroom, but she had seen him hanging around in the vicinity of Ellen's bedroom in a manner that she deemed inappropriate. A man visiting a married woman alone in her house while her husband was away was bound to start tongues wagging. The housemaid voiced her suspicions to her brother-in-law George, who relayed them to Harry. Later, while outside their bedroom door, the housemaid overheard a quarrel erupt between Harry and Ellen.

In one of his two suicide notes – that addressed to Harry Austin – Herbert Cooper denied any improper relations with Ellen Austin. He informed his former friend that he was 'sorry it came to this'. The polite, restrained tone seems strangely at odds with the situation he found himself in. It was not really what you would expect from someone who,

just a couple of hours earlier, was supposed to have been chasing Austin round the parlour trying to smash his head in with an axe. In the note, Herbert Cooper's anger is directed at Jane Beesley for her 'lies' and to a lesser extent at her brother-in-law George for spreading gossip.

Perhaps Herbert did have an affair with Ellen Austin. It's also possible he did not. George Coleman concluded that there was an affair and that Herbert was also protecting Ellen's honour. We can't say for sure. The only important thing is that Harry Austin believed, or at least strongly suspected, that Herbert Cooper was sleeping with his wife.

We don't know if George Sanger was ever aware of his favourite granddaughter's alleged adultery. It seems very likely that he was spared the details. Herbert Cooper was still working for him and had George known what was going on under his own roof he surely would have kicked Cooper off the farm, or worse. Conceivably, Harry Austin had long suspected something was going on between Cooper and his wife and he planted the idea in George Sanger's head that Cooper was a thief so that he would get rid of him. That way, he could avoid the embarrassment of having to explain his wife's infidelity. But George Sanger didn't get rid of Cooper, he kept him on. His continued presence around the farm was surely more than Harry Austin could bear.

It isn't a stretch to imagine Arthur Jackson colluding with Austin to put Herbert Cooper in the frame for the murder of George Sanger. Jackson lied at the coroner's inquest when he said he and Cooper were on friendly terms. He lied under oath again when he said he didn't know Cooper was suspected of stealing the 50 pounds. It's clear from George

Coleman's account that Jackson had baited Herbert Cooper over the stolen money and there was a lot of bad blood between them. He told the police that he saw Cooper go after Austin and Sanger with an axe. It was only in the heat of the coroner's court that he changed his mind and decided that he hadn't actually seen anyone wielding an axe after all.

What really happened at Park Farm that evening? All we know for certain is that George Sanger was found semi-conscious on the floor, bleeding from a head wound and dying. Then we run out of solid facts, but we can speculate. It almost certainly began with a trade of insults between Cooper and Jackson, which started in the kitchen and spilled over into the drawing room and escalated into a brawl in which Austin was apparently on the losing end. It seems highly likely that George Sanger joined in and was hit over the head, his skull catching the edge of the table as he slumped to the floor. Without the phantom axe, all that is left is an unhappy accident in which an old man got badly hurt in a scuffle. But Austin saw an opportunity for revenge. If the police were reasonably thorough in their search of the premises we're left no choice but to assume that he arranged for the axe to be planted later that evening when it was quiet and safe to do so. It seems very likely that the man who handed it in to the police, George Sanger's brother-in-law James Holloway, was heavily involved in the deception, but to what extent other members of the Sanger household were complicit is uncertain. Perhaps everyone in the family knew something. You couldn't rule it out.

The police report written the day after the incident con-firms that at least two-and-a-half hours elapsed before a senior

investigating team appeared at the crime scene. This delay was blamed on the remoteness of the farmhouse, but it was on a main thoroughfare no more than a couple of miles from Finchley police station. The first officer on the scene gave the job of reporting the incident to police headquarters to a random passing cyclist, who then pedalled off and was never heard of again. Eventually another officer phoned it in from a local pub. In 1911 the Metropolitan Police knew how to secure and preserve crime scenes, maintain chains of evidence, proceed in an orderly and scientific way – all the staples of procedural detective stories today. In theory, at least. Some police officers knew how to do these things better than others. The East Finchley police allowed the crime scene at Park Farm to be invaded by various members of the Sanger family. It all reads like a textbook example of how the police should not behave when a violent crime has taken place. It gave the Sanger family plenty of time to get their story together.

The police knew about Ellen Austin's alleged affair with Herbert Cooper. The housemaid told them about it in her written statement and it was mentioned again at the inquest. You may think it extraordinary therefore that the police took Harry Austin's version of events at face value. It seems to have never occurred to them that Austin might bear a grudge against Herbert Cooper. Presumably the worldwide press attention made S Division so anxious to see the case resolved as quickly as possible that they didn't mind leaving a few stones unturned. Herbert Cooper's suicide gave everyone closure.

The coroner's inquest provided an unsatisfactory account of events. Dr George Cohen was a highly intelligent man,

but at this point in his career he was relatively inexperienced. From his handwritten account, the typed depositions and press reports later, it seems that the examination lacked thoroughness. There were red flags in witness testimonies that should have begged a closer inspection, and there were points that drew unnecessary attention. The coroner focused on the razor used by Cooper to attack Austin. The blade was tied open and Cohen implied that this showed intent. But there was nothing unusual about the razor. It was a working farm and everyone in the household was aware that George Sanger always kept a few cut-throat razors with their blades open and tied back so they were always quickly available for veterinary work, perhaps to lance a horse's abscess or a swelling.

There were no questions asked about the amount of cash regularly left lying around the house in plain sight, or about George Sanger's declining mental faculties. As for the resolutely elusive axe, a sceptic might wonder why it had taken so long to spot the murder weapon, or why a member of the Sanger family was able to find it when a large team of policemen failed to. A sceptic might wonder about that, but the coroner did not. Nor did he think there was any significance to the alleged affair between Herbert Cooper and Harry Austin's wife. Everyone presumed Herbert Cooper's guilt rather than follow any other lines of enquiry. His flight and subsequent suicide were as good as an outright confession. Anything that contradicted that narrative, including the confused plea of innocence in Cooper's suicide notes, was ignored. The authorities were so heavily invested in the idea that Herbert Cooper murdered George Sanger because

he was angry about losing his job that they had closed their minds to anything that suggested otherwise. The jury asked no follow-up questions, and their deliberations in deciding that Herbert Cooper wilfully murdered George Sanger took less than a minute, or the time it took them to finish a cup of tea.

Cooper's guilt was assumed because innocent people don't run away and commit suicide. This is a flawed assumption. People wrongfully accused of a criminal offence can and often do take their own lives.[129] There is a small body of research on the psychological impacts of false allegations. Academics who have studied this subject have documented the resentment, frustration, confusion and anger felt by someone who knows they are wrongfully accused. False accusation has been compared to the trauma experienced by military veterans, refugees, disaster survivors and prisoners of war. Anxiety and panic disorders are also common in people thus accused. Coincidentally, perhaps, suicides of the innocently accused nearly always involve men. There is a suggestion that Herbert Cooper had a mental fragility which made him predisposed to suicidal thoughts. On the night of the attacks, Thomas Cooper senior predicted that if the police found his son at all, they would find him dead.

If the account in John Lukens' book as told by George Coleman is to be believed, Cooper didn't run immediately. He took refuge in his den in the farm outbuilding for at least a couple of hours before he fled. It should go without saying that this was odd behaviour from an alleged killer fleeing a murder scene. If we accept Austin and Coleman's timings as

more or less accurate, it also suggests that the first police at the crime scene were blissfully unaware that the man they were looking for was right under their noses.

What was going through Cooper's mind during that time? Was he watching the Sanger family from his hiding place, possibly even aware of what they were plotting, trying to work out what to do next? It's speculation of course, but I think it's possible he had figured out that the family were going to pin the blame on him for something terrible. At that point in Herbert's mind it was just a question of whether he would be executed by the state or killed by his own hand. In those couple of hours, I think we see a man who has resigned himself to his fate and abandoned all hope. This scenario is conjecture, but I believe it's close to the truth.

What would have happened if Herbert Cooper had not panicked and lived to face his accusers? Assuming that Arthur Jackson and Harry Austin stuck to their stories, he would have faced a trial for the murder of George Sanger and the attempted murders of Jackson and Austin. It is still possible that it would not have ended well for him. The prosecution would argue that there were compelling reasons to believe that Cooper nursed violent resentments towards his employer George Sanger, his successor Arthur Jackson and his lover's husband Harry Austin, and that he unleashed his unhinged fury in a frenzy of unprovoked attacks. Cooper's confrontation with the trespassers at Park Farm a few years earlier pointed to a history of extremely aggressive behaviour. The Crown also had the forensic pathologist Bernard Spilsbury on their side, and his word was more than persuasive, it was unimpeachable.

Herbert Cooper's chances of receiving a fair trial were also compromised. The rule of innocent until proven guilty was enshrined in law, but within hours of the alleged murder, local people were spilling potentially libellous gossip about the chief suspect to the newspapers. Apart from his well-publicised set-to with some trespassers at the farm, there were no indications that he was often aggressive or difficult to live with, or that he caused strife within his community. But people like to tell stories that put themselves in the centre of the action, and neighbours who were barely acquainted with Cooper had something negative to say about him. If the press couldn't find anyone to dish the dirt, they found another angle. One desperate correspondent reported that a local girl was so disgusted with Cooper that she tore up his picture.

This was the least of it. Some newspapers referred to Cooper as the murderer within the first 24 hours after the attacks. Not suspected murderer, not alleged murderer, but murderer. In an alarming double-page splash, the *Daily Mirror* tied the suspect to the alleged murder weapon by publishing a photo of Herbert Cooper holding a large felling axe – probably *the* felling axe – used in the attack. It was a wholly inappropriate intervention by the press in the process of justice, and anyone who saw the article could be forgiven for thinking they already knew who killed George Sanger and exactly how he did it. It wasn't the job of the Edwardian press to act as judge and jury, but the newspapers had already put a noose around Herbert Cooper's neck.

When George Sanger was a much younger man there was only one sentence for murder, an appointment with

London's public executioner. In 1911 this was John Ellis, the Rochdale hairdresser and part-time hangman who recently despatched Harvey Crippen. But the brutal morality of the Victorian age and its demands for retribution had softened in post-Edwardian Britain. The judicially sanctioned killing of a murderer was no longer considered entertainment for the mob and hangings now took place in private behind prison walls – 'private' being a flexible concept, as dozens of journalists were still allowed to attend and share the experience with their readers. The courts were also recognising new definitions of mental illness. In 1843 the Scotsman Daniel M'Naghten shot and killed Edward Drummond, secretary to former Prime Minister Sir Robert Peel, in a case of mistaken identity. Doctors testified that M'Naghten was delusional. The jury acquitted and he was sent to Bethlem Asylum. The M'Naghten case became the basis for a legal and medical landmark after it went to a highly publicised appeal. Out of that controversy emerged the question: 'Did the defendant know what he was doing, and if so, did he know what he was doing was wrong?' If he did not, he could be acquitted. Much to the distress of Queen Victoria, among others, the original verdict stood. Now juries were allowed to return a verdict of 'guilty, but insane at the time of the murder'.

A coroner's inquest had implied, on the flimsiest of evidence and without calling any expert medical witnesses, that Herbert Cooper was disposed to temporary fits of insanity because of some streak of mental illness that ran through the family on his late mother's side. Perhaps a plea of irresponsibility would have held sway and instead of

the hangman's gallows, Cooper would have been consigned to a living death in Broadmoor among Britain's criminally insane.

I think it is more likely that if a defence counsel had been allowed to test the prosecution case against Herbert Cooper there would have been compelling evidence to acquit. The questions outweighed the certainties. In the hands of a capable barrister, the strangely belated discovery of the barely concealed murder weapon alone, not to mention false and misleading information in key witness statements, should have been enough to have had the case thrown out. If the supposed affair between Cooper and Harry Austin's wife had been set before a jury it would have undermined Austin's credibility as the only witness to the attack. No one actually saw the axe blow that supposedly crushed the head of George Sanger. Without Austin's word there is no evidence that Herbert Cooper was even in the room when the fatal injury was dealt.

When John Lukens wrote *The Sanger Story*, George Coleman told him; 'Herbert Cooper didn't murder my grandfather and never intended to. He was more sinned against than sinning.'[130] But the extent to which Cooper had been wronged was much greater than anyone knew. We can never know exactly what happened at Park Farm that November night, but at the very least it seems certain some members of the Sanger household conspired to portray Herbert Cooper as a monster and drove him to his suicide. Their behaviour could be described as criminal. Perhaps Herbert Cooper's only crime was to have had an affair with a married woman and then allow himself to be goaded into a

confrontation with her husband. Perhaps the surface of this extraordinary saga has barely been scratched.

$$\backsim$$

George Sanger's life ended in a blaze of publicity as great as any he had deliberately manufactured, an irony he might have appreciated. His family hoped the story would go away, but it never did. If you type 'Lord George Sanger' into a search engine you will invariably read that he died at the hands of an axe-wielding maniac. As I write this, Wikipedia lists Herbert Cooper as one of history's 'most notable axe murderers'.

When I set out to research George Sanger it was to write a book about his extraordinary life. I hadn't thought much about his death except that it was a tragic and poignant post-script. I knew that the police files and the transcripts of the inquest into his death were held at the National Archives and at the London Metropolitan Archive and naturally I hoped that they would reveal something more than I could find out from old newspaper clippings, but I didn't antici-pate anything revelatory. At the National Archives I judged from the condition of the files and their bindings that I was the first to look at them in a very long time. In a pink folder tied with ribbon was a sheaf of brittle papers comprising dozens of legal documents, including verbatim statements from witnesses. I experienced the thrill of turning over in my hands documents that perhaps no one else had touched for more than a hundred years. When I read them it became clear that my story would go down an entirely unexpected path. But it was on a sunny day at the Metropolitan Archives

in Farringdon that I found something that made the hairs on the back of my neck stand up.

Hidden among the typed transcripts of the coroner's inquest and the original handwritten summaries of testimony there was a small scrap of grey-white paper, about two-inches wide by three-inches long, crammed on both sides with pencil handwriting complete with crossings out. With a jolt, I realised that it was Herbert Cooper's suicide note addressed to his father. I couldn't begin to imagine the torment that drove a man to write that note, then lie down in the fog and place his head on a railway line.

20

Epilogue

THE FINAL ACT of the strange drama that had absorbed so much public interest was the reading of Lord George Sanger's will. The two-year-old document reflected the confusion that clouded the last few years of his life. He bequeathed items that he didn't own and forgot family names and relationships. The will mentions his 'late daughter Julia', but the only Julia known to anyone in the family was his pet monkey. Some close relatives promised handsome endowments were disappointed; loyal employees were remembered. His bailiff Thomas Cooper and his sons Herbert and Thomas junior were each left 50 pounds. It was precisely the sum over which George Sanger had mercilessly tortured poor Herbert Cooper. To people outside the immediate Sanger family, the news that the murderer stood to benefit from the will seemed like one more cruel twist.

In February 1912 the Sanger estate was valued for probate at 29,348 pounds – around £3.5 million in 2020 terms. George's daughter Harriet Reeve got the lion's share. Not just specific items of valuable jewellery and silver plates but everything of real value, including his entire property

portfolio – the farm, the Hall by the Sea at Margate and the properties in Ramsgate including the Palace Theatre. This despite the fact that, according to his grandson, George had little affection for the Reeves and in his last years his daughter Harriet was an unwelcome visitor to Park Farm. Some members of the family suspected that Harriet had manipulated her father's will. As the sole executor, she alone had access to all his papers. On the evening of her father's death, Harriet was one of the first to arrive at Park Farm and an unnamed member of the household allegedly saw her burning documents.[131]

On 4 January 1912 the last remnants of George Sanger's show effects, including some cherished items withheld from his big sale, were sold at an auction at Park Farm by Tom Norman, nicknamed 'The Silver King' on account of the cheap jewellery dangling ostentatiously from his waistcoat.[132] The auction drew a large crowd, but it wasn't the prospect of buying some merchandise at bargain prices that had lured most of them, it was morbid curiosity. The bidding was poor. The unused *Mazeppa* equipment was sold for 26 guineas, a tiny fraction of their purchase price. Half-a-dozen lots of dresses went for 25 shillings and 'a large quantity of helmets and headgear' fetched twelve shillings and sixpence. For a team of four black ponies with a custom-built model phaeton the highest bid was 75 guineas. Thus, the great circus that had promised SOMETHING NEW UNDER THE SUN, TWICE DAILY was finally scattered to the four winds.

⌒

Under the management of Harriet and Arthur Reeve, the Hall by the Sea at Margate struggled. In 1919 they sold the

business to the amusement park magnate John Henry Iles, who redeveloped it as Margate Dreamland. Under new ownership it flourished and innovated with the country's first ever rollercoaster. The park survived Hitler, the rise of the teddy boys and the mods and rockers who fought on the seafront in the sixties, but like many seaside towns the resort's charms faded and the fairground fell silent. After decades of changing ownership, under-investment and declining visitor numbers, against all the odds, Margate Dreamland re-opened in 2015 as a heritage amusement park with public funding.

George Sanger became a wealthy man from his career in the circus, but even for his most famous performers the life rarely brought prosperity, and most retired from the ring in a state of penury. A case in point was Walter 'Watty' Hildyard, the first ever clown hired by the Sanger brothers, who continued to work with them for over 40 years. He enjoyed top billing and was regarded by his peers as one of the greatest clowns in the business, not far behind Joey Grimaldi in terms of genius. His famous creation 'the Drill Squad routine' is still seen in pantomimes everywhere today. Watty performed it at Covent Garden in front of Queen Victoria, and saw her soundly smack her son and heir Prince Albert Edward when he snatched her opera glasses. Then one day Watty received a bequest from an aunt of three pounds a week on condition that he retire from the ring and stage. Without hesitation he quit on the spot and retired to Deptford, where he died in 1901 in his 79th year.

George's great American adversary P.T. Barnum died in 1891 having suffered a stroke shortly after his greatest-ever European tour. William 'Buffalo Bill' Cody outlived Sanger

by six years, but those years were burdened with alcoholism, debts and disaster. The former millionaire died a pauper and was buried in an unmarked grave. The Barnum & Bailey Circus and successors, the Ringling Brothers, continued to use the Sanger name, billed as 'Sanger's Menagerie and Great London Show' well into the 20th century. On 21 May 2017 Ringling gave the last performance in its 146-year history, the show's signature elephants having disappeared the year before after a long campaign for animal rights.

The First World War killed the old-fashioned circus parade. Modern traffic made the slow, magnificent progress through overcrowded streets impossible. During the war, the gilt was scraped from Lord John Sanger's tableau wagons and sold for a few hundred pounds, and they stood neglected and rotting in the fields of their winter quarters at Horley in Surrey. The circus had always re-enacted wars for entertainment; now circus horses and elephants were commandeered for actual war work. Thousands of human circus performers were conscripted and many lay buried in the Flanders mud.

Harry Austin stood by his wife Ellen. He and his brother George had worked for Sanger's circus for over 30 years as a double jockey act and after their employer died they went to America to work for Ringling, Barnum and Bailey. Harry Austin served his country in the Great War and returned home in 1918. He died of a heart attack a year later, age 47, in County Durham while moving his caravan, taking the sordid family secret with him to the grave. Harry Austin's three daughters Florence, Cissy and Olive followed their parents into the performing arts and all became stars in their own right in the circus, music hall and variety theatres.

Their mother Ellen Austin survived two husbands named Harry. In 1923 the 45-year-old widow was living in Brixton with 31-year-old circus clown and comedy actor Harry Moxon. They were married in July 1940 and lived for many years on Lewisham High Street. On 20 August 1951, 59-year-old Harry Moxon fell suddenly dead in the circus ring at Chichester. Ellen lived on until her 90th year and died in 1969.

When historians of the sawdust circle describe the circus as one big family, they are being more literal than you might suppose. The Sanger family circus connections became more labyrinthian. Lord George Sanger's nephew John, who styled himself Lord John Sanger, married the ring starlet Rebecca Pinder of Pinder's Circus, perhaps the oldest circus family in the UK. John's brother James married Rebecca's sister Barbara. Another nephew, George, married his cousin, Lord George Sanger's granddaughter Georgina. Thus, George Coleman, the subject of John Lukens' book, was related to Sangers on both sides of his family.[133]

After the Great War circus owners and performers hoped to pick up where they left off, but the world had changed. Under the management of Lord George Sanger's great-nephews, Sanger's limped along, a shell of its former self, getting by on nostalgia and wounded pride, touring small towns and villages. It provided the stage debut for the young comedy duo Morecambe and Wise. The boys endured a miserable six months with Sanger's, playing to a mostly empty marquee. 'It was killed by the belief that country people were so starved of entertainment that they would accept any old rubbish,' was Ernie's withering assessment.[134]

Following a compulsory winding-up order, the Sanger travelling show left town for the last time in 1962, so ending a tradition which had spanned 117 years. One of the performers in the final show was George Coleman's daughter Vicky, who established her reputation as a first-class bareback rider before the First World War and later worked as the legendary 'Queen of the Elephants' in many more circuses all around the world. She died in 1991 aged 95, and her ashes were placed in Margate in the family grave. As a great-granddaughter of Lord George Sanger, she was the last person alive who could claim to have known the great showman upon whose knee she sat as a child in East Finchley.[135]

For Detective Inspector George Wallace and Divisional Inspector John Cundell, the Sanger case was their very last murder enquiry. In January 1912, 50-year-old Wallace took his police pension and went to live in Southend-on-Sea. Cundell retired in June that year, having also completed his 25 years' service. Detective Inspector Henry Edgar Brooks retired after 37 years policing in 1920 and became mayor of Suffolk. The Middlesex District Coroner Dr George Cohen held his position for 31 years until his death in Edgware in 1941.

George Sanger's death had a dramatic and lasting impact within the show business community to which he belonged, but for the rest of the world the story came and went in 72 hours, and even a few weeks later you wouldn't find mention of it in the local newspapers. Not that George Sanger ever disappeared completely from the news. From time to time over the next couple of years, stories about him would appear in the papers, retelling some of his famous exploits.

Though the stories would get smaller in the coming decades, his name would be invoked in just about every mention of the circus's golden age. Occasionally heirs emerged to stake claims on the Sanger estate. In 1939 an account of the murder was published in a Prague newspaper. It went on to assert that family members yet to do so had until 1940 to claim their inheritance. The report prompted a lady from Zurich, Frau Emma Hohn, to write to London Metropolitan Police claiming to represent the families of three deceased Czechoslovakian brothers, Johann, Vinzens and Carl Sanger. Identifying herself as the sister-in-law of Johann Sanger, Frau Hohn said that the three brothers had lost contact with their sibling George when he went to America as a young man. George had never been to America.

It was never over for the Cooper family. Within a couple of months, Harriet Reeve returned to the place where her father was mortally wounded and, assisted by members of her family, boxed up all his belongings and cleared out the premises. In 1912 she sold Park Farm to a bicycle manufacturer, William Vivers, and the Coopers found themselves out of work and homeless. Thomas Cooper senior used his life savings to scrape together enough money to take out a mortgage on a small dairy farm at Friern Watch in nearby North Finchley, which he worked with his two remaining sons Tom and Leonard, supplying the local area with fresh milk. The competition from local dairy businesses was fierce and they toiled up to twelve hours a day for 365 days a year without taking a day off. It took strength to remain in the community when the Coopers could have left town to escape their notoriety, but it was also perhaps a sign of

the goodwill felt by many towards the family so innocently placed in their terrible predicament.

Just when Thomas Cooper might have thought his fortunes had changed for the better, the wheel of fate turned again. In 1914, as the thunder clouds of the First World War rolled across Europe, his eldest son Thomas junior enlisted in the army, leaving his father and younger brother to work the farm alone. In February 1916 the army came for 21-year-old Leonard. Thomas Cooper was in poor health and couldn't run the business on his own. He pleaded for his son's exemption on the grounds that conscription made it impossible for him to find a replacement. The Appeal Tribunal eventually found in his favour and granted Leonard Cooper a temporary exemption, but a few months later, on 26 August 1917, Thomas Cooper senior died, aged 61. Those who knew him believed his health was destroyed by the suicide of his middle son. They lie buried side by side in Marylebone Cemetery. Thomas Cooper went to his grave never knowing that his son did not kill George Sanger.

The younger Tom Cooper and his brother Leonard returned from the war and with Leonard's new wife, Ida, they ran the dairy farm through the 1920s, but by the end of the decade the Coopers struggled to find pasture for their small herd of eleven cows and the small dairy farms were being frozen out by United Dairies. There is no trace of the Cooper dairy business after 1930. I hoped my appeals for information to the community of East Finchley would turn up more information that would allow us to fill in some of the blanks in the Cooper family story, but there the trail goes cold.

A coroner's inquiry had labelled Herbert Charles Cooper a crazed murderer. The pain and humiliation this caused his family was untold and they were never allowed to forget it. In a reprint of Sanger's ghost-written memoir *Seventy Years a Showman* published in 1926, the author Kenneth Graham wrote in his introduction: 'In 1911 a manservant in his employ, of a sullen and revengeful disposition, fired by some real or fancied grievance over which he had probably brooded long, suddenly ran amok, as it were, attacked two fellow-menservants, wounding one of them severely, and battered the life out of poor old Mr Sanger with a hatchet.'

Having helped seal Herbert Cooper's undeserved repu-tation as a cold-blooded murderer, Dr Bernard Spilsbury went on to enjoy a career unparalleled in the history of forensic medicine. The Crippen case projected him into the limelight, but the Brides in the Bath investigation made him a household name. In 1915 the police exhumed the first of three bodies, that of 38-year-old Margaret Lofty, a vicar's daughter from Bristol. All three women were assumed to have accidentally drowned after fainting or having a fit in the bath. Suspicions were aroused when it emerged that they had been married to the same man, 43-year-old George Joseph Smith, a smooth-talking con man with a long criminal record and a gift for exploiting vulnerable women. The police were certain that Smith was the killer, but they couldn't figure out how he despatched his victims. There was no bruising nor any signs of struggle on their bodies and they appeared to have drowned while unconscious. Spilsbury speculated that the women were drowned in their baths before they had time to put up a fight. All Smith had to do was grab their

legs and pull them under the surface and the sudden rush of water into nose and throat meant that they would quickly lose consciousness and drown. Spilsbury tested his murder theory on a policewoman in a bath set up in his Home Office laboratory. It worked so well that it took half an hour to revive her. At Smith's trial the jury found Spilsbury's explanation convincing, and it took them just 22 minutes to find the accused guilty.

The 'magnificent Spilsbury' became a national celebrity. He acted for the prosecution in more than 200 murder trials, in which his mere presence in the court room was almost enough to condemn a defendant. There was a name for his invincibility, coined by 25-year-old Norman Thorne, accused of killing his girlfriend in 1915. Thorne claimed she had committed suicide but Spilsbury said she was murdered. The evidence was circumstantial, but Spilsbury's reputation was enough to sway the jury and Thorne was sentenced to death. There was a public outcry and Arthur Conan Doyle among others voiced grave doubts about the verdict. As Norman Thorne sat awaiting death for a murder he may not have committed, he wrote to his father: 'Never mind, Dad ... I am a martyr to Spilsburyism.'

Spilsbury could never admit to making a mistake, and for 40 years his word was enough to see a man hanged, but as he got older his courtroom cool deserted him. Small ripples of doubt about his conclusions began to spread. With hindsight, some of his supposedly watertight murder theories began to look as though they were invented on the spur of the moment. The long and distinguished career of the giant of forensic pathology ended somewhere near to

humiliation, as Spilsbury was reduced to hanging around the coroner's office in the hope of picking up a death for autopsy. Shortly before Christmas 1947, following a couple of minor strokes, he closed the windows and doors in his laboratory at University College London, turned on the gas taps and waited to die.

In the decades that followed, the crucial forensic evidence that Spilsbury used to send men and women to the scaffold was re-examined and many of his observations were found to be flawed. The science that condemned Harvey Crippen was similarly tainted. Crippen had maintained his innocence throughout and mounted an unsuccessful appeal on the grounds that the identity of the body in the cellar had not been established beyond doubt. His guilt turned almost entirely on a piece of skin identified by Spilsbury as the lower part of Cora Crippen's abdomen, but a DNA test has since shown that it was tissue removed from a male body. To the list of victims of Spilsburyism we could also now add the name Herbert Charles Cooper.

Appendix

Advertisement for Lord George Sanger's circus in the *Rushden Argus*, 8 October 1897

Lord George Sanger
THE WORLD'S GREATEST SHOWMAN
THE ORIGINAL SANGER,
Will visit Rushden
on Tuesday, October 12th 1897

For 50 years a London Theatrical and Circus Manager, and 60 years an Artist and Proprietor throughout the Provinces of the United Empire and the Continents of Europe and America.

(This World-Renowned Establishment is in no way connected with Lord Sanger or Lord John Sanger and Sons Limited)

The confidence confided in LORD GEORGE SANGER has risen his Establishment from the One Horse Penny Circus to the Largest Exhibition in the world, and proof of the public favour bestowed upon the reliable trading of the Proprietor and the patronage given, the resources of this World-famed Showman has extended, not only to the great travelling Exhibition, as announced, but

LORD GEORGE SANGER'S ROYAL CIRCUS, EARL'S COURT, LONDON, that gave the Royal Diamond Jubilee Performance to 11,000 Children at the Royal Agricultural Hall, London, on Friday, June 11th 1897, his company being specially selected by the London School Board; and as there are three Circuses by the name of Sanger – and being the Original Sanger and Founder of the Circus by name of Sanger – will respectfully ask the Public to distinguish and remember the Name. If you ask for LORD GEORGE SANGER, THE ORIGINAL SANGER, you will not be deceived.

In celebration of the Record Reign of Her
Illustrious Majesty the Queen,

it has been determined by LORD GEORGE SANGER to effect two purposes, two great events at the same time, Sixty Years of unequalled and glorious prosperity. Sixty Years has THE QUEEN reigned, and Sixty Years upon the Coronation Day of the present year has LORD GEORGE SANGER appeared before the Nations of Europe and America as a PERFORMER. It will be interesting for the Public to know at the time HER MAJESTY was receiving the high honours from the Bishops, Nobles and High Officials at Westminster Abbey, that LORD GEORGE SANGER at the precise time was performing his Equestrian and Acrobatics Feasts at the Fair in Hyde Park, London, for the first time. It was thought by the authorities that holding of a National Fair in the Park would have a tendency to clear the streets through which the Royal Procession would have to pass from Buckingham Palace to Westminster Abbey, and the large Exhibition which at the time frequented the provincial towns to hold their Annual Festivities, assembled in the Great Metropolis to assist in the Royal Hyde Park Fair.

THE QUEEN
Has ruled her people prosperously and happily, and

LORD GEORGE SANGER
Has appeared before the public dating not only from the same day, but absolutely from the same hour. Sixty Years the just beloved QUEEN, and Sixty Years the most Renowned and Reliable Showman, and to immortalize the double event, the Queen and the Showman,

HER MAJESTY
will receive in high and un-heard-of Magnificence the leading lights of the Empire, and most renowned men of her Colonies; at the same time LORD GEORGE SANGER has made special arrangements to receive all Classes of the Community, yes, from HER MAJESTY to the humble peasant, and with the greatest regard to what is most essential to Exhibitions where the Clergy, the Aristocracy, and the wives and families are catered for, nothing of an objectionable nature will form any item in this
GLORIOUS GRAND EXHIBITION.

Appendix

THE GRAND PROCESSION

More Grand and Extensive than upon any former occasion, will embrace representatives and Characters in Costume of the Dominions of the Queen from every part of the Explored Globe where her majesty's Crown and Sceptre hold the sway. There will be Men and Women in Costume who will represent people from those Vast Dominions, that is an unheard-of-Sight for the British Public, and to complete the Goliath-like Exhibitions, the

DROMEDARIES AND CAMELS

From the Indian Exhibition, Earl's Court, London, have been purchased to and to the number of those Sheep of the Desert that will represent Egypt, and among the many specimens will be found the

BLACK SACRED MADHI CAMEL

This beautiful animal is the only one of its kind that has ever been seen in this country, so much spoken of by Mr Bennett Burleigh, the special War Correspondent of the *Daily Telegraph*, and in addition the

12 HUGE ROYAL ELEPHANTS

From Rangoon. These splendid animals have been specially imported to represent India for the Record Celebration.
Africa – its Herd of

MAGNIFICENT OSTRICHES,

With their Hottentots and attendants; and in like from the Colonies will be represented. There is no Exhibition in any part of the world that will bear comparison.

LORD GEORGE SANGER will not use the old familiar words – 'The Biggest Thing on Earth' – but publicly Challenges any Show, whether it shall be on the other side of the Atlantic or elsewhere, to produce anything half so grand and original.

Now then to the Performers – the very best of English, American, and Continental Artistes have been secured, Magnificent Bands, Hundreds of Horses and Ponies and a Great Menagerie.

Grand Cavalcade at one o'clock – Two performances : At 2.30 and 7.30.

Notes

1. In heavily populated areas policemen's beats were much shorter. By day the constable would patrol on the kerb side of the pavement, but by night he switched to the inner side of the pavement so he could check more easily the security of bolts and fastenings on the various buildings that fell under his protection. A beat bobby usually stayed on his beat for a couple of months, then he was moved to another within his section. When he'd covered all the beats in his section, the cycle would start over again. The routine was prescribed to avoid the temptations of familiarity while ensuring a degree of local knowledge. PC White was also expected to know every shop and public house as well as the occupier of every premises on his beat.

2. There is no traceable birth certificate for George Sanger but according to (1) his wedding certificate, (2) the 1861 census, (3) his surviving daughter and the inscription on his headstone, George Sanger was born in 1825.

3. According to Sanger family folklore, George Sanger's uncle John married the daughter of William Bacon, proprietor of Bacon's Genuine Patent Medicine Warehouse and became his business partner before taking over after his death. As John Sanger & Sons he founded a famous dynasty of wholesale druggists, succeeded by his son, another John Sanger, whose sons Charles and William Albert were admitted to partnership in 1862. The renamed business Sanger Ltd. was still operational in the late 20th century. The connection between the two branches of the Sanger family however is unproven.

4. *An Essay on the Most Effectual Means of Preserving the Health of Seamen*, James Lind, 1762.

5. According to his memoir, *Seventy Years a Showman*, for

service to his country, George Sanger was awarded a pension of ten pounds a year for his war injuries and a letter from the government, a Royal Prescription, giving the holder the right to pursue any lawful trade he wished, without restraint, in any part of the kingdom and immunity to certain legal restrictions. James called it his 'Freedom of England' document. According to the navy records, however, there was no pension ever awarded and his 'Royal Prescription' was probably just an ordinary discharge certificate.

6. *The English Illustrated Magazine.*

7. *Our Mutual Friend*, Charles Dickens, 1997.

8. *Seventy Years a Showman*, 'Lord' George Sanger, 1910.

9. *Old Bailey Proceedings Online* (www.oldbaileyonline.org).

10. *London Evening News*, 29 November 1911.

11. Ibid.

12. The anecdote as told in George Sanger's memoir relates to the actual murder of 40-year-old widow Ann Pullen, landlady of the White Hart, Wantage, by nineteen-year-old farmhand George King on 30 August 1833. That Friday evening King had entered the White Hart public house in a drunken state and, finding the proprietor alone, demanded some supper. Pullen went to cut him a rasher of bacon and he followed her into the kitchen, where he propositioned her. She threatened to give him a knock on his head with a poker and King left. Much later in the evening King returned and took his revenge, removing her head with a clean wipe of his sickle. He claimed it was self-defence and he'd not meant to decapitate her. The following morning, Ann's twelve-year-old son stumbled over his mother's head lying on the kitchen floor. There were no witnesses to the crime and the facts as reported are based entirely on George King's full confession.

13. *Seventy Years a Showman*, Sanger.

14. Ibid.

15. Ibid.

16. George's memory betrayed him. According to his memoir he was at Newport for the annual Whitsuntide fair, but this event

always took place in May, not November, the month of the actual Newport Rising.

17. *Seventy Years a Showman*, Sanger.

18. Ibid.

19. Ibid.

20. *Days Of My Years*, Sir Melville Macnaghten, 1914.

21. *Poses plastiques* began as social entertainment whereby actors struck certain static poses, perhaps impersonating statues or scenes in famous paintings, but they left the private salon and became public displays of full- or semi-nudity.

22. *The Sporting Review*, Volume XIV.

23. *The Victorian Clown* by Jacky Bratton contains the previously unpublished memoirs of the circus performer James Frowde, who first saw young George Sanger at a fair in North Shields, dressed as Hamlet, performing conjuring tricks from his living carriage. Frowde recalled his experience of sharing digs with other performers and described the round of clowning work in circuses and other venues around the country as akin to slavery.

24. George Bernardo Eagle was an ex-British-army officer. His chief rival Anderson was billed as The Great Wizard of the North. As far as records show there was a still a vacancy for a 'Wizard of the East'.

25. *Seventy Years a Showman*, Sanger.

26. The King's Cross Dust Heap became a valuable export. It was taken down and shipped to Russia for the manufacture of bricks.

27. *Seventy Years a Showman*, Sanger.

28. A servant in a living wagon. William Manders, a one-time spieler for Hilton's menagerie, raised the money to buy Manders Grand National Star Menagerie from his old employer by passing his hat around at the end of each performance. He became one of the greatest showmen of the era.

29. Nellie Sanger was probably the second-ever female lion trainer. Thomas Frost names Polly Hilton, niece of the proprietor of Hilton's menagerie, as the first to step into a lion's cage in 1839–40.

30. *Liverpool Mercury*, 2 April 1847.

31. In George Sanger's memoir the banter between Nellie, the Queen and the Prince Consort goes on over a couple of pages. In reality the meeting was probably much briefer and less intimate than George would have us believe. Queen Victoria's journal entry for 28 October 1947 confirms that Her Majesty declined the offer to see Nellie's lion taming act, possibly because as the Queen was four months pregnant it was thought the excitement might be too much for her, but the legend persisted that the Lion Queen had performed before the actual Queen.

32. Usually known as Ellen Blight, but also as Helen (or Ellen) Bright.

33. Alfred Harmsworth was known as Lord Northcliffe from 1905.

34. *Daily Mirror*, 29 November 1911.

35. *Daily Telegraph*, 29 November 1911.

36. *Birmingham Daily Mail*, 29 November 1911.

37. *Aberdeen Journal*, 30 November 1911.

38. *Leicester Post*, 30 November 1911.

39. *Birmingham Daily Mail*, 29 November 1911.

40. *Daily Mirror*, 29 November 1911.

41. *Daily Mirror*, 29 November 1911.

42. *Birmingham Daily Mail*, 29 November 1911.

43. *Birmingham Daily Mail*, 29 November 1911.

44. *Evening News*, 30 November 2011.

45. *Birmingham Daily Mail*, 29 November 1911.

46. *Birmingham Daily Gazette*, 29 November 1911.

47. *Daily Telegraph*, 29 November 1911.

48. *Birmingham Daily Gazette*, 29 November 1911.

49. *The West Australian*, December 1911.

50. *New Zealand Post*, 12 January 1912

51. *Melbourne Argus*, 30 November 1911.

52. *New York Times*, 30 November 1911.

53. *New York Times*, 30 November 1911.

54. *Evening News*, 1 December 1911.

55. *Evening News*, 1 December 1911.

56. *Daily Mirror*, 30 November 1911.

57. *Leicester Post*, 30 November 1911.

58. *Evening News*, 1 December 1911.

59. *Morning Post*, 30 November 1911.

60. *Hendon & Finchley Times*, 1 December 1911.

61. Rev. Howse occasionally also took his work home with him. When he died in 1842, human bones were discovered beneath his kitchen floor.

62. Census.

63. *Sketches by Boz*, Charles Dickens, 1995.

64. *The Times*, 12 October 1851.

65. *Seventy Years a Showman*, Sanger.

66. The first side of the Beatles' *Sergeant Pepper's Lonely Hearts Club Band* album ends with a song whose lyrics are taken verbatim from the poster for a performance at Pablo Fanque's Circus Royal in Rochdale, dated 14 February 1843, exactly eleven years to the day before Kite's debut with Sanger's circus.

67. *Seventy Years a Showman*, Sanger.

68. *Mazeppa*; or the Wild Horse of Tartary was a hugely popular equestrian drama featuring live horses, loosely based on Lord Byron's poem 'Mazeppa' (1819).

69. In his memoir George Sanger states that the new Astley's opened with a Christmas pantomime, but his memory let him down again.

70. George Sanger's shameless hijacking of the Queen's Thanksgiving Day parade, as described in his memoir, is uncorroborated. According to the extensive press coverage, his circus parade followed a couple of hours after the official parade.

71. Henry Bertrand worked as road manager and ringmaster for Sanger's circus for eighteen years. His famous great-grandson is the comedian, actor, author and musician Eric Idle.

72. *Studio and Stage*, Joseph Harker, 1924.

73. *Suicide: Its History Literature, Jurisprudence, Causation, and Prevention*, W.W. Westcott, 2019.

74. *The Railway Workers*, F. McKenna, 1976.

75. *The Times*, 1 December 1911.

76. *Evening News*, 1 December 1911.

77. *Tewkesbury Register*, 9 December 1911.

78. *Hendon & Finchley Times*, 1 December 1911.

79. *Personal Recollections and Observations of General Nelson A. Miles, Embracing a Brief View of the Civil War*, Nelson Miles, 1897.

80. *Illustrated London News*, 10 May 1887.

81. *The Life and Adventures of Buffalo Bill*, Buffalo Bill and William Lightfoot Visscher, 1917.

82. *Seventy Years a Showman*, Sanger.

83. In his autobiography George Sanger blamed his lawyers, claiming that they had advised him that there were certain irregularities when the injunction was served and that he could ignore it and carry on as before.

84. In the delusional account of his skirmish with Cody in his memoir, George Sanger imagined that he emerged the clear victor; '[the verdict] reached me just towards the close of the afternoon performance, in the shape of a telegram to say I had won the day. I read that telegram to the audience, who cheered me heartily, and I promised to put the facts before them in a special bill.'

85. *The Sanger Story*, John Lukens, 1956. According to his grandson, George Coleman, George Sanger was known for his colourful language, but this was the only time anyone ever heard him swear in front of his wife Nellie.

86. His rivals were keen to jump on the bandwagon, as the circus historian Rupert Croft-Cooke explains in *The Sawdust Ring*: 'the effect of this on the other circus proprietors of the time was amusing ... Cooke became Sir John Henry Cooke, Bob Fossett was transformed into Sir Robert Fossett, and the acrobat head of one of the smallest tenting shows went one better and styled himself King Ohmy. Lion tamers became captains and even grooms hinted at aristocratic connections.'

87. *The Daily Mail*, 5 December 1911.

88. *Seventy Years a Showman*, Sanger.

89. *A History of the Circus*, George Speaight, 1980.

90. *The Era*, November 1899.

91. *Barnum: An American Life*, Robert Wilson, 1982.

92. *From Barnum & Bailey to Feld: The Creative Evolution of the Greatest Show on Earth*, Ernest Albrecht, 2014.

93. *Cardiff Evening Express*, May 1899.

94. John Holtum caught his first cannonball in 1872 and lost a finger, but he and his wife Anna went on to become 'King and Queen of the Cannonball'. Annoyed by accusations that he was a fraud, Holtum offered a generous cash prize to anyone who could replicate his act on stage. No one ever did, but in Leeds in 1880 he was brought up on remand before magistrates for 'unlawfully wounding' a member of his audience, one Elijah Fenton, who accepted the challenge and received a fractured skull. Neither were deterred by the fate of their contemporary, an Italian strongman who attempted to deflect a live grenade with his powerfully muscled chest, only to be blown to pieces. Another cannonball catcher Alexandrini caught a steel ball fired directly at him but was fatally injured in 1885. Gaston Richards, who was himself a human cannonball, on the occasion of his last performance, fell short of the net when the spring mechanism failed and was killed.

95. 'The lynx that escaped the other day from a menagerie near Liverpool has not been recovered. It is still, in fact, the missing lynx.' *Huddersfield Chronicle*, 15 January 1870.

96. *The Times*, 11 September 1911.

97. White elephants are extremely rare and held sacred in parts of Asia, although the few that exist are only nominally 'white' and appear greyish pink.

98. Barnum added a couple of feet to Jumbo's height in his press releases and on the posters he was magnitudes larger, but if the American's measurements were elastic, so were George's. Both men knew that claims of that kind were impossible to fact check.

99. Charlie the elephant was stuffed and placed in the Crystal Palace, where he remained until he and the building were destroyed by fire in 1936.

100. Wood, J.G. *The Boy's Own Magazine: An Illustrated Journal of Fact, Fiction, History and Adventure*, 1862, vol. 8, issue 45, p. 177.

101. Ibid.

102. *The Sanger Story*, Lukens.

103. In his memoir George Sanger says that the escaped wolves caused such a furore that 'questions were asked in parliament'. There's no mention in Hansard that it ever did.

104. *My Life with Animals and Other Reminiscences*, Garrard Tyrwhitt-Drake, 1939.

105. *The Greatest Show on Earth*, Willson Disher, 1937. Ned Hannaford, knife-thrower, equestrian and later circus proprietor, held his employer in such high esteem that he named one of his sons William George Sanger Hannaford.

106. The Victorian circus was relatively very inclusive and featured a great many talented black performers. One of the most well-known is Pablo Fanque, a third-generation black British equestrian, acrobat and slack-roper performer who later became the first black circus owner in Britain. It is fair to say that the experiences of black performers in Britain were markedly better than those operating in the United States.

107. *Observer*, 3 December 1911.

108. In the early-19th century, birth, marriage and death records were not regulated to a national system and were the responsibility of the local parishes. To this day, George Sanger's birth record has yet to be found, but our most informed guess is that his daughter Harriet was correct in stating that her father died a few weeks short of his 86th birthday.

109. The prevailing view among physicians of the time who specialised in mental illness was that most madness was hereditary and that the maternal side was the most likely source.

110. The primrose was thought to be Disraeli's favourite

flower, at least it was by Queen Victoria, who bombarded him with bunches of primroses from Osborne House.

111. *Seventy Years a Showman*, Sanger.

112. In 1888 the government introduced the Moveable Dwellings Bill, calling for the registration of all caravans, compulsory school attendance for travellers' children and regulations limiting the number of occupants in a caravan. The most controversial clause gave local authorities the right of entry into any caravan at any daylight hour to inspect for overcrowding, disease and 'moral irregularity'. For the showmen, Smith's bill was a declaration of war. George Sanger mobilised the biggest circus proprietors of the day and organised a campaign to protest the legislation, crucially winning the support of Henry 'Inky' Stephens, Conservative MP for Hornsey. In February 1891 the showmen met at Astley's Amphitheatre for the first meeting of the new United Kingdom Van Dwellers Protection Association to protest Smith's bill with George Sanger elected their first president. After five years of vigorous campaigning, the Bill was defeated. The Van Dwellers Association continued to represent travelling showmen with George Sanger as their president for the next eight years. He gave his time and his money to the cause generously and his stalwart efforts in the defence of showman's rights cemented his place as the industry's most respected and influential leader. In 1917 the association he helped found became the Showmen's Guild of Great Britain, the first ever organisation set up to protect the rights of people in the entertainment industry, a service it provides to this day.

113. In Polari, which was once the private language of showmen and travelling folk, a josser was someone who worked in the trade but wasn't born into it. In Romany, a josser is literally an outsider.

114. Queenvictoriasjournals.org

115. Ibid. On 17 July 1899 at Windsor Castle the Queen wrote in her diary: 'At ¼ to 5 drove with Lenchen & Beatrice to the Lawn below the Terrace, to see Sanger's Circus pass in procession.

It was a wonderful sight. The horses were nothing remarkable, but there was a very pretty team of 23 ponies, driven from the box & various others. Amongst the procession were 5 elephants & several camels. Mr G. Sanger himself was brought up to me carriage & expressed his thanks. He does not exhibit in London, his Circus always travelling about the country. The lions & tigers in the cages, seemed very fine.'

116. In 1933 the monument was dismantled to make way for a car park. In 1966 it was relocated to Victoria Park, but without the second female figure.

117. *Hendon and Finchley Times*, October 1905.

118. Or possibly J. Odell. By 1890 George's friend Tom Norman 'the Silver King' had moved on from exhibiting 'human novelties' and made a successful career as a showman's auctioneer and would enjoy a long career conducting all the principal circus auctions. In 1905 Sanger wrote to him at short notice and offered him the job of organising the sale of his travelling circus effects. However, as Tom Norman explains in his memoirs, he was away on business and the invitation was sent to an old address and it was not forwarded to him until it was too late. Presumably Norman's name was still on the sale catalogue because there wasn't time to print new copies. Hence the mistaken assumption ever since that Tom Norman was the auctioneer.

119. *Hendon and Finchley Times*, November 1905.

120. George Robert Sims was a man of wide cultural interests but perhaps best known for a series of sensational articles about the living conditions of the poor, published under titles such as 'How the Poor Live' and 'Horrible London'. He also wrote extensively about Jack the Ripper, and such was his dedication to Ripperology that some believed Sims was the killer. The writer was also a playboy and gambler and he either lost or gave most of his money away to charity, so he was probably happy to take on any commission that paid well. Sims's authorship of the book has never been corroborated. Sims's autobiography *My Life – Sixty Years' Recollections of Bohemian London* was published in 1917

but contains no mention of the author ever having met George Sanger.

121. According to the transcripts of the trial of George King for the murder of Ann Pullen at Wantage there were no eyewitnesses and either James Sanger or his son George almost certainly made the story up. James probably put it together from local rumours or lifted it wholesale from another peep-show operator.

122. The story about the gingerbread man George claimed he saw murdered in broad daylight at Stalybridge is also apocryphal. It's reasonable to assume that a violent murder committed in broad daylight at a public event would have been worth a mention in at least one newspaper but there were none. The local press covered the fair, noting a rare ascent in a balloon but reported little drunkenness and no violence. You could argue that the old showman's memory was faulty 60 years after the event and his recollection of dates or places was muddled, but he was very specific about the time and place because he said it happened on the same day that he found out that his father had died. George's anecdote is now cited by academics as a textbook case of myth uncritically repeated as historical fact. E.H. Carr, *What is History?*, 1976 (originally pub. 1961), pp. 12–13.

123. Charles Dickens was already an accomplished horse rider when George Sanger was still a small boy.

124. The Sanger family, in keeping with the custom of the time, dealt out names so sparingly that it is impossible to keep track of all the Georges, Johns and Williams without a spreadsheet. 'Lord' George Sanger's grandson was George Sanger Coleman but to avoid confusion here he is simply George Coleman.

125. Maurice Willson Disher was a respected author and critic who wrote extensively about the Victorian circus. His anecdote about George Sanger sleeping in a wooden box however is probably apocryphal. If such a box existed, it would surely have been mentioned in the police crime-scene reports of George Sanger's death. I can find no reference to it anywhere else either, so I'm

inclined to believe that it is another of the misleading literary flourishes that often coloured Willson Disher's writings.

126. In fact, the *This is Spinal Tap* Stonehenge scene, but in reverse.

127. *The World's Fair*, Charles Hughes.

128. *The Sanger Story*, Lukens.

129. 'Psychological impact of being wrongfully accused of criminal offences: A systematic literature review', Samantha K. Brooks, Neil Greenberg, *Medicine, Science and the Law*, Sage, 2020.

130. *The Sanger Story*, Lukens.

131. Ibid.

132. Tom Norman was a highly respected showman who once exhibited the freak show performer Joseph Merrick. This relatively brief episode in Norman's career was featured in a book written by the surgeon Frederick Treves and a film on which it was based, *The Elephant Man*. In the book, Treves portrays Norman as ruthless drunkard, a 'vampire showman' who treated Merrick 'like a dog'. These assumptions were refuted in Tom Norman's memoir. He asserted that Merrick chose to exhibit himself and established an equal financial partnership with Norman and was treated very well when the alternative was abandonment to the horrors of the workhouse. Norman claimed that Merrick hated his time with Frederick Treves at the London Hospital and much preferred to be displayed discreetly while being paid, not stripped naked and 'exhibited like an animal in a cattle market'.

133. The circus historian W.S. Meadmore described 19th-century circus genealogy as 'bewildering'. The Sangers married into the Pinder, Coleman, Austin, Hoffman, Freeman and Ginnett circus families: the Kayes with the Bakers, the Bakers with the Paulos, the Paulos with the Fossetts, the Fossetts with the Yeldings and the Yeldings with the Barretts.

134. *Little Ern: The Authorised Biography of Ernie Wise*, Robert Sellers and James Hogg, 2011.

135. *The Daily Telegraph: Third Book of Obituaries*, Hugh Massingberd, 1997.

Select bibliography

Archives
The National Archives, Kew
ADM 73/1-35 MEPO 3/216B, MEPO 4/335/73159, MEPO
4/346/52, MH 47/85/15, Trafalgar ancestors database, UK,
Naval Medal and Award Rolls 1793–1972

London Metropolitan Archives
COR/MC/1911

Newspapers and journals
Birmingham Daily Mail
Daily Mirror
Daily Telegraph
The Era
Hendon & Finchley Times
Illustrated London News
Leeds Mercury
Leicester Post
Lloyd's Weekly Newspaper
Music Hall & Theatre Review
New York Times
The Observer
The Scotsman
Smithsonian Magazine
The Times

Books
Assael, Brenda, *The Circus and Victorian Society*, University of
   Virginia Press: 2005
Bratton, Jacky, *The Victorian Clown*, Cambridge University
   Press: 2006

Croft-Cooke, Rupert, *The Sawdust Ring*, Odhams Press: 1950

Evans, Colin, *The Father of Forensics: The Groundbreaking Cases of Sir Bernard Spilsbury, and the Beginnings of Modern CSI*, Icon Books: 2008

Frost, Thomas, *Circus Life and Circus Celebrities*, Tinsley Brothers: 1875

Frost, Thomas, *The Old Showmen and the Old London Fairs*, Tinsley Brothers: 1875

Harker, Joseph, *Studio and Stage*, Nisbet and Co., London: 1924

Lavery, Brian, *Nelson's Fleet at Trafalgar*, Naval Institute Press: 2004

Lukens, John, *The Sanger Story*, Hodder & Stoughton: 1956

Nicolson, Juliet, *The Perfect Summer*, John Murray: 2007

Norman, Tom, *The Penny Showman: Memoirs of Tom Norman 'Silver King'*, G.B. Norman-Noakes: 1985

Rose, Andrew, *Lethal Witness: Sir Bernard Spilsbury, Honorary Pathologist*, The History Press Ltd: 2007

Speaight, George, *History of the Circus*, Gazelle Books: 1981

Sanger, George, *Seventy Years a Showman*, C.A. Pearson: 1910

Turner, J.T., *The Performers: V1 & 2: A Dictionary of British Circus Biography*, Lingdales Press: 1995

Tyrwhitt-Drake, Sir Hugh Garrard, *The English Circus and Fairground*, Methuen & Co. Ltd: 1947

Tait, Peta, *Fighting Nature: Travelling Menageries, Animal Acts and War Shows*, Sydney University Press: 2016

Velten, Hannah, *Beastly London. A History of Animals in the City*, Reaktion Books: 2016

Acknowledgements

Every period in the development of the circus seems to have been dominated by one particularly colourful character. In the second half of the 19th century that person was Lord George Sanger. I found out about George and his amazing story while I was researching the life of the original circus showman Philip Astley, so I owe thanks to the people who helped put me on that trail, especially Andrew Van Buren and his family. I am also indebted to the authors of numerous books who helped me discover the 19th century circus. Most of all I am indebted to my agent Laura and to Icon for having faith.

Index

Index